SUMMIT ROUTES

WASHINGTON'S 100 HIGHEST PEAKS

SUMMIT ROUTES

WASHINGTON'S 100 HIGHEST PEAKS

ROUTES FOR HIKERS, SCRAMBLERS, & CLIMBERS

SCOTT STEPHENSON
BRIAN BONGIOVANNI

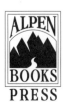

ALPEN BOOKS PRESS

Published by AlpenBooks Press, LLC
4602 Chennault Beach Road, B-1
Mukilteo, WA 98275 USA
(425) 493-6380

Edited by Julie Van Pelt
Book design and layout by Jennifer Shontz
Maps by Jennifer Shontz
Route overlays by Scott Stephenson

Front cover photograph by Lowell Skoog: *Climber on Chiwawa Mountain at sunrise; Clark Mountain in background*
Back cover photograph by Lowell Skoog: *Scramblers on Dumbell Mountain; Chiwawa Mountain, Fortress Mountain and Glacier Peak in background*
Frontispiece photograph by Cliff Leight: *Climbers on Eldorado Peak*

Library of Congress Cataloging-in-Publication Data
Stephenson, Scott 1967-
   Summit routes : Washington's 100 highest peaks : routes for hikers, scramblers, and climbers / Scott Stephenson and Brian Bongiovanni.-- 1st ed.
       p. cm.
   Includes bibliographical references and index.
   ISBN 0-9669795-8-3 (pbk.)
   1. Mountaineering--Washington (State)--Guidebooks. 2. Washington (State)--Guidebooks.
I. Bongiovanni, Brian, 1963- II. Title.
   GV199.42.W2S73 2004
   796.52'2'09797--dc22
                                                     2004022621

Contents

○

Climb the mountains and get their good tidings. Nature's peace will flow into you as sunshine flows into trees. The winds will blow their own freshness into you, and the storms their energy, while cares will drop off like autumn leaves.

— John Muir, 1901

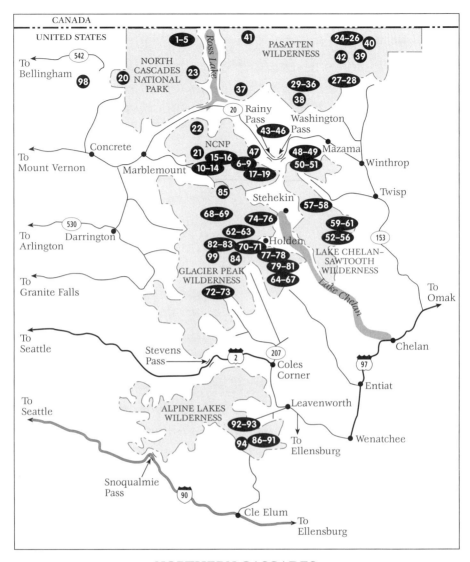

NORTHERN CASCADES

LEGEND

Interstate	90	Country boundary	— · · — · · —
U.S. highway	97	State boundary	— · — · —
State route	530	Park or wilderness boundary	— · · — · —
City	●	Body of water	
Pass	)(	River	

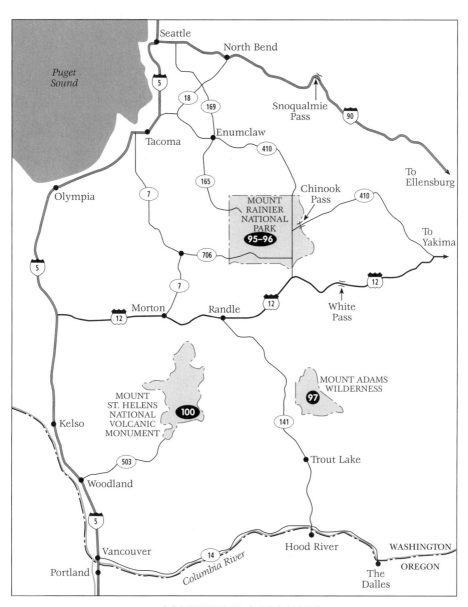

SOUTHERN CASCADES

Acknowledgments

○

SCOTT DEDICATES THIS BOOK TO JANE WOODS, without whose companionship—both in life and on the trails—friendship, insightful ideas, seemingly endless patience, and editorial and compositional skills this book would never have been written. Thanks also to Ellen and John, my parents, who first introduced to me the wilderness and started me on this great journey.

The authors wish to thank those who contributed to this project with their boundless enthusiasm, suggestions, reviews, and endless encouragement. It was this support that kept us going when the task seemed insurmountable.

We wish to thank Fred Beckey (and The Mountaineers Books) for permission to reprint the route descriptions for the Southeast Spire of the Mox Peaks and Storm King Mountain from his amazing *Cascade Alpine Guides*. Our utmost appreciation to John Lixvar, John Plimpton, and John Roper for compiling the original "Bulger List" of the 100 highest peaks. We fully comprehend the enormity of that task.

We are grateful to Paul Parker for his extremely helpful and timely advice in the early stages of the publishing process. Our sincerest appreciation to Paul Klenke and Chris Nowak, whose exhaustive reviews of the manuscript provided a key element of its accuracy and completeness.

We extend a special thanks to Lowell Skoog, Chris Nowak, Ron Sheets, Paul Klenke, and Don Beavon for providing helpful approach and route information. We are also indebted to Paul Klenke, Lowell Skoog, Paul McClellan, Eric Willhite, Sam Avaiusini, and Cliff Leight for generously contributing photographs of some of the included peaks.

We wish to thank Bob Koch at AlpenBooks Press for truly believing in this project and for seeing it through. Also thanks to Julie Van Pelt for her amazing editing skills and well-timed pep talks, and to Jennifer Shontz, whose wonderful cover and interior design make this book such a pleasure to read.

Without the help of all of these people, and many others, this book would never have been what we hoped: a reliable reference for those seeking to hike, scramble, or climb one or more of Washington's 100 highest peaks.

Introduction

○

THE PURPOSE OF *SUMMIT ROUTES: WASHINGTON'S 100 HIGHEST PEAKS* is to provide you, the reader, with a comprehensive guide to reaching the geographically and geologically diverse high points of Washington. This book arose out of necessity. As climbing partners, we, the authors, have spent literally thousands of hours sitting at the kitchen table, surrounded by precarious stacks of maps and books so high that a collapse promised sure death. The irony of our circumstances didn't escape us. To climb the high points of Washington is to get away from it all and experience the grandeur and beauty of its wonderful wilderness. Yet here we were, before every outing, engaged in a laborious activity that would do a federal bureaucrat proud. We persevered because we knew the great reward that awaited us when we left the trailhead, and we have never been disappointed. But each time, upon our return, we faced the task of planning the next outing with some dread. "Wow," we thought, "I really wish there was a book on this." Well, here is that book! It's the product of our near-death experiences at the kitchen table and the life-giving, real-world experiences of ourselves and many friends and fellow climbers whose feet have tramped the trails, slogged the scree, and glided the glaciers to the remote corners of the Washington Cascades. We think that all but the most ardent bibliophiles will appreciate the information that will get you away from *your* kitchen table and out into the mountains where you really want to be anyway. Whether you are interested in summiting all 100 of these peaks or just in selecting individual ones, this guide is for you. It contains a wealth of information to help you embark on an incredible journey through the Cascades, one of America's greatest alpine mountain ranges.

WHY THESE PEAKS AND ROUTES?

To determine the 100 highest mountains in Washington, an initial list was generated using available maps that contained the summits with 400 feet or more of clean prominence. Clean prominence is defined as the number of feet a peak rises above the lowest contour that entirely encircles the peak without including any others. The following adjustments were then made to this list:

- Volcanic subpeaks were removed so that each volcano (apart from Mount Rainier) has one summit.
- Little Tahoma was included because of its impressive size and prominence even on a peak as large as Mount Rainier.
- Seven Fingered Jack and Blackcap Mountain were included because their clean prominence was within the margin of error ($\pm$ 39 feet).

This methodology produced a wonderfully varied and interesting list of peaks that includes all of the major summits of Washington.

Routes on the peaks were then chosen based on two primary criteria: difficulty and grouping potential. For difficulty, the emphasis was on hiking or scrambling routes over technical climbing routes, wherever possible. For grouping potential, the routes and their approaches were chosen to maximize the ability to combine them with other high points into a joint trip.

HOW TO USE THIS BOOK

The peaks in this book are grouped into the six main regional areas in which they are found, starting in the north and moving south, with the exception of the Cascade volcanoes. The volcanoes appear in their own section because these peaks have a distinctly different feel from most of the others in this book and require similar skills to climb, so grouping them together seems natural. In addition, they are located in four separate wilderness areas, two of which contain no other high points.

Within these seven distinct sections, the high points are further subdivided into **Slams** and **Free Agents.** A **Slam** is simply a group of peaks that can be logically combined into one trip using a common trailhead and approach. Within a Slam, the high points are ordered by elevation from highest to lowest. Each Slam begins with the following summary:

- Peaks and routes to be climbed (and the order to climb them in)
- Maximum difficulty for the overall Slam (including type of terrain encountered)
- Roundtrip (car-to-car) duration for the trip, including all routes in the Slam
- Total roundtrip mileage from trailhead to base camp and back (on and off-trail)
- Total elevation gain (car-to-car) for the journey, including all routes in the Slam
- Required USGS 7.5-minute quadrangles for the routes
- Required Green Trails 15-minute maps for the approach
- Name of trailhead
- Recommended climbing season

This is followed by a suggested itinerary for completing the Slam, to help you plan your trip. Note that the Slams are simply recommended groupings of peaks; peaks can still be summited individually or can be removed from Slams.

A **Free Agent** is a peak that can't be logically grouped with others into a Slam, typically because the peak is too isolated or its primary route doesn't share a common approach with another peak's primary route. These peaks are grouped for each section, following the Slams, and are ordered by elevation from highest to lowest.

Each individual peak begins with its elevation and list ranking, with 1 being the highest peak and 100 the lowest. Recommended routes on the peak follow, with a summary of approach and route information:

For the Approach

- Time from trailhead to base camp
- Mileage one-way from trailhead to base camp (on and off-trail)
- Elevation change (gain and loss) from trailhead to base camp
- Required Green Trails 15-minute maps for the approach
- The ranger station or agency to contact for information (all listed in Appendix E)

For the Route

- Route difficulty (including type of terrain encountered)
- Time from base camp to summit, one-way
- Elevation change (gain and loss) from base camp to summit
- Required USGS 7.5-minute quadrangles for the route
- Recommended climbing season

Where possible, a photograph of the route is also provided. Together, this information gives an excellent overview for each peak to help you select a trip that's appropriate for you, given your desired type of route (rock, snow, glacier, etc.), skill, experience, and available time.

Finally, to further help you select a Slam or individual peak, Appendices A and B categorize the Slams and peaks by difficulty and duration.

Elevation Change

Elevation change captures the net gain and loss from the starting point to the ending point of the journey and includes the feet ascended and descended along the way. For example, consider a hypothetical (but typical) approach to base camp: the trail begins at 2,500 feet, crosses a pass at 3,500 feet, descends into a valley at 2,000 feet and makes a final climb to base camp at 2,500 feet. The elevation change for this approach would be calculated as follows:

Elevation gain = 3,500 ft - 2,500 ft + 2,500 ft - 2,000 ft = + 1,500 ft
Elevation loss = 2,000 ft - 3,500 ft = - 1,500 ft

This example illustrates that although the elevation of the trailhead and base camp are the same (2,500 ft), the elevation change experienced by a hiker on this approach is not zero feet! In fact, using this trail, the hiker must walk uphill on the way to base camp and uphill on the way back. Computing elevation change with this method avoids misleading statistics and, taken alongside the mileage, provides an accurate idea of the effort required for the trip. Elevation gain and loss from base camp to summit is calculated in exactly the same way.

Topographic Maps

As a general rule, the USGS 7.5-minute quadrangles (quads) listed for the peaks are those required for coverage of the routes on the peak but not the approach. Exceptions to this rule (e.g., Snowfield Peak) are made where the approach requires significant off-trail travel with potentially challenging routefinding.

Green Trails 15-minute maps were used extensively in the preparation of the approach descriptions and are highly recommended. They are generally more up-to-date than the USGS quads and include mileage, elevations, trail numbers and names, and other useful information.

Appendix C provides a complete list of all the Green Trails maps and USGS quads required for all of the Slams and peaks in this guide.

Rating System

This guide uses the Roman numeral grading system to assess the overall effort, commitment, and expertise a route requires. This system takes into account the time required, overall difficulty, routefinding challenges, and objective hazards. Of course, all ratings are by their very nature subjective. For example, if conditions on the route are poor or if your climbing party isn't sufficiently skilled or experienced, a grade III route can become a grade V experience. The following grading system is intended to give you a good idea what to expect on the route under normal conditions:

Grade I: The entire route can be completed in less than half a day, with easy scrambling or climbing and minimal exposure to objective hazards. Escape is quick.

Grade II: Technical portions of the route will take less than half a day, with increased difficulty and exposure to objective hazards. Escape is reasonably quick.

Grade III: Technical portions of the route will require more than half a day, with moderate difficulty and exposure to objective hazards. Escape is time-consuming and involved.

Grade IV: Technical portions of the route will take all day, with a high degree of difficulty and exposure to objective hazards. Escape is very difficult (possible bivouac). There are no routes of this grade in this guide.

Grade V: Technical portions of this route will take more than one day, requiring a bivouac, with extreme difficulty and exposure to objective hazards. Escape is extremely difficult. There are no routes of this grade in this guide.

For rock climbing, this guide uses the following standard system developed in the European Alps:

Class 1: Hiking.

Class 2: Easy scrambling where hands are not always required.

Class 3: Exposed scrambling requiring the use of hands but not a rope.

Class 4: Highly exposed scrambling where a rope is used for belays and intermediate protection may be placed.

Class 5: Technical rock climbing where protection is placed between belays.

Class 5 ratings are made more precise using the Yosemite Decimal System (YDS), now standard in the United States:

Class 5.0 through 5.3: Easy climbing where protection is placed occasionally. In this guide, this is referred to as **low-fifth class.**

Class 5.4 through 5.6: Moderate climbing where protection is placed more frequently. In this guide, this is referred to as **mid-fifth class.**

Class 5.7 and above: Challenging climbing requiring a high degree of skill. There are no routes 5.7 or above in this guide.

WHAT TO KNOW BEFORE YOU GO
Route Difficulty

This book's routes cover a wide range of difficulties, from walk-ups to challenging technical rock and glacier climbs requiring significant skill and experience to scale. The majority of the routes, though, are scrambles. Scrambling is perhaps best defined as moving through the mountains, over rock, snow, and ice without use of ropes or other cumbersome technical equipment. Scrambles range from boulder hopping or easy rock climbing (class 2) to steep, exposed rock climbing on technically easy terrain (class 4). They may also include snow/ice climbing, where knowledge of how to use an ice ax and crampons is required. Some of the most challenging scrambles (easiest technical climbs) in this guide require rappelling, a potentially dangerous activity that must be learned from an experienced climber or guide service.

No one but you can decide what is appropriate for your skill, experience, and comfort level. If you're new to scrambling and climbing, we recommend starting with the easier Slams and peaks listed in Appendices A and B and working your way up. Or better yet, take a course through a local climbing club or respected guide service to get you off to a solid start. Slams and peaks are defined as easier (▲), intermediate (▲▲), or advanced (▲▲▲). The associated icons will help you to quickly assess a route's difficulty.

Equipment

Always, always wear a helmet. It could save your life, either from rock or icefall or, perish the thought, if you happen to fall. Many of the routes in this book involve ascending high mountain gullies. Due to active erosion (wind, ice, and water), these gullies often tend to be littered with loose rock debris that can "let go" without warning. Even a small piece of debris impacting your naked head could do some serious damage. So do yourself a favor and put a cap on your cranium, a bucket over your brain, a lid on your life. We're big fans of fast and light too, but take your helmet and leave something else behind instead.

Choice of footwear depends on the route selected. For scrambling, a pair of moderately stiff above-the-ankle leather hiking boots with a good, hard, Vibram-type sole is perfect. If your route involves extended periods on glaciers and/or snow (e.g., Icecap Slam), you might consider wearing plastic boots. They are stiffer than hiking boots, which helps when kicking steps in snow, and keep your feet dryer and warmer because they don't absorb water. If you don't own a pair, some outdoor stores rent them. It's a trade-off though, as plastic boots tend to be heavy, hot, and uncomfortable on long trail approaches. For technical rock climbs, take along a pair of rock shoes and put them on at the base of the rock pitches.

Depending on the chosen route and season, an ice ax and crampons may be required for many of the ascents in this book. It's left to you to decide whether or not to bring them.

For technical climbs, it's assumed that you are capable of deciding what gear to bring based upon the types of terrain to be encountered on the approach and route. This includes, but is not limited to, ice axes, crampons, ropes, harnesses, carabiners, rock protection (cams, chocks, etc.), ice screws, runners, belay devices, extra webbing for rappel anchors, glacier rigs, and snow pickets/flukes. If you're not familiar with this gear (and how to use it) or are uncomfortable deciding what to bring, consider choosing a different route.

Wilderness Navigation Skills

This book assumes you have a map, compass, and altimeter and, more importantly, that you know how to use them. The routes in this book are generally in remote areas and almost all require at least some off-trail travel and navigation. The approach and route descriptions have been written assuming you know how to do at least the following:

- Read a map, including topographic lines (contours)
- Orient a map both to the surrounding topography and using a compass
- Take a compass bearing, both from the map and surroundings, and follow it
- Locate your position on the map using compass bearings, surrounding topography, and elevation information
- Choose the "best" route through unfamiliar surroundings

There are numerous excellent books available on orienteering, and many outdoor equipment shops offer weekend courses that can teach you these skills in a fun atmosphere. Trust us, by the time you've attempted a handful of the routes in this book, you'll either be a good navigator or you won't have made it to many of the summits.

Physical Fitness

The Washington Cascades are, in general, a remote and rugged wilderness. As such, most of the summits in this book require lengthy, often strenuous, approaches. To make your outings as safe and enjoyable as possible, we recommend a regular workout program that includes weight lifting and aerobic exercise. Spend an hour a few times a week exercising and your weekend adventures in the mountains will be that much more rewarding.

First Aid

Let's face it, scrambling and climbing are potentially dangerous activities and many of the routes in this book are in remote areas far from civilization. Rescue from any of these peaks would be involved and time-consuming affairs. As such, a standard course in first aid (preferably mountain oriented) is highly recommended before undertaking any of the routes in this book. Hopefully you'll never need it, but if you do, it could mean the difference between life and death.

SAFETY DISCLAIMER

Scrambling and climbing are sports in which you may be injured or die. This guidebook is a compilation of information, some of it unverified, from many different climbers. The authors and the publisher cannot assure the accuracy of any of the information in the book, including the route descriptions and difficulty ratings. There are no warranties, whether expressed or implied, that this guidebook is accurate or that the information contained in it is reliable. Your safety depends upon your own good judgment, based on experience and a realistic assessment of your own ability. If you have any doubt about your ability to safely do a route described in this book, don't attempt it.

NORTH CASCADES NATIONAL PARK

•

WHEN PETER JACKSON WAS SEARCHING FOR A LOCATION to film the *Lord of the Rings,* he need have looked no further than North Cascades National Park. The majesty of the jagged peaks and immense glaciers, the beauty of its crystal clear alpine lakes and cascading waterfalls, and the wild expanses of ancient forest make this park the true unsung hero of the national park system.

In contrast to the likes of Yellowstone, Glacier, and Smokey Mountains national parks, the North Cascades' lack of roads and its difficult, steep, vegetated terrain help keep the *wild* in wilderness. Though Highway 20 (North Cascades Highway) showcases the beautiful peaks of the Liberty Bell massif, the most spectacular landscapes can only be discovered on foot. Access to the interior can often be arduous, but for those determined travelers who persevere, their rewards are wild, remote country and often a healthy dose of peace and solitude.

North Cascades was designated a national park in 1968 and today encompasses more than 684,000 acres. The heavy precipitation results in deep snows and immense glaciers (more than 700). Twenty-three of this guide's high points are within the park. Of the twenty-three, nineteen of them can be climbed in five distinct Slam itineraries, leaving only four Free Agent peaks to be climbed individually. Summit these North Cascades peaks and you will journey to some of the most remote corners of this remarkable wilderness and, in doing so, appreciate all of its many wonders as few others have.

● Chilliwack Slam

Peaks & routes	Mount Spickard (Silver Glacier—Northeast Ridge), Mount Redoubt (South Face), Mount Custer (South Ridge), Mox Peaks—Southeast Spire (West Face), Mox Peaks—Northwest Spire (Northeast Ridge)
Max difficulty	▲▲▲ Grade III; steep snow; glacier travel; mid-fifth class rock
Duration	6 days
Roundtrip to camp	18 miles
Elevation gain	+15,600 ft
USGS 7.5-minute	Mount Redoubt, Mount Spickard
GT 15-minute	n/a
Trailhead	Depot Creek Trail
Season	July–September

The Chilliwack Range is a remote, heavily glaciated, and extraordinarily striking area encompassing some of the most challenging summits to reach in this guide. All this beauty, peace, and solitude is guarded by a difficult approach, dubious highlights of which include an unguarded crossing of the U.S.–Canadian border and a scramble up a waterfall. The base camps at Ouzel Lake and on the Redoubt Glacier are set smack in the middle of all this grandeur, though, and it just doesn't get much better than this.

	ITINERARY	
Day	**Elevation change**	**Instructions**
1	+3,200 ft; -0 ft	Follow the approach for Mount Spickard to Ouzel Lake and camp (5,680 ft).
2	+3,700 ft; -2,100 ft	Move camp to the flat area at 7,300 ft on the Redoubt Glacier near the Depot–Redoubt Creek divide (see Mox Peaks—Southeast Spire). Climb Mount Redoubt and return to camp.
3	+2,500 ft; -2,500 ft	Get a very early start, climb Mox Peaks—Southeast Spire and return to camp.
4	+1,800 ft; -3,400 ft	Get a very early start, climb Mox Peaks—Northwest Spire and move camp back down to Ouzel Lake.
5	+4,600 ft; -4,600 ft	Climb Mounts Spickard and Custer and return to camp.
6	+0 ft; -3,200 ft	Hike out.

Notes: This is a very strenuous itinerary. If the Mox Peaks are not in your plan, keep your base camp at Ouzel Lake. The routes for Mounts Spickard and Custer share a common point at the pass above Silver Lake.

1 Mount Spickard

8,979 ft; 16th highest

Mount Spickard is the highest summit in the Chilliwack Range. It's a massive, heavily glaciated, rugged mountain with numerous radiating ridges and subpeaks. The southwest ridge spans almost 2 miles, connecting with the twin spires of the Mox Peaks and forming an impressive backdrop high above Ouzel Lake. The Silver Glacier sweeps down Spickard's northern flank and empties into Silver Lake, nestled in an awesome cirque.

SILVER GLACIER—NORTHEAST RIDGE

This is a beautiful climb with fantastic alpine ambience. You'll ascend the moderate Silver Glacier and be treated to fantastic views of the Silver Lake cirque over your shoulder as you climb. The scrambling finish on the northeast ridge is a great way to wrap up this Cascade classic. The glacier gets icy, particularly in late season, so don't forget the crampons.

APPROACH

Time to camp	5–6 hours
Mileage	6 miles
Elevation change	+3,200 ft; -0 ft
GT 15-minute	n/a
Contact	North Cascades NP, Headquarters or Marblemount Ranger Station

ROUTE

Difficulty	▲▲ Grade II; moderate or steep snow; glacier travel; class 3–4 rock
Time to summit	3–4 hours
Elevation change	+3,300 ft; -0 ft
USGS 7.5-minute	Mount Redoubt, Mount Spickard
Season	June–September

Approach: As mentioned, access to the Chilliwacks via Depot Creek Trail requires an unguarded crossing of the U.S.-Canadian border. Your use of this route indicates your assumption of the risks associated with this crossing. Bring your passport and any other required identification so you at least have some proof of identity and citizenship—you'll need it at the guarded border crossing anyway if you're coming from the United States.

Although permits are technically required for overnight outings in the park, there is simply no convenient way to obtain one for entry via the Depot Creek

Mount Spickard from the north (Mount Custer) Photo by Lowell Skoog

Trail; there is a trail register at the border crossing. Please practice minimum-impact camping techniques to protect this fragile alpine environment.

Ouzel Lake is shown but not labeled on the Mount Redoubt USGS quad. It's the small lake at the head of the Depot Creek drainage beneath the toe of the Redoubt Glacier.

From Interstate 5 near Bellingham, take exit 255 (Mount Baker). Drive 10 miles east on Highway 542 to Nugents Crossing and the junction with Highway 9. Turn left (north) onto Highway 9 and drive 14 miles to Sumas. Cross the U.S.-Canadian border and proceed toward Abbotsford and the junction with Trans-Canada Highway 1. Turn right (east) onto Highway 1 toward Hope and proceed 17 miles to exit 119 (Sardis/Vedder Road). Drive south on Vedder Road to Vedder Crossing. Just before crossing the Chilliwack River Bridge, turn left (east) onto Chilliwack Lake Road and drive approximately 32 miles, past numerous camping options and turnoffs, to the junction with Depot Creek Road. Turn onto Depot Creek Road and drive approximately 1 mile to the first fork in the road. Unless you have a high-clearance vehicle, park your car here as the final section of road is very rough.

Stay left at the first fork and walk 1 mile on the road to reach a second fork. Stay left again and hike another mile to the end of the road on the north side of Depot Creek and the trailhead for the Depot Creek Trail (approx. 2,500 ft). This "trail" is more appropriately called a climber's path as it is not maintained and is quite overgrown and muddy in sections.

Hike the climber's path through dense forest. Near the edge of the forest, watch carefully for where the path turns left and ascends onto the slope above the creek. Continue on the path as it traverses the slopes for approximately 1 mile and leaves the forest. Follow the path across the brushy slopes, keeping a sharp lookout for an obvious waterfall above (you'll hear it long before you see it); continue on the path as it climbs steeply to the falls (approx. 4,000 ft). Ascend a short, slippery rock step making use of a hand line that is often present. Locate a gap in the brush on the left side of the falls that leads to a talus slope and ascend it, keeping a sharp lookout for the exit path above and right. Follow the path through steep brush to reach the top of the slope and the edge of a basin (approx. 4,800 ft). Traverse across talus along the left side of the basin to avoid brush and a boggy stream. Continue up the valley to Ouzel Lake at its head and good camping (5,680 ft).

Route: From the north end of Ouzel Lake, ascend along the inlet stream northeasterly to a pass overlooking Silver Lake at the rim of the massive Silver Lake cirque (approx. 7,400 ft). From the pass, make a rising traverse easterly to the center of the Silver Glacier. Ascend the glacier southeasterly into a cirque beneath Mount Spickard's upper north face. Climb along the left (east) side of the glacier to reach a prominent notch at the base of Spickard's northeast ridge (approx. 8,600 ft) about 175 feet below a large bergschrund. Scramble up a series of gullies and ribs (class 3–4), staying on or closely left (east) of the ridge crest, to the summit (8,979 ft). Alternatively, from near the notch, ascend steep snowslopes (can be icy in late season) to just below the large bergschrund, then scramble up rock to gain the crest of the northeast ridge and continue to the summit as previously described.

Descent: Descend the route using a combination of rappels and downclimbing.

2 Mount Redoubt

8,969 ft; 18th highest

Mount Redoubt is an ice-clad, craggy peak with a spectacular, perfectly alpine, north face covered by the impressive Redoubt and Depot glaciers. Its southern flank rises high above Bear Lake and features the sheer, unmistakable rock face of the Flying Buttress. Your approach and climb will get you up close and personal with many of the striking features of this beautiful peak.

SOUTH FACE

This superb route begins with a moderate crossing of the Redoubt Glacier on the way to a traverse beneath the intimidating Flying Buttress. Then the real fun begins: you'll climb a steep couloir into a hanging cirque, ascend its slopes, and finish with an exposed scramble to the summit. The views down the north face are truly dizzying.

Mount Redoubt from the south   Photo by Lowell Skoog

APPROACH

Time to camp	5–6 hours
Mileage	6 miles
Elevation change	+3,200 ft; -0 ft
GT 15-minute	n/a
Contact	North Cascades NP, Headquarters or Marblemount Ranger Station

ROUTE

Difficulty	▲▲ Grade II+; steep snow; glacier travel; class 3–4 rock
Time to summit	4–5 hours
Elevation change	+3,500 ft; -200 ft
USGS 7.5-minute	Mount Redoubt
Season	June–September

Approach: Follow the approach for Mount Spickard to Ouzel Lake and good camping (5,680 ft).

Route: From Ouzel Lake, ascend a rocky shoulder westerly, then south-westerly to reach the toe of the Redoubt Glacier. Ascend the glacier west-southwesterly, staying left (south) of a rock rib at 7,400 feet, to reach a broad col (approx. 7,800 ft) in Redoubt's south ridge. This col is just right (north) of Point 8090 and just left (south) of the Flying Buttress. Cross the col and descend westerly past the Flying Buttress until able to bear rightward (northwest) and ascend to the base of a steep, narrow couloir.

Climb the couloir into a cirque beneath Redoubt's upper south face. Scramble left to gain a broad snow/scree rib on the left side of the cirque and ascend it to reach the upper left corner of a snowfield beneath the summit area. There is a sporadically visible climber's path in these sections that can help to show the way. Scramble a ledge and ramp rightward into an exposed gully and climb it (class 3) to reach a notch near the summit. Scramble along the very exposed crest to the summit (8,969 ft).

Descent: Descend the route using a combination of rappels and downclimbing.

3 Mount Custer

8,630 ft; 38th highest

Mount Custer and its long northeast ridge forms the picturesque western boundary of Silver Lake cirque. Its steep north face harbors the Custer Glacier, and the Maselpanik Glacier clothes the western flank of the northeast ridge.

SOUTH RIDGE

This scramble gets you high up on the rim of the Silver Lake cirque. There's a lot of loose rock so be careful, particularly when passing outcrops.

APPROACH

Time to camp	5–6 hours
Mileage	6 miles
Elevation change	+3,200 ft; -0 ft
GT 15-minute	n/a
Contact	North Cascades NP, Headquarters or Marblemount Ranger Station

Summit

Mount Custer from the south; route ascends the ridge that begins in the foreground Photo by Lowell Skoog

ROUTE

Difficulty   ▲▲ Grade II; moderate snow; class 3 rock
Time to summit 3–4 hours
Elevation change +3,000 ft; -0 ft
USGS 7.5-minute Mount Redoubt, Mount Spickard
Season   June–September

Approach: Follow the approach for Mount Spickard to Ouzel Lake and good camping (5,680 ft).

Route: From the north end of Ouzel Lake, ascend along the inlet stream northeasterly to a pass overlooking Silver Lake at the rim of the massive Silver Lake cirque (approx. 7,400 ft). Cross the pass and ascend easy snow and boulder slopes northerly to join Mount Custer's south ridge. Scramble northerly along the loose and rocky ridge crest (class 3), negotiating outcrops, to the summit (8,630 ft).

Descent: Descend the route.

4 Mox Peaks—Southeast Spire

8,504 ft; 55th highest

The Mox Peaks are imposing, vertiginous spires whose rugged forms are a stunning terminus to Mount Spickard's long southwest ridge. The Southeast Spire, the taller of the two, features a precipitous 1,500-foot east face that rises sheer above the Perry Creek drainage. A glacier occupies a basin on its southwestern flank, bordered on the south by the serrated Ridge of Gendarmes. This is surely one of the great alpine sights in the Cascades and an impressive example of the power of glaciers.

WEST FACE

According to Fred Beckey, "the summit of the Southeast Spire is one of the most difficult to attain in the Cascade Range" (Beckey 1995, p. 128). Forewarned is forearmed, we figure. To summit this imposing peak is definitely venturing off the beaten track, with challenging routefinding, loose rock, and plenty of exposure. All this just adds to the satisfaction you'll feel when you reach the top.

APPROACH

Time to camp	5–6 hours
Mileage	6 miles
Elevation change	+3,200 ft; -0 ft
GT 15-minute	n/a
Contact	North Cascades NP, Headquarters or Marblemount Ranger Station

ROUTE

Difficulty	▲▲▲ Grade III; moderate snow; mid-fifth class rock
Time to summit	7–10 hours
Elevation change	+3,500 ft; -600 ft
USGS 7.5-minute	Mount Redoubt
Season	July–September

Summit

Southeast Spire from the Ridge of Gendarmes; route ascends left-hand skyline
Photo by Lowell Skoog

Approach: Follow the approach for Mount Spickard to Ouzel Lake and good camping (5,680 ft).

Route: From Ouzel Lake, ascend a rocky shoulder westerly, then southwesterly to reach the northern terminus of the Redoubt Glacier. Ascend the glacier west-southwesterly to the base of a rock rib at 7,200 feet. Bear south across the glacier through a flat area (approx. 7,300 ft; good camping) to reach the right (west) end of a craggy ridge that forms the southern border of the glacier at the Depot–Redoubt Creek divide (7,200 ft; additional good camping). Leave the glacier and round the ridge to its south side. Traverse easterly across heather and moraine slopes at the head of the Redoubt Creek drainage to the glacier remnant between the Mox Peaks. Ascend the glacier and rock to the central col between the Southeast and Northwest spires (aka Twin Spires; approx. 7,840 ft) and follow Beckey's directions (compass directions are given in capital letters):

From near the col between the Twin Spires, ascend obliquely S on ledges c. 200 ft toward the Ridge of Gendarmes. Then ascend the left side of the major E-W gully to its head on a rib crest that extends from the Spires col to the Ridge of Gendarmes.

Climb a 10-ft vertical step and continue working up and S toward the most prominent notch in the Ridge of Gendarmes (150 vertical ft of class 3 scrambling), where one gains an intimidating view of the massive summit tower. Now work obliquely down and E for 200 vertical ft toward a major snow-filled gully that trends SE from the Ridge. Descend this gully another 100 vertical ft to a ledge that enables one to cross to the next gully E (this places one at the base of two additional SE-running gullies from the Ridge). Take the rightmost (eastern) gully, closest to the W face of the [Southeast] Spire, first staying on the right side (E) for the first 150 ft (class 3–4), then ascend the gully to the high notch on the crest of the Ridge (200 ft vertical gain, loose class 3). This gully is at first a chimney with blocks, then a loose gully. One's position is now beyond the last pinnacle on the Ridge and at the base of the Spire's W face.

Serious climbing begins here: make a short right traverse (5.5 or more) then climb c. 80 ft to the right side of a detached white column (class 4). From a belay behind the column, climb up and right to belay slings (140 ft—5.2). The third pitch is 60 ft of class 4 to within easy summit scrambling. The now-standard route party (Bryce Simon and Tim Place, 1974) continued on an exposed and somewhat loose left side of the steep corner for 165 ft above the belay stance of the white pillar. (Beckey 1995, p. 130)

Descent: Make "three rappels on the spire and one in the gully" (Beckey 1995, p. 130). Retrace your route back to the central col and descend the remainder of the route.

5 Mox Peaks—Northwest Spire

8,407 ft; 70th highest

The rugged Northwest Spire of the Mox Peaks, shorter but just as impressive as its neighbor, bookends Mount Spickard's long southwest ridge high above Ouzel Lake. Its steep northwestern flank adjoins the Redoubt Glacier and a narrow, steep glacier descends from the central col between the spires into the Perry Creek drainage.

NORTHEAST RIDGE

Like its neighbor the Southeast Spire, the Northwest Spire is a difficult summit to reach. Don't expect lichen-free rock to lead you to the summit, as this
peak sees few ascents. Do expect wonderful alpine ambience, some heart-
pumping exposure, and a healthy dose of routefinding challenge, all of which
add to the appeal of this exciting climb.

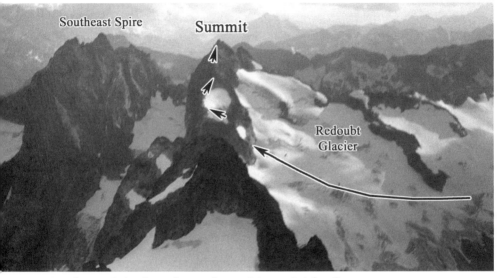

Northwest Spire from the northeast (Mount Spickard) Photo by Brian Bongiovanni

APPROACH

Time to camp	5–6 hours
Mileage	6 miles
Elevation change	+3,200 ft; -0 ft
GT 15-minute	n/a
Contact	North Cascades NP, Headquarters or Marblemount Ranger Station

ROUTE

Difficulty	▲▲▲ Grade III; steep snow; mid-fifth class rock
Time to summit	5–6 hours
Elevation change	+2,800 ft; -0 ft
USGS 7.5-minute	Mount Redoubt
Season	July–September

Approach: Follow the approach for Mount Spickard to Ouzel Lake and
good camping (5,680 ft).

Route: From Ouzel Lake, ascend a rocky shoulder westerly, then southwesterly to reach the northern terminus of the Redoubt Glacier. At approximately 7,000 feet, traverse easterly across the glacier passing below a rock rib. Aim for the point at which the glacier reaches nearest to the crest of the northeast ridge of the Northwest Spire. A snow finger may provide a boost onto the rock, depending on conditions. Alternatively, it may be necessary to begin climbing rock to the left of the remnant snow finger to avoid wet rock. Ascend a corner system that requires careful rock climbing (mid-fifth class) before climbing out of it to the right to reach easier, blockier ground. Continue climbing to reach the crest of the northeast ridge.

Once on the northeast ridge, climb easy rock (class 2–3) along the ridge crest to reach an elegant snow crest atop the ridge. Continue along this crest enjoying fine views of Mount Spickard and the Southeast Spire of the Mox Peaks. About 200 feet below the summit (approx. 8,200 ft), leave the ridge via a semi-obvious ramp/gully to the left. Traverse easily along the south side of the ridge to the base of the summit structure. Climb one steep rock pitch (low-fifth class) less than 100 feet to a good belay ledge below the ridge crest. Finish with an easier and shorter pitch to the summit (8,407 ft).

Descent: Make two short rappels from near the summit back to the ridge crest. Downclimb the ridge until able to make a long rappel back to the Redoubt Glacier, then retrace the remainder of the route.

Chinook Slam

Peaks & routes	Mesahchie Peak (West Ridge), Katsuk Peak (East Ridge), Kimtah Peak (West Route), Cosho Peak (East Ridge)
Max difficulty	▲▲ Grade II; class 4 rock
Duration	5 days
Roundtrip to camp	20 miles
Elevation gain	+16,200 ft
USGS 7.5-minute	Mount Arriva, Mount Logan
GT 15-minute	Mount Logan (No. 49)
Trailhead	Easy Pass
Season	June–September

This Slam combines the high points of the rugged Ragged Ridge, a crest of rocky peaks located between Fisher and Panther creeks and northeast of Mount Logan. The approach via Easy Pass is far from easy, but it's definitely one of the most beautiful hikes in the park and there's good camping in the Fisher Creek valley. The view of Mount Logan from each of the summits will have you dreaming of the Thunder Slam, if you aren't already.

ITINERARY

Day	Elevation change	Instructions
1	+2,800 ft; -1,300 ft	Follow the approach for Mesahchie Peak to Fisher Camp and camp (5,200 ft).
2	+4,500 ft; -5,900 ft	Climb Mesahchie and Katsuk peaks and return to camp. Move camp down to Cosho Camp, following the approach for Kimtah Peak (3,800 ft).
3	+4,800 ft; -800 ft	Climb Kimtah Peak and bivi at the high notch just east of Thieves Peak (7,800 ft). If time allows, and for a little more sheltered spot, return to the central gully on Cosho's south slopes and ascend it to approximately 7,600 ft. Scout around the area to find a small bench that provides decent bivi accommodation.
4	+1,400 ft; -5,400 ft	Climb Cosho Peak and return to Cosho Camp and camp (3,800 ft).
5	+2,700 ft; -2,800 ft	Hike out.

Notes: All but the most physically fit parties should break this Slam into two outings. For day 2, Mesahchie and Katsuk peaks share a common point on the rock rib 300 feet below Katsuk's east summit (8,200 ft). For day 3 and 4, Kimtah and Cosho peaks share a common point in the central gully at 7,000 feet. However, a combined ascent of these peaks would be a very long day (not possible for most parties). Therefore, it's best to spend a night at a high bivi, using snow patches for water (scarce in late season).

6 Mesahchie Peak

8,795 ft; 28th highest

Mesahchie Peak is the highest and easternmost of the major summits on Ragged Ridge. Its name means "wicked" in Chinook Jargon (Phillips 1912; Shaw 1909), but don't be deterred by the name; it's not really all that bad. The northern flank harbors the Mesahchie Glacier and the easternmost section of the Katsuk Glacier, while the southern flank is mostly scree and talus.

WEST RIDGE

This ascent features a lengthy scramble along a rocky rib crest, mercifully above the talus and scree, and finishes with some interesting routefinding to gain the gully that leads to the summit.

APPROACH

Time to camp	3–4 hours
Mileage	6 miles
Elevation change	+2,800 ft; -1,300 ft
GT 15-minute	Mount Logan (No. 49)
Contact	North Cascades NP, Marblemount Ranger Station

ROUTE

Difficulty	▲▲ Grade II; class 3–4 rock
Time to summit	4–5 hours
Elevation change	+3,800 ft; -200 ft
USGS 7.5-minute	Mount Arriva, Mount Logan
Season	June–September

Approach: Permits are required for overnight outings in the park and can be obtained a maximum of 24 hours in advance. Obtain your permit from the Marblemount Ranger Station, signposted on the west side of town. A Northwest Forest Pass is required to park at the trailhead.

From Interstate 5 north of Mount Vernon, take exit 230 (Anacortes/Burlington). Drive 96 miles east on Highway 20 (North Cascades Highway) to the signed trailhead for Easy Pass on the south side of the highway (3,700 ft).

Hike the very steep trail 3.5 miles southwesterly along Easy Pass Creek to Easy Pass (6,500 ft). Cross the pass and descend Fisher Creek Trail's steep switchbacks for 2.1 miles to Fisher Camp and good camping (5,200 ft).

Route: From Fisher Camp, descend west on the Fisher Creek Trail to approximately 5,000 feet. Leave the trail and ascend easy terrain northwesterly to reach a flat basin northeast of a knob (approx. 6,600 ft). Ascend slopes west-northwesterly to gain the crest of a south-trending rock rib above the obvious buttress of Point 7430. This rock rib originates at Katsuk Peak's east summit. Scramble northerly along the rib, staying on or left (west) of the crest, until approximately 300 feet below Katsuk's east summit (8,200 ft). Leave the rock rib and contour easterly across exposed terrain to reach the Mesahchie-Katsuk col at the base of Mesahchie's west ridge (8,200 ft). Cross the col and contour northerly for less than 50 yards. From this point, a large couloir can be seen above that weaves its way up Mesahchie's west ridge. Choosing your route carefully, climb up to enter the couloir and ascend it to the summit ridge. Scramble a short distance easterly along the exposed crest to the summit (8,795 ft).

Descent: Descend the route.

7 Katsuk Peak

8,680 ft; 36th highest

Katsuk Peak's name means "center" in Chinook Jargon (Phillips 1912; Shaw 1909), stemming, undoubtedly, from its central location on Ragged Ridge. Its steep northern flank is clad by the mile-wide Katsuk Glacier, while its southern flank features extensive talus and scree.

EAST RIDGE

This route ascends the same rocky rib crest as the route for Mesahchie Peak before finishing with a lofty rising traverse to the summit.

APPROACH

Time to camp	3–4 hours
Mileage	6 miles
Elevation change	+2,800 ft; -1,300 ft
GT 15-minute	Mount Logan (No. 49)
Contact	North Cascades NP, Marblemount Ranger Station

ROUTE

Difficulty	▲▲ Grade II; class 3–4 rock
Time to summit	4–5 hours
Elevation change	+3,700 ft; -200 ft
USGS 7.5-minute	Mount Arriva, Mount Logan
Season	June–September

Approach: Follow the approach for Mesahchie Peak to Fisher Camp and good camping (5,200 ft).

Route: From Fisher Camp, descend west on the Fisher Creek Trail to approximately 5,000 feet. Leave the trail and ascend easy terrain northwesterly to reach a flat basin northeast of a knob (approx. 6,600 ft). Ascend slopes west-northwesterly to gain the crest of a south-trending rock rib above the obvious buttress of Point 7430. This rock rib originates at Katsuk Peak's east summit. Scramble northerly along the rib, staying on or left (west) of the crest, until approximately 300 feet below the east summit (8,200 ft). Leave the rib and make an airy rising traverse west-northwesterly, crossing multiple rock ribs, to gain the upper east ridge. Scramble westerly along the ridge, bypassing small gendarmes, to the summit (8,680 ft).

Descent: Descend the route.

8 Kimtah Peak

8,600 ft; 43rd highest

Kimtah Peak's name means "behind or after" in Chinook Jargon (Phillips 1912; Shaw 1909), most likely referring to its position relative to other summits along Ragged Ridge. Its northeast ridge divides the Katsuk and Kimtah glaciers, while on its southern flank one finds numerous alternating minor rock ribs and gullies.

WEST ROUTE

This is primarily a moderate scramble up the rocky and desolate south slopes, apart from a short section of challenging scrambling over a ridge separating the upper drainages.

APPROACH

Time to camp	5 hours
Mileage	10 miles
Elevation change	+2,800 ft; -2,700 ft
GT 15-minute	Mount Logan (No. 49)
Contact	North Cascades NP, Marblemount Ranger Station

ROUTE

Difficulty	▲ Grade I+; class 4 rock
Time to summit	6 hours
Elevation change	+4,800 ft; -0 ft
USGS 7.5-minute	Mount Logan
Season	June–September

Approach: Follow the approach for Mesahchie Peak to Fisher Camp. Continue west on the trail along Fisher Creek and beneath Ragged Ridge to Cosho Camp and good camping (3,800 ft), 9.7 miles from the trailhead.

Route: From Cosho Camp, follow the Fisher Creek Trail west to where it crosses Fisher Creek on a log bridge. Continue on the trail approximately a quarter mile (450 yards) farther west from the crossing. From here, to the north can be seen the summits of Cosho Peak (left) and Kimtah Peak (right), as well as the route up the central gully. Leave the trail and cross to the north side of Fisher Creek on a fallen tree. Bushwhack northerly through unpleasant vine maple and slide alder to reach a stream flowing south from the central gully. Stay either left or right of the stream along the edge of the forest to avoid the worst of the brush. Once the central gully has been reached, ascend it northerly, sometimes in the gully and sometimes on a rib crest on the left (west), to 7,000 feet. Climb out of the gully on the right (east) and scramble over a south-trending ridge (class 4) that originates at Thieves Peak, a prominent 8,120-foot subpeak midway between Kimtah and Cosho peaks. Ascend northerly to a notch just right (east) of Thieves Peak (approx. 7,800 ft). Contour across the southern slopes staying below the ridge crest, then make a gradual rising traverse on a course that stays well below Kimtah's false (west) summit. Once past the false summit, ascend an easy scree/talus slope to the true (east) summit (8,600 ft). To avoid more difficult terrain, resist the temptation to gain elevation too quickly during the traverse.

Descent: Descend the route.

9 Cosho Peak

8,332 ft; 90th highest

Cosho Peak is the lowest and westernmost of the major summits on Ragged Ridge. Its name means "hog" or "pig" in Chinook Jargon (Phillips 1912; Shaw 1909), but it's not that ugly, really. The northern flank of the mountain forms the western boundary of the Kimtah Glacier and the southern slopes are predominantly scree and talus.

EAST RIDGE

Like its neighbors, this route is primarily about talus and scree. Watch your step and keep an eye out for rockfall.

APPROACH

Time to camp	5 hours
Mileage	10 miles
Elevation change	+2,800 ft; -2,700 ft
GT 15-minute	Mount Logan (No. 49)
Contact	North Cascades NP, Marblemount Ranger Station

ROUTE

Difficulty	▲ Grade I+; class 3 rock
Time to summit	5–6 hours
Elevation change	+4,600 ft; -0 ft
USGS 7.5-minute	Mount Logan
Season	June–September

Approach: Follow the approach for Mesahchie Peak to Fisher Camp. Continue west on the trail along Fisher Creek and beneath Ragged Ridge to Cosho Camp and good camping (3,800 ft), 9.7 miles from the trailhead.

Route: From Cosho Camp, follow the Fisher Creek Trail west to where it crosses Fisher Creek on a log bridge. Continue on the trail approximately a quarter mile (450 yards) farther west from the crossing. From here, to the north can be seen the summits of Cosho Peak (left) and Kimtah Peak (right), as well as the route up the central gully. Leave the trail and cross to the north side of Fisher Creek on a fallen tree. Bushwhack northerly through unpleasant vine maple and slide alder to reach a stream flowing south from the central gully. Stay either left or right of the stream along the edge of the forest to avoid the worst of the brush. Once the central gully has been reached, ascend it northerly, sometimes in the gully and sometimes on a rib crest on the left (west). When the gully forks up high, take the left (west) branch and ascend it to a notch (approx. 7,900 ft) just left (west) of Thieves Peak, a prominent 8,120-foot subpeak midway between Cosho and Kimtah peaks. Turn left (west), and scramble loose rock and ledges (class 3) along Cosho's east ridge to the summit (8,332 ft).

Descent: Descend the route.

Icecap Slam

Peaks & routes	Eldorado Peak (East Ridge), Primus Peak (South Route), Klawatti Peak (South Route), Dorado Needle (Northwest Ridge), Austera Peak (South Route)
Max difficulty	▲▲▲ Grade III; steep snow; glacier travel; mid-fifth class rock
Duration	5 days
Roundtrip to camp	14 miles
Elevation gain	+12,900 ft
USGS 7.5-minute	Cascade Pass, Eldorado Peak, Forbidden Peak
GT 15-minute	Diablo Dam (No. 48), Cascade Pass (No. 80)
Trailhead	Eldorado Peak
Season	April–September

Comprised of the Eldorado, Inspiration, McAllister, Klawatti, and North Klawatti glaciers, the Eldorado Icecap is a tremendous volume of ice and a textbook lesson in glaciology. Undertaking this adventurous Slam gets you up close and personal with this starkly beautiful environment. You'll live on the glaciers for 5 days and traverse the full length of the icecap, summiting all of its major peaks along the way. This Slam is a must for anyone who wants to experience the best of the Cascades. Don't miss it!

ITINERARY

Day	Elevation change	Instructions
1	+5,700 ft; -300 ft	Follow the approach for Eldorado Peak to the Eldorado Glacier and camp (7,500 ft).
2	+2,100 ft; -1,800 ft	Break camp and climb Eldorado Peak, leaving your packs at the base of the east ridge. Join Klawatti Peak's approach to Klawatti Col and camp (7,800 ft). Climb Klawatti Peak and return to camp.
3	+1,500 ft; -1,500 ft	Climb Dorado Needle and return to camp.
4	+3,500 ft; -3,500 ft	Get an early start, climb Austera and Primus peaks and return to camp (this is a full day).
5	+300 ft; -6,000 ft	Hike out.

Eldorado Icecap from the east (Klawatti Peak) Photo by Brian Bongiovanni

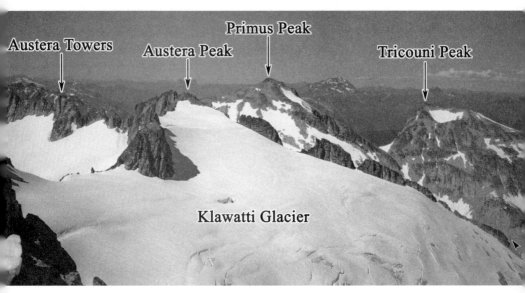

Eldorado Icecap from the south (Klawatti Peak) Photo by Brian Bongiovanni

10 Eldorado Peak

8,868 ft; 25th highest

Eldorado Peak may be, for climbers at least, the fabled lost city of gold. As the gateway to the stupendous Eldorado Icecap, the mountain's eastern flank harbors the 3-mile wide Inspiration Glacier. On the west, the summit rises more than 6,000 feet in less than 2 miles from the Marble Creek drainage. The long, radiating ridges of this gigantic peak stretch north to Tepeh Towers, southwest to The Triad, and east, disappearing beneath Inspiration Glacier.

EAST RIDGE

This route is one of the most popular climbs in the Cascade Pass area and rightly so. Get the lung-busting, thigh-burning approach behind you and you'll be treated to a well-deserved, scenic base camp and an enjoyable climb. The highlight of the ascent is the exhilarating finish on the classic knife-edge snow arête.

APPROACH

Time to camp	6–8 hours
Mileage	5 miles
Elevation change	+5,700 ft; -300 ft
GT 15-minute	Diablo Dam (No. 48), Cascade Pass (No. 80)
Contact	North Cascades NP, Marblemount Ranger Station

ROUTE

Difficulty	▲▲ Grade II; 35-degree snow; glacier travel
Time to summit	2–3 hours
Elevation change	+1,400 ft; -0 ft
USGS 7.5-minute	Cascade Pass, Eldorado Peak, Forbidden Peak
Season	April–September

Eldorado Peak from the northeast (Klawatti Peak) Photo by Lowell Skoog

Approach: Permits are required for overnight outings in the park and can be obtained a maximum of 24 hours in advance. Obtain your permit from the Marblemount Ranger Station, signposted on the west side of town. A Northwest Forest Pass is required to park at the trailhead.

From Interstate 5 north of Mount Vernon, take exit 230 (Anacortes/Burlington). Drive 46 miles east on Highway 20 (North Cascades Highway) to Marblemount. Continue a short distance east on Highway 20 to a fork in the road and take the right fork over a bridge onto Cascade River Road. Drive 19 miles on the narrow road to a large parking area on the right side of the road (approx. 2,200 ft).

From the parking area, follow a climber's path that leads down to the Cascade River and scout for a suitable place to cross. This crossing can be dangerous when the water level is high. Once across, scout again to find the path. It's best to spend the extra time locating the path near the river to avoid an unnecessary bushwhack in the steep woods. Follow the path upstream along the river and then north along the left (west) side of Eldorado Creek as it climbs steeply through forest. Continue up the path, crossing a talus field, to the base of a second talus field. Follow the path up and right (east) across the talus to reach a stream at the base of small waterfalls (approx. 5,000 ft). Continue a short distance to a large cairn, cross to the right (east) side of the stream and proceed up switchbacks to an open basin and potential camping (approx. 5,500 ft).

Ascend switchbacks to the ridge crest (approx. 6,100 ft) on the left (west). About 200 yards beyond, locate and descend a gully with a large boulder at its head (class 3) left (west) into the Roush Creek drainage. Bear right (north) over talus, then ascend slabs, moraine and easy snowslopes to a large, flat area on the Eldorado Glacier and good camping (7,500 ft).

Route: From the large, flat area (7,500 ft), continue 1 mile across the gentle glacier to the base of Eldorado Peak's east ridge. Starting on the right (north) side of the ridge, climb the ridge westerly to the narrow (2-foot-wide) exposed snow arête and follow it to the summit (8,868 ft).

Descent: Descend the route.

11 Primus Peak

8,508 ft; 54th highest

Primus Peak is a moderate, glaciated summit situated in a spectacular alpine environment at the northern end of the Eldorado Icecap. On the mountain's southern flank is the North Klawatti Glacier and on the northern flank is the Borealis Glacier, bounded on the east by Tricouni Peak.

SOUTH ROUTE

This is a moderate climb, the crux of which is the long approach traversing the Eldorado Icecap. It's beautiful country though, so take your time and enjoy it. Not many folks make it out this far, so you'll probably have it all to yourself.

APPROACH

Time to camp	7–9 hours
Mileage	7 miles
Elevation change	+6,000 ft; -300 ft
GT 15-minute	Diablo Dam (No. 48), Cascade Pass (No. 80)
Contact	North Cascades NP, Marblemount Ranger Station

Primus Peak from the south in spring Photo by Paul Klenke

ROUTE

Difficulty   ▲▲ Grade II; moderate snow; glacier travel; class 2 rock
Time to summit 4 hours
Elevation change +1,900 ft; -1,100 ft
USGS 7.5-minute Cascade Pass, Forbidden Peak
Season   April–September

Approach: Follow the approach for Eldorado Peak to the flat area on the Eldorado Glacier (7,500 ft). Continue 1 mile across the gentle glacier to the base of Eldorado's east ridge. Contour northerly, then northeasterly at 7,800 feet, weaving around crevasses, along the base of the south side of Tepeh Towers to Klawatti Col and good camping (approx. 7,800 ft).

Route: From Klawatti Col, traverse the McAllister Glacier north-north-easterly, along the base of the western flank of Klawatti Peak, to a small notch at the base of Klawatti's north ridge (7,900 ft). Cross the notch and descend to the Klawatti Glacier using a short rappel if necessary (consider leaving a fixed rope to simplify the return journey). Contour the glacier north-north-easterly at 7,800 feet until able to descend east-northeasterly along the south side of Austera Peak's east ridge. Continue descending until past the last of the ridgetop crags (approx. 6,800 ft), then cross the ridge to gain the North Klawatti Glacier. Ascend the glacier westerly to 7,200 feet, then contour northerly across the glacier to reach the broad south slopes of Primus Peak. Ascend northerly up the moderate slopes to the summit (8,508 ft).

Descent: Descend the route.

12 Klawatti Peak

8,485 ft; 57th highest

Klawatti Peak is surrounded by the Inspiration, McAllister, and Klawatti glaciers. The mountain has been carved by the crushing forces of these glaciers into a spectacular chunk of rock. Perhaps its most unique feature is The Smokestack, an obvious tower on the north ridge that bears an uncanny resemblance to its namesake.

SOUTH ROUTE

This is an exciting climb in the black-and-white world of rock, snow, and ice. Start with a fantastic journey into the heart of the Eldorado Icecap, then finish with steep snow or rock guaranteed to get your heart pumping, especially on the descent.

Klawatti Peak from the southwest in winter Photo by Sam Avaiusini

APPROACH

Time to camp	6–8 hours
Mileage	5 miles
Elevation change	+5,700 ft; -300 ft
GT 15-minute	Diablo Dam (No. 48), Cascade Pass (No. 80)
Contact	North Cascades NP, Marblemount Ranger Station

ROUTE

Difficulty	▲▲ Grade II; steep snow; glacier travel; class 3–4 rock.
Time to summit	3–4 hours
Elevation change	+1,000 ft; -0 ft
USGS 7.5-minute	Cascade Pass, Forbidden Peak
Season	April–September

Approach: Follow the approach for Eldorado Peak to the flat area on the Eldorado Glacier and good camping (7,500 ft).

Route: From the large, flat area (7,500 ft), continue 1 mile across the gentle glacier to the base of Eldorado's east ridge. Contour northerly, then northeasterly at 7,800 feet, weaving around crevasses, along the base of the south side of Tepeh Towers to Klawatti Col and good camping (approx. 7,800 ft).

From Klawatti Col, traverse easterly to the base of a steep snowfield on Klawatti's south-southeast face. Ascend the steep snow (45–50 degrees) to its end and scramble easy rock northerly for a few hundred feet to the summit (8,485 ft). In late season there are potential moat problems halfway up the snowfield. The moat can be bypassed on the right by ascending a broad, gray gully (class 3–4) to the summit.

Descent: Descend the route.

13 Dorado Needle

8,440 ft; 64th highest

Dorado Needle is a rugged, pyramidal peak located on the brink of the Marble Creek cirque and the head of the huge McAllister Glacier. The impressive southwest rock face and ridge rise nearly 1,000 feet above a series of small western glacier remnants.

NORTHWEST RIDGE

This route features enjoyable rock climbing on good quality rock in a superb alpine setting. Just getting onto the rock can be the crux of the route, as a moat/bergschrund is often very difficult to cross after early August.

APPROACH

Time to camp	6–8 hours
Mileage	5 miles
Elevation change	+5,700 ft; -300 ft
GT 15-minute	Diablo Dam (No. 48), Cascade Pass (No. 80)
Contact	North Cascades NP, Marblemount Ranger Station

Dorado Needle from the north in spring Photo by Lowell Skoog

ROUTE

Difficulty   ▲▲▲ Grade III; moderate snow; glacier travel; mid-fifth class rock
Time to summit 4–6 hours
Elevation change +1,600 ft; -600 ft
USGS 7.5-minute Cascade Pass, Eldorado Peak, Forbidden Peak
Season   April–September

Approach: Follow the approach for Eldorado Peak to the flat area on the Eldorado Glacier and good camping (7,500 ft).

Route: From the large, flat area (7,500 ft), continue 1 mile across the gentle glacier to the base of Eldorado's east ridge. Bear 1 mile northerly toward Dean's Spire to a pass leading to the McAllister Glacier (8,200 ft). Cross the pass and traverse left (west), then descend to a flat area on the glacier (7,600 ft). Ascend the glacier northwesterly to its terminus at a notch beneath several gendarmes high on Dorado Needle's northwest ridge. In late season, a moat/bergschrund that forms halfway up the final snowslope can be difficult to cross. From the notch, cross another moat to gain the rock, then climb a short pitch (low-fifth class) to the crest of the northwest ridge. Finish with two more rock pitches (mid-fifth class) along the ridge crest, including a section of exposed *au cheval,* to the summit (8,440 ft).

Descent: Downclimb the ridge until able to rappel back to the glacier, then retrace the remainder of the route.

14 Austera Peak

8,334 ft; 88th highest

Austera Peak is the highpoint of Austera Towers, also known as Austera Ridge. The rock of the towers has been carved by the immense combined forces of the McAllister, Klawatti, and North Klawatti glaciers into a narrow crest of serrated arêtes, particularly impressive northwest of the summit.

SOUTH ROUTE

This is primarily a glacier climb except for a final short but exposed rock scramble to the summit.

APPROACH

Time to camp	7–9 hours
Mileage	7 miles
Elevation change	+6,000 ft; -300 ft
GT 15-minute	Diablo Dam (No. 48), Cascade Pass (No. 80)
Contact	North Cascades NP, Marblemount Ranger Station

ROUTE

Difficulty	▲▲ Grade II; moderate snow; glacier travel; class 4 rock
Time to summit	2–3 hours
Elevation change	+700 ft; -100 ft
USGS 7.5-minute	Cascade Pass, Forbidden Peak
Season	April–September

Approach: Follow the approach for Eldorado Peak to the flat area on the Eldorado Glacier (7,500 ft). Continue 1 mile across the gentle glacier to the base of Eldorado's east ridge. Contour northerly, then northeasterly at 7,800 feet, weaving around crevasses, along the base of the south side of Tepeh Towers to Klawatti Col and good camping (approx. 7,800 ft).

Route: From Klawatti Col, traverse the McAllister Glacier north-northeasterly, along the base of the western flank of Klawatti Peak, to a small notch at the base of Klawatti's north ridge (7,900 ft). Cross the notch and descend to the Klawatti Glacier using a short rappel if necessary (consider leaving a fixed rope to simplify the return journey). Contour the glacier north-northeasterly at 7,800 feet until able to make a rising traverse northerly to the head of the glacier. Make a short traverse northwesterly across the false summit crest to a small notch separating it from the true summit. Scramble down into the notch, dropping to the southwest side of the crest, to

Austera Peak summit chimney from the south in spring Photo by Paul Klenke

the base of a narrow, 50-foot chimney with a chockstone halfway up. Climb the chimney (class 4), then scramble a short stretch of exposed rock to the summit (8,334 ft).

Descent: Descend the route.

● Sahale Slam

Peaks & routes	Mount Buckner (Southwest Route), Boston Peak (Southeast Face)
Max difficulty	▲▲ Grade II; steep snow; glacier travel; class 4 rock
Duration	3 days
Roundtrip to camp	12 miles
Elevation gain	+9,900 ft
USGS 7.5-minute	Cascade Pass, Goode Mountain
GT 15-minute	Cascade Pass (No. 80)
Trailhead	Cascade Pass
Season	June–October

This Slam takes you to some of the most impressive scenery in the North Cascades. You'll see jagged Ripsaw Ridge, the Boston Glacier (the largest in the region), graceful Forbidden Peak, and Sharkfin Tower, to name a few highlights. The approach hike up Sahale Arm is nothing short of spectacular, passing through a veritable alpine garden with stunning views in all directions. And the high camp! It's one of the best, with a "loo with a view" that's hard to beat.

ITINERARY

Day	Elevation change	Instructions
1	+ 4,000 ft; -0 ft	Follow the primary approach for Mount Buckner to Sahale Glacier Camp and camp (7,600 ft).
2	+ 4,000 ft; -4,000 ft	Climb Mount Buckner and return to camp.
3	+ 2,000 ft; -6,000 ft	Climb Boston Peak and hike out.

15 Mount Buckner

9,112 ft; 11th highest

Mount Buckner is the highest summit in the Cascade Pass area and is perhaps the most accessible of the ten nonvolcanic peaks over 9,000 feet. The massive Boston Glacier lies on Buckner's northern flank, and the jagged Ripsaw Ridge adjoins Buckner's west ridge. The east summit has been triangulated at 9,112 feet. The west summit, although not triangulated, is essentially of equal height.

SOUTHWEST ROUTE

The crux of this ascent is likely just reaching upper Horseshoe Basin, no matter which way you choose to go about it. Once there, you'll be treated to great

Mount Buckner from the southwest (Pelton Peak); the west and east summits are close together and are labeled simply "Summit" Photo by Lowell Skoog

views of the entire basin and spectacular Ripsaw Ridge. This route is primarily snow/talus, finishing with a short rock scramble to the summit.

APPROACH

	Primary	Alternate
Time to camp	4 hours	5 hours
Mileage	6 miles	9 miles
Elevation change	+4,000 ft; -0 ft	+3,000 ft; -1,800 ft
GT 15-minute	Cascade Pass (No. 80)	Cascade Pass (No. 80)
Contact	North Cascades NP, Marblemount Ranger Station	North Cascades NP, Marblemount Ranger Station

ROUTE

Difficulty	▲▲ Grade II; steep snow; glacier travel; class 4 rock
Time to summit	4 hours (primary approach); 5–6 hours (alternate approach)
Elevation change	+2,800 ft, -1,200 ft (primary approach); +4,400 ft, -0 ft (alternate approach)
USGS 7.5-minute	Cascade Pass, Goode Mountain
Season	May–October

Primary Approach: Permits are required for overnight outings in the park and can be obtained a maximum of 24 hours in advance. Obtain your permit from the Marblemount Ranger Station, signposted on the west side of town. A Northwest Forest Pass is required to park at the trailhead.

After snow cover on the steep, glacier-polished slabs beneath the terminus of the Sahale Glacier has melted, this approach becomes more dangerous (August–September).

From Interstate 5 north of Mount Vernon, take exit 230 (Anacortes/Burlington). Drive 46 miles east on Highway 20 (North Cascades Highway) to Marblemount. Continue a short distance east on Highway 20 to a fork in the road and take the right fork over a bridge onto Cascade River Road. Drive 22.3 miles on the narrow road to its end at a large parking area and the trailhead for the Cascade Pass Trail (3,600 ft).

Follow the trail for 3.7 miles as it climbs to Cascade Pass (5,400 ft). Pick up the trail up Sahale Arm approximately 100 yards east of the pass and climb steeply along the broad mountain ridge. At 7,000 feet, the grade steepens and the trail switchbacks up scree and talus to Sahale Glacier Camp (7,600 ft), 2.2 miles from Cascade Pass. There's good camping here and composting toilets are provided.

Alternate Approach: Follow the primary approach to Cascade Pass (5,400 ft). Cross the pass and follow the trail east for 3.7 miles into the upper Stehekin River valley to the junction with the Horseshoe Basin Trail (3,600 ft). Turn left onto the Horseshoe Basin Trail and hike 1.5 miles to its end at cliffs below the upper basin at the Black Warrior Mine and good camping (approx. 4,800 ft).

Route: If coming via the primary approach, from Sahale Glacier Camp make a gradual descending traverse easterly to the lower end of Sahale Glacier (7,200 ft). Make a descending traverse across the glacier to reach a rock rib descending from Sahale Peak. Downclimb the rib (loose class 4) and/or steep snowslopes approximately 600 feet into Horseshoe Basin, watching out for icefall and rockfall, until able to round the cliffs at the base of the rib. Traverse easterly across the basin on a system of broad ledges at approximately 6,400 feet to gain Mount Buckner's southwest slopes.

If coming via the alternate approach, locate an abandoned mining trail on the right (east) side of Basin Creek. Follow the old trail as it ascends rightward (east) to reach the route of the old mining cableway. Ascend the route of the cableway (class 4), through cliff bands and steep brush, to reach the upper basin. Bear northeasterly to gain Mount Buckner's southwest slopes.

Ascend talus/snow and a steep snow gully northeasterly up Mount Buckner's southwest slopes to just below the summit. Scramble rock (class 3) to the west summit (9,112 ft).

Descent: Descend the route.

16 Boston Peak

8,894 ft; 23rd highest

Boston Peak straddles the scenic divide between Boston Basin and the Quien Sabe Glacier on the west and the Boston Glacier on the east and north. The fantastic views from the summit take in all the peaks of the Cascade Pass area and surpass even those from nearby Sahale Peak.

SOUTHEAST FACE

Boston Peak has a deserved, even somewhat notorious, reputation for loose rock. Let's just say that Boston doesn't see a lot of repeat ascents, so take your time and enjoy the views from the summit just that little bit more. Our best bit of advice is to definitely bring a rope for the rappel back to the Boston Glacier. No sane person would want to downclimb this route.

APPROACH

Time to camp	4 hours
Mileage	6 miles
Elevation change	+4,000 ft; -0 ft
GT 15-minute	Cascade Pass (No. 80)
Contact	North Cascades NP, Marblemount Ranger Station

ROUTE

Difficulty	▲▲ Grade II; moderate snow; glacier travel; class 4 rock
Time to summit	3–4 hours
Elevation change	+1,700 ft; -400 ft
USGS 7.5-minute	Cascade Pass
Season	June–October

Approach: Follow the primary approach for Mount Buckner to Sahale Glacier Camp and good camping (7,600 ft).

Route: From Sahale Glacier Camp, ascend the glacier to the rocky south ridge of Sahale Peak (8,400 ft). Scramble (class 2) up the ridge for approximately 100 yards until you are able to traverse right (northerly) onto loose, slabby rock directly above a gully that drops steeply away. Scramble up (exposed class 3) to a notch (approx. 8,600 ft) about 50 feet below the summit of Sahale Peak between the main summit crag on the left and a smaller outcrop on the right. Cross the notch and descend to the Boston-Sahale col (8,500 ft). Be prepared for moderate snowslopes along the way.

From the col the traverse to Boston Peak is very loose and exposed. Follow the path of least resistance northerly along the exposed ridge (class 3) toward

Boston Peak from the south (Sahale Peak) Photo by Brian Bongiovanni

Boston Peak. When possible, descend to the edge of the Boston Glacier and the southeast corner of Boston's south face.

Scramble up a short distance to reach a major ledge and traverse it northeasterly to near its end. Ascend the rubbly face (class 4) working up and occasionally right for 250 feet to the summit ridge. Scramble the exposed crest southerly to the summit (8,894 ft). The rock is very loose so choose your handholds and footholds carefully.

Descent: Do three single-rope rappels (after carefully inspecting/backing up the existing anchors) down the south face and back to the Boston Glacier. Retrace the remainder of the route.

Thunder Slam

Peaks & routes	Mount Goode (Southwest Couloir–Southeast Ridge), Mount Logan (Fremont Glacier), Storm King Mountain (South Route)
Max difficulty	▲▲ Grade II+; glacier travel; low-fifth class rock
Duration	5 days
Roundtrip to camp	13 miles
Elevation gain	+13,600 ft
USGS 7.5-minute	Goode Mountain, Mount Logan
GT 15-minute	McGregor Mountain (No. 81)
Trailhead	Park Creek Trail
Season	June–September

This Slam combines three fantastic peaks that lie in the remote heart of the park. Mounts Goode and Logan are members of the exclusive club of ten nonvolcanic peaks over 9,000 feet in elevation. The nearby Thunder Creek valley is blessed with one of the last stands of old-growth forest in the Cascades. It's an involved, time-consuming approach to make it in here, but it's definitely worth the effort. The views from the summit of Mount Logan are among the best in the entire range, encompassing many of the high points of the park. Make the effort. You won't regret it.

ITINERARY

Day	Elevation change	Instructions
1	+1,700 ft; -0 ft	Follow the approach to Fivemile Camp and camp (4,000 ft).
2	+4,600 ft; -1,200 ft	Follow the route for Mount Goode to the flat area at 7,400 feet and bivi (7,400 ft). Climb Storm King Mountain and return to camp.
3	+1,800 ft; -5,200 ft	Climb Mount Goode and descend back to Fivemile Camp and camp (4,000 ft).
4	+5,600 ft; -5,600 ft	Climb Mount Logan and return to camp.
5	+0 ft; -1,700 ft	Hike out.

Notes: For day 5, remember to arrive back at the trailhead in time to catch the shuttles back to Stehekin and, subsequently, the ferry back down the lake.

17 Mount Goode

9,200 ft; 9th highest

Mount Goode's remarkable northeast face rises more than a vertical mile above the North Fork Bridge Creek valley in less than 2 miles. The lower portion of the face is clad by the Goode Glacier.

SOUTHWEST COULOIR–SOUTHEAST RIDGE

Like exposure? Then this route is for you. There's plenty in the southwest couloir and, if that's not enough, the traverse above the east face will put some serious air beneath your derrière. Watch for loose rock in the couloir and definitely don't climb beneath another party.

APPROACH

Time to camp	3 hours
Mileage	5 miles
Elevation change	+1,700 ft; -0 ft
GT 15-minute	McGregor Mountain (No. 81)
Contact	North Cascades NP, Golden West Visitor Center

ROUTE

Difficulty	▲▲ Grade II +; much class 3–4 rock and some low-fifth class rock
Time to summit	5–7 hours
Elevation change	+5,200 ft; -0 ft
USGS 7.5-minute	Goode Mountain
Season	June–September

Approach: Permits are required for overnight outings in the park and can be obtained a maximum of 24 hours in advance. Obtain your permit from the Golden West Visitor Center in Stehekin.

This approach requires use of commercial transportation to reach Stehekin at the northern tip of Lake Chelan. The *Lady of the Lake* ferry (or a high-speed catamaran run by the same company) departs from Fields Point Landing on the west shore or from the town of Chelan at the lake's southern tip. Contact the Lake Chelan Boat Company in Chelan for the current boat schedule (see Appendix E for all company contact information). Or, if you've got less time and a lot more money, a floatplane to Chelan or Stehekin might be an option worth considering. In the Seattle area, try Kenmore Air or Seattle Seaplanes, and in Chelan, contact Chelan Airways. From Stehekin, there's a shuttle bus to High Bridge ($6 per person one-way; bring exact change) that

Mount Goode from the southwest Photo by Paul McClellan

connects with a shuttle van (schedules synchronized) to the trailhead for the Park Creek Trail (another $6 per person one-way; bring exact change). Contact the Golden West Visitor Center for the current shuttle schedule. Make sure you synchronize your transport options so that you don't get stuck in Stehekin overnight.

If catching the ferry at Fields Point Landing, drive US 2 east to Alternate US 97 at Wenatchee. Continue north on Alternate US 97 to the town of Entiat. Drive another 9 miles on Alternate US 97, turn left (north) onto Highway 971 (Navarre Coulee Road) and continue to Lake Chelan State Park. Bear left (north) onto South Lakeshore Road and drive 8 miles to Fields Point Landing. If catching the ferry at Chelan, drive US 2 east to Alternate US 97 at Wenatchee. Continue on Alternate US 97 to Chelan at the southern tip of the lake. From either landing, take the *Lady of the Lake* ferry to Stehekin on the northern tip of the lake, then the shuttle bus and van to the trailhead for the Park Creek Trail (2,300 ft). (The road was severely damaged in the October 2003 floods and repairs may take some time; call ahead.)

From the trailhead, follow the Park Creek Trail up the valley for 5 miles to Fivemile Camp and good camping (4,000 ft).

Route: From Fivemile Camp, backtrack and descend the trail approximately 1 mile southeasterly to a cairn marking the start of the climber's path up Mount Goode's southwest slopes. (If you leave the woods and enter a large open area, you've gone too far. The path starts in the woods just west of the open area.) Leave the trail and follow the initially faint path as it ascends northeasterly through forest. The path becomes quite pronounced on or near the ridge crest at approximately 4,500 feet. Continue following the path (good bivi sites at 6,400 ft) as it leaves the forest and ascends scree/snow to a flat area at the base of Goode and good bivi sites (7,400 ft).

Ascend into a small basin and up moraine slopes to the edge of a snow/talus field in a small cirque beneath Goode's southwest face (approx. 7,700 ft). Ascend the snow/talus field easterly along the base of the southwest face until able to locate and traverse an easy ledge leading leftward to the base of the southwest couloir (approx. 8,200 ft). Climb the southwest couloir (class 3–4), following black rock on the left to avoid rockfall, to the base of a narrow chimney (approx. 8,800 ft). Bypass the chimney by climbing a white slab (low-fifth class) until able to traverse right on a ledge (class 4) past rappel slings around a large block. Scramble a loose gully/ramp up and left for approximately 100 feet, past more rappel slings, to a notch in the sharp ridge crest (upper southeast ridge) near the Black Tooth. This is Black Tooth Notch. Take careful note of the location of all rappel slings on the way up. Cross the notch and traverse a very exposed dirt ledge high above the east face. At the end of the ledge, climb exposed rock (class 4) toward the ridge crest. Scramble upward on the upper crest of the northeast buttress for one rope length to the base of a tower with an alcove at its center. Traverse right at the base of the alcove, then bear up and left over gradually easier terrain to the summit (9,200 ft).

Descent: Rappel and/or downclimb the route back to the Black Tooth Notch. Scramble down the loose gully approximately 20 feet to rappel slings and rappel (single rope) to reach the large block with rappel slings. Rappel (single rope) into the southwest couloir and descend the remainder of the route.

18 Mount Logan

9,087 ft; 13th highest

Mount Logan is a heavily glaciated massif and one of the largest mountains in the North Cascades. The peak's northern flank harbors the Banded Glacier, the western flank the Fremont Glacier, and the eastern flank the Douglas Glacier. Logan's commanding central position provides an outstanding, seemingly endless panorama, taking in many of the high points of the North Cascades.

FREMONT GLACIER

It's a complex undertaking to get to this remote peak. However, the views from the summit are extraordinary and there's enjoyable climbing to be had. But don't take our word for it, go and see for yourself. We're sure you won't regret it.

APPROACH

Time to camp	3 hours
Mileage	5 miles
Elevation change	+1,700 ft; -0 ft
GT 15-minute	McGregor Mountain (No. 81)
Contact	North Cascades NP, Golden West Visitor Center

ROUTE

Difficulty	▲▲ Grade II; glacier travel; class 4 rock
Time to summit	5–7 hours
Elevation change	+5,400 ft; -300 ft
USGS 7.5-minute	Goode Mountain, Mount Logan
Season	June–September

Mount Logan from the southwest (Sahale Peak) Photo by Brian Bongiovanni

Approach: Follow the approach for Mount Goode to Fivemile Camp and good camping (4,000 ft).

Route: From Fivemile Camp, ascend the trail 2.2 miles to Park Creek Pass (6,040 ft). Cross the pass and descend the Thunder Creek Trail north for 0.4 mile to a rocky flat with a small stream (5,800 ft). Locate a climber's path that travels north-northeasterly in an ascending traverse through the alp and across a sandy gully. Ascend to 7,600 feet to cross a southwest-trending spur ridge and continue to the south edge of the Fremont Glacier (approx. 8,000 ft). Ascend northerly, bypassing a huge wind cirque/bowl in the glacier, to a high spot at 8,600 feet. Climb a rock gully approximately 200 feet to a notch in the ridge above (class 3). Traverse ledge systems on the right (east) side of the south ridge, staying below the ridge crest, approximately 0.3 mile northerly (class 3–4), past a couple of notches, to the summit (9,087 ft).

Descent: Descend the route.

19 Storm King Mountain

8,520 ft; 50th highest

Storm King Mountain is a wonderfully named peak sandwiched between, and overshadowed by, its more famous and loftier neighbors, Mounts Logan and Goode. On Storm King's western flank is the Wyeth Glacier. Like Mount Goode, the northeast aspect drops precipitously into the North Fork Bridge Creek valley. Stand atop Storm King and fantasize, if just for a moment, that you're in charge of the fickle Cascade weather. Trust us, you'll feel better for it, especially the next time you're drenched to the skin by the perpetual drizzle. And if that isn't enough, the views of Mount Goode from the summit will knock your socks off. The true summit is the easternmost tower of the east peak, despite the USGS quad showing the summit as the 8,515-foot west peak.

SOUTH ROUTE

This is a challenging route with exposed scrambling, many loose sections, and a short stretch of exposed crack climbing just below the summit. To avoid plentiful scree and talus, consider an early summer ascent.

APPROACH

Time to camp	3 hours
Mileage	5 miles
Elevation change	+1,700 ft; -0 ft
GT 15-minute	McGregor Mountain (No. 81)
Contact	North Cascades NP, Golden West Visitor Center

ROUTE

Difficulty	▲▲ Grade II; moderate snow; mostly class 4 rock with some low-fifth class
Time to summit	5 hours
Elevation change	+4,600 ft; -0 ft
USGS 7.5-minute	Goode Mountain
Season	June–September

Storm King Mountain from the south in spring Photo by Lowell Skoog

Approach: Follow the approach for Mount Goode to Fivemile Camp and good camping (4,000 ft).

Route: From Fivemile Camp, backtrack and descend the trail approximately 1 mile southeasterly to a cairn marking the start of the climber's path up Mount Goode's southwest slopes. (If you leave the woods and enter a large open area, you've gone too far. The path starts in the woods just west of the open area.) Leave the trail and follow the initially faint path as it ascends northeasterly through forest. The path becomes quite pronounced on or near the ridge crest at approximately 4,500 feet. Continue following the path (good bivi sites at 6,400 ft) as it leaves the forest and ascends scree/snow to a flat area at the base of Goode and good bivi sites (7,400 ft).

Turn left (northwest) and contour at 7,400 ft across slopes and heather benches for about 1 mile to enter a snow/scree/talus basin below and south of Storm King Mountain. From here, one can see the west peak and the two prominent towers of the east peak, the easternmost of which is the true summit. Ascend snow/scree/talus slopes north-northeasterly until directly beneath a gully that leads to the notch between the east peak's towers (approx. 8,300 ft). Begin scrambling up the loose gully toward the notch, then follow Fred Beckey's directions (compass directions are given in capital letters):

When slabs with loose rock/debris are encountered, traverse right across a

ledge to the SW face. Ascend short face via loose class 3–4 rock. Be prepared to climb this section without being able to place protection due to the rotten rock. Continue on low-angle slabs to just below the summit block. Climb a 20-ft crack (class 4) to a notch just N of the summit, then scramble a short distance southward to touch the summit spire. (Beckey 2003, p. 340)

Descent: Make three single-rope rappels down the slabs, watching out for rockfall, and descend the remainder of the route.

● Free Agents

20 Mount Shuksan

9,131 ft; 10th highest

Mount Shuksan is one of the most rugged, challenging, and striking mountains in the Cascade Range, boasting no fewer than six large glaciers and four imposing faces. It's located east of Mount Baker on the west side of the park. This massive mountain complex exemplifies all that is amazing about climbing in Washington: huge active glaciers, gaping crevasses, challenging routefinding, physically demanding approaches, highly changeable weather, and often poor visibility.

SULPHIDE GLACIER

Climbing Mount Shuksan is a challenge by any route. Fortunately, the Sulphide Glacier provides a route to the summit that is only moderately technical. But remember: this is a serious mountain, so come prepared.

APPROACH

Time to camp	5 hours
Mileage	5 miles
Elevation change	+4,000 ft; -0 ft
GT 15-minute	Mount Shuksan (No. 14)
Contact	North Cascades NP, Headquarters

ROUTE

Difficulty	▲▲ Grade II +; moderate snow or ice; glacier travel; class 3–4 rock
Time to summit	4–5 hours
Elevation change	+2,700 ft; -0 ft
USGS 7.5-minute	Mount Shuksan
Season	May–September

Skier descending Sulphide Glacier Photo by Lowell Skoog

Approach: Permits are required for overnight outings in the park and can be obtained a maximum of 24 hours in advance. Obtain your permit from park headquarters in Sedro-Woolley. A Northwest Forest Pass is required to park at the trailhead.

From Interstate 5 north of Mount Vernon, take exit 230 (Anacortes/Burlington). Drive 28 miles east on Highway 20 (North Cascades Highway) to the junction with Baker Lake Road. Turn left onto Baker Lake Road and follow it for approximately 25 miles to Shannon Creek Campground at the junction with Shannon Creek Road (Forest Road 1152). Turn left onto Shannon Creek Road (Forest Road 1152) and drive 4.5 miles to the junction with Forest Road 1152-014. Turn right onto Forest Road 1152-014 and drive to the end of the road and the trailhead for the Shannon Ridge Trail (approx. 2,500 ft).

Hike the trail/road for approximately 2 miles to the base of an old clearcut where the road becomes a trail (3,200 ft). Follow the trail as it climbs steeply up through the clearcut, enters the forest and gains the ridge crest (4,600 ft). Continue on the trail along the open ridge to reach a col at timberline and good camping (5,400 ft). From the col, traverse northeasterly across steep snow/talus to reach gradual terrain below the toe of the Sulphide Glacier and more campsites (5,700 ft). Ascend to the glacier (approx. 6,000 ft) and continue to additional good camping on its west edge (6,500 ft).

Route: From the high campsites (6,500 ft), ascend the left (west) edge of the Sulphide Glacier, weaving around crevasses, to reach a flat area (7,600 ft). Continue along the left (west) side of the glacier and proceed past a notch at the head of the upper Curtis Glacier (labeled "The Hourglass" on the USGS quad). Climb the final snowslopes to the base of the summit pyramid. Scramble the central gully of the pyramid (class 3–4) to the summit (9,131 ft).

Descent: From the summit, downclimb (watch out for dangerous downsloping holds) and/or rappel back to the Sulphide Glacier. Descend the remainder of the route.

21 Forbidden Peak

8,815 ft; 27th highest

Forbidden Peak is arguably the most coveted ascent of the Cascade Pass area. Its heavily glaciated form and graceful, sweeping ridges are immediately recognizable from other nearby summits. The mountain's long north and east ridges cradle the western edge of the massive Boston Glacier, while on the northern flank is the Forbidden Glacier and on the southern flank is an unnamed glacier.

WEST RIDGE

This is a distinctly alpine climb on excellent rock and a great opportunity to follow in the footsteps of the pioneering Beckey brothers (see Beckey 2003, p. 322). This is a popular route that's often crowded in summer, so don't be surprised if you have company.

APPROACH

Time to camp	4 hours
Mileage	3 miles
Elevation change	+3,200 ft; -0 ft
GT 15-minute	Diablo Dam (No. 48), Cascade Pass (No. 80)
Contact	North Cascades NP, Marblemount Ranger Station

ROUTE

Difficulty	▲▲▲ Grade III; steep snow or ice; glacier travel; mid-fifth class rock
Time to summit	4–6 hours
Elevation change	+2,500 ft; -0 ft
USGS 7.5-minute	Cascade Pass, Forbidden Peak
Season	May–September

Forbidden Peak from the south-southeast (Sahale Peak) Photo by Brian Bongiovanni

Approach: Permits are required for overnight outings in the park and can be obtained a maximum of 24 hours in advance. Obtain your permit from the Marblemount Ranger Station, signposted on the west side of town. A Northwest Forest Pass is required to park at the trailhead.

From Interstate 5 north of Mount Vernon, take exit 230 (Anacortes/Burlington). Drive 46 miles east on Highway 20 (North Cascades Highway) to Marblemount. Continue a short distance east on Highway 20 to a fork in the road and take the right fork over a bridge onto Cascade River Road. Drive 21.7 miles on the narrow road to the trailhead at a small pullout area (3,200 ft). This pullout forms the beginning of an abandoned road.

Follow the abandoned road less than 1 mile past a mine site and pick up a trail that climbs steeply up open slopes. Continue on the trail through dense forest, traversing west across a hillside and crossing multiple streams (difficult in early season). Ascend switchbacks through the forest to Boston Basin and good camping (5,800 ft). Alternatively, follow a trail northerly up the moraine and traverse left (west) to higher campsites (6,400 ft). Both campsites have toilets.

Route: From Boston Basin, ascend a small glacier toward the base of the west ridge couloir. Ascend the 500-foot couloir (50-degree snow or ice) for as much as 400 feet until forced to exit leftward onto rock, then scramble (class 4) to a notch on the ridge crest. The length and quality of snow in the couloir will vary throughout the season and there's the possibility of a bergschrund about halfway up. Climb the exposed ridge easterly for 1,200 linear feet and 500 vertical feet on and sometimes left (north) of the crest. Just west of the summit, an imposing tower can be bypassed by traversing around its left (north) side to reach a small notch. From the notch, scramble (class 4) to the summit (8,815 ft). With the occasional pitch of mid-fifth class rock, running belays work well for this route.

Descent: Descend the route using a combination of rappels and downclimbing back to the head of the west ridge couloir. Downclimb or rappel (two ropes useful) the couloir and retrace the remainder of the route.

22 Snowfield Peak

8,347 ft; 86th highest

Snowfield Peak is a rocky, glaciated mountain located just south of Diablo Dam. Snowfield is an appropriate name for this summit that sits at the south end of the large Neve Glacier. The Neve, in turn, is only marginally separated from the Colonial Glacier to its north. All this ice is surrounded by Colonial Peak, Pyramid Peak, The Needle, and numerous other summits. It's Cascade alpine scenery at its best.

NEVE GLACIER

This ascent is guarded by a long, dry approach, so take along some extra water. The crossing of the Colonial and Neve glaciers will definitely leave you questioning whether most glaciers in the Cascades are truly receding.

APPROACH

Time to camp	5–6 hours
Mileage	6 miles
Elevation change	+5,000 ft; -0 ft
GT 15-minute	Diablo Dam (No. 48)
Contact	North Cascades NP, Marblemount Ranger Station

ROUTE

Difficulty	▲▲ Grade II; glacier travel; class 3–4 rock
Time to summit	4–5 hours
Elevation change	+2,500 ft; -200 ft
USGS 7.5-minute	Diablo Dam, Ross Dam
Season	May–September

Approach: Permits are required for overnight outings in the park and can be obtained a maximum of 24 hours in advance. Obtain your permit from the Marblemount Ranger Station, signposted on the west side of town. A Northwest Forest Pass is required to park at the trailhead.

From Interstate 5 north of Mount Vernon, take exit 230 (Anacortes/Burlington). Drive 46 miles east on Highway 20 (North Cascades Highway)

Snowfield Peak approach from the northeast Photo by Scott Stephenson

Snowfield Peak from the north (Colonial Peak) Photo by Eric Willhite

to Marblemount. Continue east on Highway 20 for another 21 miles to a pull-out on the left (north) side of the highway 1.5 miles east of the Gorge Lake Bridge. The trailhead for the Pyramid Lake Trail is on the opposite side of the highway just east of the creek (1,150 ft).

Follow the trail 2.1 miles to Pyramid Lake (2,640 ft). Despite the water's brackish appearance, top off your bottles here as it's usually the last until 5,900 feet. Follow a climber's path around the right side of the lake and up a steep climb to the ridge crest (approx. 4,500 ft). Continue along the ridge to a steep, alder-covered rock step. Negotiate the difficult step (class 3) via the brush-covered climber's path up its center. Proceed a short distance to another step and pass it on the right (4,700 ft). Continue ascending along the ridge crest to possible campsites at approximately 5,400 feet (no running water; use snow patches). Ascend rocky slopes to the base of Pyramid Peak, then descend and traverse snow/talus (5,700 ft) to the toe of the Colonial Glacier. Traverse the right side of a meltwater lake at 5,900 feet (appears by midsummer) to good campsites in the Colonial Glacier basin (6,100 ft).

Route: From camp in the Colonial Glacier basin, hike up moraine slopes to the Colonial Glacier. Ascend the glacier southerly to a col (6,900 ft), then descend approximately 200 feet to the Neve Glacier. Make an ascending traverse southerly up the Neve Glacier to its upper left (southeast) edge (7,800 ft). Climb scree and talus to the base of a prominent gully bearing easterly toward the summit. Ascend the gully (class 3) to within 100 feet of its end, then climb/scramble over a rib on the left (north) to reach a sloping ramp and follow it to its end at a notch. Cross the notch and continue ascending through boulders for another 30–40 feet to a defined ledge leading right (south) to the base of another gully. Ascend the gully (class 3) to the summit (8,347 ft).

Descent: Descend the route.

23 Luna Peak

8,311 ft; 97th highest

Luna Peak is the highest mountain in the Picket Range, a wild and remote portion of the North Cascades that has to be seen to be believed. This is some of the most rugged and inaccessible mountain country anywhere, and the summit of Luna provides an incredible viewpoint from which to gaze out over all of this splendor. When you see the jagged "fence" of peaks that surround the McMillan and Luna Creek cirques, lined up one after another, you'll know how this range got its name.

SOUTHWEST RIDGE

All routes in the Pickets have difficult, even horrendous, approaches and Luna Peak is no exception. The approach is likely the crux of the trip. Trust us though, it'll all be worth it when you've seen the views from the summit—they're truly incredible.

APPROACH

Time to camp   1–2 days
Mileage   14 or 20 miles
Elevation change + 2,700 ft; -0 ft
GT 15-minute   Ross Lake (No. 16), Diablo Dam (No. 48)
Contact   North Cascades NP, Marblemount Ranger Station

ROUTE

Difficulty   ▲▲ Grade II; class 4 rock
Time to summit 5–6 hours
Elevation change + 4,100 ft; -0 ft
USGS 7.5-minute Mount Challenger, Mount Prophet
Season   June–September

Approach: Permits are required for overnight outings in the park and can be obtained a maximum of 24 hours in advance. Obtain your permit from the Marblemount Ranger Station, signposted on the west side of town. A Northwest Forest Pass is required to park at the trailhead.

This approach has two options. The first option, recommended, is to save your energy (you'll need it later) and take a water taxi ($25, maximum six people) from above Ross Dam to Big Beaver Camp and walk 0.4 mile to Big Beaver Horse Camp; contact Ross Lake Resort (see Appendix E) in advance for scheduling/booking information. The second option is to hike approximately 6 miles along the west shore of Ross Lake on the Big Beaver Trail to Big Beaver Horse Camp.

From Interstate 5 north of Mount Vernon, take exit 230 (Anacortes/Burlington). Drive 46 miles east on Highway 20 (North Cascades Highway) to Marblemount. Continue 29 miles farther east on Highway 20 to the parking area and trailhead for Ross Dam/Ross Lake Resort (2,100 ft) on the left (north) side of the highway.

Walk 0.8 mile down the Ross Dam Trail to Ross Lake. If you're taking a water taxi, follow the sign. If you're walking, continue to Ross Dam and the trailhead for Big Beaver Trail (1,600 ft). Cross the dam and hike approximately 6 miles along the west shore of the lake to Big Beaver Horse Camp, just beyond the crossing of Big Beaver Creek.

From Big Beaver Horse Camp (1,600 ft), follow the Big Beaver Trail 9.4 miles west to Luna Camp and good camping. Continue approximately 1.5 miles beyond Luna Camp to a point just north of where a creek known among climbers as "Access Creek" flows into Big Beaver Creek (see Beckey 1995, p. 385 and Nelson and Potterfield 1993, p. 199). Leave the trail and carefully cross Big Beaver Creek on a log (scout for the best spot to cross). Ascend westerly up the valley along the right (north) side of Access Creek through patchy brush. As the valley gradient lessens, slide alder and thick brush is encountered. Cross to the south side of the creek and bushwhack your way through this very unpleasant section to reach open talus and scree slopes at the head of the valley and good camping (approx. 4,300 ft).

Route: From the head of the valley (4,300 ft), bear southerly and ascend steep snow/scree slopes to reach a notch in Luna Peak's southeast ridge above (approx. 6,100 ft). Cross the notch and contour westerly across Luna's steep, snow/heather-covered south slopes to reach a high col in Luna's southwest ridge (approx. 7,200 ft). From the col, turn right (northeast) and ascend talus along the ridge, then make a short rock scramble (class 3) to the false (southwest) summit. Scramble northeasterly along the exposed, loose ridge crest (class 4) to the true (northeast) summit (8,311 ft).

Descent: Descend the route.

PASAYTEN
WILDERNESS

•

STRETCHING EAST FROM THE CASCADE CREST along more than 50 miles of the U.S.-Canadian border, the Pasayten Wilderness encompasses an astounding variety of landscapes, plants, and animals. The wilderness contains 150 peaks over 7,500 feet in elevation and more than 160 lakes. In the west, along the Cascade Crest, sculpted summits rise high above dense, wet forests of fir, cedar, and western hemlock. In contrast, the eastern side of the wilderness features gentle, rolling summits and dry forests of fir, pine, and larch. The wilderness also provides a critical wildlife corridor. Deer, moose, gray wolves, black bears, and grizzly bears roam the woods and hills, while mountain goats and bighorn sheep scale the rocky heights. The wilderness is within the Okanogan National Forest.

The wilderness encompasses nineteen of this guide's high points. Although these peaks as a whole tend to be gentler and more weathered than their western counterparts, they are still fantastic ascents in beautiful surroundings. They are also great destinations in early or late season, when conditions aren't favorable in the west, particularly in fall when the land seems ablaze with the gold of turning larches. Thirteen of the high points can be climbed in five distinct Slam itineraries, leaving only six Free Agent peaks to be climbed individually.

● Cathedral Slam

Peaks & routes	Cathedral Peak (West Ridge), Amphitheater Mountain (West Route), Apex Mountain (North Route)
Max difficulty	▲ Grade I+; class 4 rock
Duration	4 days
Roundtrip to camp	36 miles
Elevation gain	+8,600 ft
USGS 7.5-minute	Remmel Mountain
GT 15-minute	Coleman Peak (No. 20)
Trailhead	Cathedral Driveway Trail
Season	June–October

This is a joyous Slam that might just have you whistling along the way. You'll hike through ancient forest along the banks of the fish-filled Chewuch River before emerging into the meadows and rolling parkland of the Cathedral area. The sheer south face of Cathedral Peak is a sight to behold and the campsite at upper Cathedral Lake is truly gorgeous. Bring along some of your nonclimber friends. They'll enjoy it just as much as you will. If you've got more time, Andrews Peak can be climbed in a day from Remmel Lake. Remmel Mountain can be included by hiking out via the Chewuch Trail. And finally, Windy Peak can be climbed in a day from the same trailhead.

ITINERARY

Day	Elevation change	Instructions
1	+2,500 ft; -1,300 ft	Follow the approach for Cathedral Peak to the junction with the Boundary Trail and camp (6,800 ft).
2	+3,500 ft; -2,900 ft	Break camp and ascend to Apex Pass. Climb Apex Mountain, leaving your packs at the pass. Continue to upper Cathedral Lake and camp (7,400 ft). Climb Amphitheater Mountain and return to camp.
3	+1,300 ft; -4,000 ft	Break camp and climb Cathedral Peak, leaving your packs at Cathedral Pass. Continue hiking out and camp near the junction with the Chewuch Trail (4,700 ft).
4	+1,300 ft; -400 ft	Finish hiking out.

24 Cathedral Peak

8,601 ft; 42nd highest

Cathedral Peak is a remarkable mountain whose sheer and imposing 1,000-foot south face, interestingly, exceeds the north face in both vertical relief and steepness. There are several excellent alpine rock climbs on this face. Southwest of the peak is the jewel-like upper Cathedral Lake, nestled just beneath the cliffs of Amphitheater Mountain. Walk another few miles north and you'll be in Canada.

WEST RIDGE

This is an exciting scramble with a few exposed moves near the summit that are guaranteed to get your heart pumping.

APPROACH

Time to camp	2 days
Mileage	18 miles
Elevation change	+3,400 ft; -1,600 ft
GT 15-minute	Coleman Peak (No. 20)
Contact	Okanogan/Wenatchee NF, Tonasket Ranger District

ROUTE

Difficulty	▲ Grade I+; class 4 rock
Time to summit	2 hours
Elevation change	+1,300 ft; -0 ft
USGS 7.5-minute	Remmel Mountain
Season	June–October

Approach: Backcountry self-registration permits are required for the Pasayten Wilderness and may be obtained at the trailhead. A Northwest Forest Pass is required to park at the trailhead.

From Loomis, drive 2.2 miles north on Sinlahekin Valley Road (County Route 9425) to the junction with Toats Coulee Road (Forest Road 39). Turn left (west) onto Toats Coulee Road and continue approximately 20.5 miles to the junction with Forest Road 300 near the Long Swamp Campground. Bear right onto Forest Road 300 and drive approximately 3 miles to the trailhead for the Cathedral Driveway Trail (5,600 ft).

Hike the Cathedral Driveway Trail 2.2 miles west to the junction with the Chewuch Trail (4,300 ft). Turn right (north) onto the Chewuch Trail and hike approximately 3.9 miles to the junction with the Tungsten Trail (4,700 ft). (This junction is not well signed. It occurs in a small meadow immediately

Cathedral Peak from the southwest Photo by Scott Stephenson

before the trail crosses the river on two single-tree bridges.) Turn right onto the Tungsten Trail and hike 6.2 miles to the junction with the Boundary Trail and good camping approximately 100 yards right of the junction (6,800 ft). Turn left (west) onto the Boundary Trail and hike approximately 5.5 miles over Apex and Cathedral passes to upper Cathedral Lake and additional good camping (7,400 ft).

Route: From upper Cathedral Lake, follow the Boundary Trail north and then east to Cathedral Pass (approx. 7,620 ft). Leave the trail and ascend heather and scree slopes northerly, aiming for the prominent notch in Cathedral Peak's west ridge. Continue ascending until beneath cliffs at approximately 8,300 feet. There's a well-defined climber's path in this section. Turn right (east), scramble through a notch in a rock rib and bear left (north) up a gully to gain the crest of the next rock rib. Scramble to the head of the rock rib, then cross a notch on the right (south) to reach an exposed gap just below the summit. Cross the gap (class 4) using good handholds and scramble easy terrain to the summit (8,601 ft).

Descent: Descend the route.

25 Amphitheater Mountain

8,358 ft; 85th highest

Amphitheater Mountain is a unique, heavily glaciated, lanky massif. Two east spur ridges cradle a large basin beneath the steep east face and sheer cliffs on the north drop swiftly to the shores of sparkling upper Cathedral Lake. Two high subpeaks rise nearly as tall as the summit, one at the end of the west spur and the other at the south end of the summit plateau.

WEST ROUTE

This is a straightforward ascent, mostly on trail and with gentle cross-country, with an easy final rock scramble to the summit.

APPROACH

Time to camp	2 days
Mileage	18 miles
Elevation change	+3,400 ft; -1,600 ft
GT 15-minute	Coleman Peak (No. 20)
Contact	Okanogan/Wenatchee NF, Tonasket Ranger District

ROUTE

Difficulty	▲ Grade I; hiking
Time to summit	2 hours
Elevation change	+1,200 ft; -200 ft
USGS 7.5-minute	Remmel Mountain
Season	June–October

Amphitheater Mountain from the south (Remmel Mountain)
Photo by Scott Stephenson

Approach: Follow the approach for Cathedral Peak to upper Cathedral Lake and good camping (7,400 ft).

Route: From upper Cathedral Lake, follow the trail aproximately 0.5 mile southeasterly around Amphitheater Mountain's west spur ridge and west summit to an unsigned trail junction (approx. 7,200 ft). Turn left and follow the trail as it ascends into a basin between the west summit and the true summit (approx. 7,500 ft). Continue on the trail up scree and grassy slopes northeasterly to the head of the basin and the north end of the summit plateau (approx. 8,000 ft). (This point can also be reached by scrambling up a loose class 2–3 gully from east of upper Cathedral Lake.) Turn right (south) and hike up the easy north slopes to the summit (8,358 ft).

Descent: Descend the route.

26 Apex Mountain

8,297 ft; 100th highest

Apex Mountain's northeastern aspect is steep and forms a confined cirque that cradles Tungsten Lake. The other flanks of the mountain are comparatively gentle.

NORTH ROUTE

This ascent is entirely a hike up scree slopes dotted with small colonies of delicate alpine vegetation.

APPROACH

Time to camp	1 day
Mileage	13 miles
Elevation change	+2,500 ft; -1,300 ft
GT 15-minute	Coleman Peak (No. 20)
Contact	Okanogan/Wenatchee NF, Tonasket Ranger District

ROUTE

Difficulty	▲ Grade I; hiking
Time to summit	2 hours
Elevation change	+1,500 ft; -0 ft
USGS 7.5-minute	Remmel Mountain
Season	June–October

Approach: Follow the approach for Cathedral Peak to the junction with the Boundary Trail and good camping (6,800 ft) approximately 100 yards right of the junction.

Apex Mountain from the north (Apex Pass) Photo by Scott Stephenson

Route: Turn left (west) onto the Boundary Trail and ascend to Apex Pass (approx. 7,100 ft). Leave the trail and ascend Apex Mountain's easy north slopes southerly to the summit (8,297 ft).

Descent: Descend the route.

Craggy Slam

Peaks & routes	Big Craggy Peak (South Route), West Craggy Peak (South Route)
Max difficulty	▲ Grade I+; class 2–3 rock
Duration	2 days
Roundtrip to camp	8 miles
Elevation gain	+5,400 ft
USGS 7.5-minute	Billy Goat Mountain
GT 15-minute	Billy Goat Mountain (No. 19), Mazama (No. 51)
Trailhead	Copper Glance Lake Trail
Season	May–October

The Craggies, along with Isabella Ridge and Sherman Peak, make up a picturesque palisade hemming in Copper Glance basin. Base camp in a beautifully situated upper basin puts you right in the heart of all this vertical wilderness.

ITINERARY

Day	Elevation change	Instructions
1	+2,700 ft; -0 ft	Follow the approach for Big Craggy Peak to the upper basin and camp (6,600 ft).
2	+2,700 ft; -5,400 ft	Climb Big Craggy Peak and West Craggy Peak. Hike out.

Notes: You can traverse from the summit of Big Craggy Peak to West Craggy Peak by descending Big Craggy's west ridge (loose rock) to a pronounced saddle (approx. 7,600 ft). From the saddle, contour westerly at 7,600 feet beneath cliffs (class 2–3) and over minor rock ribs until able to scramble scree/talus slopes (class 2–3) northwesterly to the crest of Isabella Ridge (approx. 8,000 ft) and join the route for West Craggy.

27 Big Craggy Peak

8,470 ft; 58th highest

Big Craggy Peak is the highest summit in a massif of rocky mountains that includes West Craggy Peak and the subsummits of beautiful Isabella Ridge. The mountain has a steep northern flank, particularly on the northwest above No Dice Lake.

SOUTH ROUTE

This is a straightforward scramble with plenty of scree and talus to go around. Alternatively, do it in the spring when the snowslopes often make for good cramponing.

APPROACH

Time to camp	3–4 hours
Mileage	4 miles
Elevation change	+2,700 ft; -0 ft
GT 15-minute	Billy Goat Mountain (No. 19), Mazama (No. 51)
Contact	Okanogan/Wenatchee NF, Methow Valley Ranger District

ROUTE

Difficulty	▲ Grade I+; class 2–3 rock
Time to summit	2–3 hours
Elevation change	+1,900 ft; -0 ft
USGS 7.5-minute	Billy Goat Mountain
Season	May–October

Big Craggy Peak from the west in spring Photo by Scott Stephenson

Approach: Backcountry self-registration permits are required for the Pasayten Wilderness and may be obtained at the trailhead. A Northwest Forest Pass is required to park at the trailhead.

From Winthrop, drive West Chewuch Road (Forest Road 51) north for 9.3 miles to the junction with Eightmile Creek Road (Forest Road 5130). Turn left onto Eightmile Creek Road and follow it 12.4 miles, past several national forest campgrounds, to the trailhead for the Copper Glance Lake Trail and park in the small pullout on the right (3,900 ft).

Hike the abandoned Forest Road 505 approximately 1.5 miles to its end and the start of the Copper Glance Lake Trail (approx. 5,200 ft). Continue on the Copper Glance Lake Trail for approximately 1.7 miles to where it crosses Copper Glance Creek (approx. 6,100 ft). Leave the trail a few hundred yards west of the crossing and ascend northwesterly through largely open terrain to reach the upper basin and good camping (approx. 6,600 ft). When you leave the trail, stay as far left (west) as possible, skirting along the foot of a talus slope, to avoid thick brush and windfall.

Route: From camp in the upper basin, hike northeasterly across the basin to talus and rocks at the base of Big Craggy Peak's south slopes. Ascend the scree/talus/snow slopes northerly (class 2–3) to the summit (8,470 ft).

Descent: Descend the route.

28 West Craggy Peak

8,366 ft; 80th highest

West Craggy Peak is the high point of the spectacular Isabella Ridge, a craggy ridge with many unnamed subsummits above 8,000 feet. The mountain has a precipitous eastern flank above No Dice Lake.

SOUTH ROUTE

This is an enjoyable, moderate scramble with plenty of scree and talus, followed by a scenic ridge walk to the summit. Spring is a good time for this ascent, when the debris is often covered by nice, crampon-friendly snow—just watch out for the cornices on Isabella Ridge.

West Craggy Peak from the east (Big Craggy Peak) in spring
Photo by Scott Stephenson

APPROACH

Time to camp	3–4 hours
Mileage	4 miles
Elevation change	+2,700 ft; -0 ft
GT 15-minute	Billy Goat Mountain (No. 19), Mazama (No. 51)
Contact	Okanogan/Wenatchee NF, Methow Valley Ranger District

ROUTE

Difficulty	▲ Grade I+; class 2–3 rock
Time to summit	2–3 hours
Elevation change	+1,800 ft; -0 ft
USGS 7.5-minute	Billy Goat Mountain
Season	May–October

Approach: Follow the approach for Big Craggy Peak to camp in the upper basin (approx. 6,600 ft).

Route: From camp in the upper basin, ascend west-northwesterly along the north side of the creek into the steep-walled basin beneath rugged Isabella Ridge (approx. 7,200 ft). Turn right (northwest) and scramble up a broad talus/scree/snow-filled gully (class 2–3) to the crest of Isabella Ridge (approx. 8,000 ft). In spring, be wary of large cornices that form on the crest above. Turn right (north) and follow the easy ridge and open slopes to the summit (8,366 ft).

Descent: Descend the route.

Lago Slam

Peaks & routes	Mount Lago (Southeast Ridge), Mount Carru (Southeast Ridge), Osceola Peak (Southwest Ridge)
Max difficulty	▲ Grade I+; class 3 rock
Duration	3 days
Roundtrip to camp	23 miles
Elevation gain	+11,500 ft
USGS 7.5-minute	Mount Lago
GT 15-minute	Pasayten Peak (No. 18), Washington Pass (No. 50)
Trailhead	Buckskin Ridge Trail
Season	June–October

Lago Slam peaks from the southeast (Shellrock Pass) Photo by Brian Bongiovanni

This Slam is a fantastic outing with enjoyable scrambling, great views, a stunning campsite, and a healthy dose of peace and solitude. If you've got more time and energy or want a different grouping of routes, you can mix and match peaks from the Ptarmigan Slam that shares a nearby base camp.

ITINERARY

Day	Elevation change	Instructions
1	+2,100 ft; -2,100 ft	Follow the approach for Osceola Peak to Lake Doris and camp (6,975 ft).
2	+5,800 ft; -5,800 ft	Climb Mounts Lago and Carru. Return to camp.
3	+3,700 ft; -3,700 ft	Climb Osceola Peak and hike out.

Notes: For day 2, from the summit of Mount Lago, follow Lago's alternate descent route via the west ridge to 7,000 feet and join the route for Mount Carru.

---

29 Mount Lago

8,745 ft; 31st highest

Mount Lago is the highest peak in the Pasayten Wilderness. The northern and eastern flanks are steep, the latter cradling a broad cirque situated between rugged spur ridges. The southern flank is largely talus and scree punctuated by two main spur ridges.

SOUTHEAST RIDGE

This moderate scramble is very enjoyable, particularly the airy section of the upper southeast ridge with its dizzying views down the precipitous east face.

APPROACH

Time to camp	2 days
Mileage	17 miles
Elevation change	+2,700 ft; -3,200 ft
GT 15-minute	Pasayten Peak (No. 18), Washington Pass (No. 50)
Contact	Okanogan/Wenatchee NF, Methow Valley Ranger District

ROUTE

Difficulty	▲ Grade I +; class 3 rock
Time to summit	3–4 hours
Elevation change	+2,400 ft; -0 ft
USGS 7.5-minute	Mount Lago
Season	June–October

Mount Lago from the southeast (Shellrock Pass) Photo by Brian Bongiovanni

Approach: Backcountry self-registration permits are required for the Pasayten Wilderness and may be obtained at the trailhead. A Northwest Forest Pass is required to park at the trailhead.

From Winthrop, drive west on Highway 20 (North Cascades Highway) to Mazama and turn north onto the Mazama Cutoff Road. Cross the river, turn left (west) onto Harts Pass Road (County Road 1163), and continue approximately 9.8 miles (road becomes Forest Road 5400) to the junction with the River Bend Access Road. Turn right to continue on Forest Road 5400 to Harts Pass and the junction with Forest Road 200. Turn right onto Forest Road 200 and follow it for 2 miles to Slate Pass and the trailhead for the Buckskin Ridge Trail (approx. 6,900 ft). The trail starts at a road switchback.

Hike the Buckskin Ridge Trail 1.3 miles, past the junction with the Slate Pass Trail, to the junction with the Whistler Trail (approx. 6,500 ft). Turn right (east) onto the Whistler Trail and hike 2.7 miles, descending into the Middle Fork Pasayten River valley, to the junction with the Robinson Creek Trail (approx. 5,200 ft). Turn left (north) onto the Robinson Creek Trail and hike 5.1 miles to the junction with the Eureka Creek Trail (approx. 5,000 ft), just before the trail crosses Berk Creek. There's ample camping all along the Middle Fork Pasayten River valley and at Berk Creek.

Turn right (east) onto the Eureka Creek Trail (becomes the Shellrock Trail) and hike approximately 7 miles past Freds Lake (6,507 ft), over a pass (approx. 7,100 ft), past Lake Doris (6,975 ft; good camping) and across the head of the Eureka Creek valley to a meadow at the western base of Shellrock Pass and good camping (approx. 6,400 ft).

Route: From the base of Shellrock Pass, ascend the trail east to the pass (7,500 ft). Leave the trail and ascend easy talus northwesterly up Mount Lago's long southeast-trending ridge, crossing a stretch of slabby terrain (class 3), to reach a large northwest-trending ledge (approx. 8,000 ft). Follow the ledge northwesterly to reach a south-trending spur ridge and scramble to its crest (class 3). Scramble the crest of the spur ridge (class 3) northerly to reach Lago's summit ridge east of the summit. Turn left (west) and enjoy a beautiful scramble (class 3) on decent rock to the summit (8,745 ft).

Descent: Descend the route. Alternatively, descend the talus-covered west ridge to the Carru-Lago col (approx. 7,600 ft), then turn left (south) and descend to 7,000 feet (where you meet the route for Carru). Bear southeasterly and continue descending through the forest to pick up a climber's path that traverses the cliffy slopes and enters a gully at 6,600 feet. Descend the gully (class 2) back to the Shellrock Trail (6,200 ft), then turn left (east) and follow the trail back to camp.

30 Mount Carru

8,595 ft; 44th highest

Mount Carru has a short but steep northern flank. The east face of the southeast ridge drops abruptly to the Carru-Lago col. The southern flank is predominantly scree and talus interspersed with rock ribs and gullies.

SOUTHEAST RIDGE

This route keeps you out of the worst of the talus and scree. Be careful though, as there's still plenty of loose rock.

APPROACH

Time to camp	2 days
Mileage	17 miles
Elevation change	+2,700 ft; -3,200 ft
GT 15-minute	Pasayten Peak (No. 18), Washington Pass (No. 50)
Contact	Okanogan/Wenatchee NF, Methow Valley Ranger District

ROUTE

Difficulty	▲ Grade I +; class 3 rock
Time to summit	3–4 hours
Elevation change	+2,500 ft; -300 ft
USGS 7.5-minute	Mount Lago
Season	June–October

Mount Carru from the south Photo by Brian Bongiovanni

Approach: Follow the approach for Mount Lago to the meadow at the western base of Shellrock Pass and good camping (approx. 6,400 ft).

Route: From the base of Shellrock Pass, hike the Shellrock Trail westerly to approximately 6,200 feet at the base of a gully. Ascend the gully (class 2) to 6,600 feet, then exit the gully and pick up a climber's path that traverses the cliffy slopes and ascends northwesterly through the forest to 7,000 feet. Bear northerly and ascend to 7,200 feet, then angle north-northwesterly and ascend scrub and rocky slopes, staying just left (west) of the ridge that drops sharply to the Carru-Lago col, to reach a shoulder (8,100 ft). Work northwesterly, negotiating outcrops along the ridge crest (class 3), to the summit (8,595 ft).

Descent: Descend the route.

31 Osceola Peak

8,587 ft; 47th highest

Osceola Peak has steep north and east faces. Pleasant Valley is nearly enclosed by its long, protruding northwest and north ridges, the eastern flanks of both being markedly steeper than their western counterparts. Lake Doris lies nestled in a narrow basin at the base of the southwest ridge.

SOUTHWEST RIDGE

This fun, straightforward scramble is a remarkably quick ascent from Lake Doris.

Osceola Peak from the southwest (Lake Doris) Photo by Brian Bongiovanni

APPROACH

Time to camp	6 hours
Mileage	12 miles
Elevation change	+2,100 ft; -2,100 ft
GT 15-minute	Pasayten Peak (No. 18), Washington Pass (No. 50)
Contact	Okanogan/Wenatchee NF, Methow Valley Ranger District

ROUTE

Difficulty	▲ Grade I+; class 2 rock
Time to summit	2 hours
Elevation change	+1,700 ft; -0 ft
USGS 7.5-minute	Mount Lago
Season	June–October

Approach: Follow the approach for Mount Lago down the Middle Fork Pasayten River valley to the junction with the Eureka Creek Trail (approx. 5,000 ft), just before the trail crosses Berk Creek. Turn right (east) onto the Eureka Creek Trail and hike approximately 2.1 miles past Freds Lake (6,507 ft) and over a pass (approx. 7,100 ft) to Lake Doris and good camping (6,975 ft).

Route: From Lake Doris, ascend alp slopes northerly to a saddle in Osceola Peak's southwest ridge just right (northeast) of Point 7598. From the saddle, turn right (northeast) and ascend a climber's path and solid rock (class 2) along the easy ridge crest to the summit (8,587 ft).

Descent: Descend the route.

Monumental Slam

Peaks & routes	Monument Peak (Southeast Ridge), Lake Mountain (South Route)
Max difficulty	▲▲ Grade II; class 3 rock
Duration	3 days
Roundtrip to camp	23 miles
Elevation gain	+10,600 ft
USGS 7.5-minute	Mount Lago
GT 15-minute	Billy Goat Mountain (No. 19), Washington Pass (No. 50), Mazama (No. 51)
Trailhead	Monument Creek Trail
Season	June–October

This is a physically demanding Slam featuring a steep, hot, and dry approach and extensive talus and scree. The reward for your labor includes a journey to the remote and infrequently visited summit of Monument Peak, which possibly didn't see its first ascent until 1978 (Beckey 1995, p. 213). The base camp at Lake of the Woods is a welcome oasis set in a larch grove. It's a great destination in fall when the days are cooler and the larches are ablaze with color.

ITINERARY

Day	Elevation change	Instructions
1	+ 4,700 ft; -500 ft	Follow the approach for Monument Peak to Lake of the Woods and camp (6,600 ft).
2	+ 5,400 ft; -5,400 ft	Climb Monument Peak and Lake Mountain. Return to camp.
3	+ 500 ft; -4,700 ft	Hike out.

Notes: Note that the ascent to Pistol Pass is long, steep, hot, and without water throughout much of the summer, so bring extra along. The routes for Monument Peak and Lake Mountain share a common point northwest of the col on Lake's south ridge (approx. 7,400 ft).

32 Monument Peak

8,592 ft; 45th highest

Monument Peak is a large and remote summit, isolated by its neighbors Blackcap and Lake mountains and a steep western escarpment above the wild Eureka Creek valley. The mountain has a steep north face and a long, sweeping southeast ridge with a rugged eastern aspect.

SOUTHEAST RIDGE

This route requires a healthy dose of cross-country travel, over plentiful scree and talus, followed by a long scramble along the ridge crest to the summit.

APPROACH

Time to camp	6–7 hours
Mileage	12 miles
Elevation change	+4,700 ft; -500 ft
GT 15-minute	Billy Goat Mountain (No. 19), Washington Pass (No. 50), Mazama (No. 51)
Contact	Okanogan/Wenatchee NF, Methow Valley Ranger District

ROUTE

Difficulty	▲▲ Grade II; class 3 rock
Time to summit	4–5 hours
Elevation change	+3,200 ft; -1,200 ft
USGS 7.5-minute	Mount Lago
Season	June–October

Approach: Backcountry self-registration permits are required for the Pasayten Wilderness and may be obtained at the trailhead. A Northwest Forest Pass is required to park at the trailhead.

From Winthrop, drive west on Highway 20 (North Cascades Highway) to

Monument Peak from the southeast Photo by Brian Bongiovanni

Labels on photo: Summit, North Ridge, East Ridge, Blackcap Mountain

Monument Peak from the east-southeast (Lake Mountain) Photo by Paul Klenke

Mazama and turn north onto the Mazama Cutoff Road. Cross the river, turn left (west) onto Harts Pass Road (County Road 1163), and continue 7 miles to the trailhead for the Lost River Trail/Monument Creek Trail (approx. 2,400 ft), just beyond the Lost River Airstrip.

Hike the Monument Creek Trail north along the Lost River. At 3.6 miles the trail crosses Eureka Creek, the last source of water in summer until Lake of the Woods, approximately 8 miles farther on. From Eureka Creek, the poorly maintained trail climbs steeply up the slopes of Pistol Peaks to Pistol Pass (approx. 7,100 ft), 10.7 miles from the trailhead. Cross the pass and descend the trail to 6,600 feet, then pick up a path that contours northerly to Lake of the Woods and good camping (approx. 6,600 ft).

Route: From Lake of the Woods, ascend talus and scree westerly to a col in Lake Mountain's south ridge (approx. 7,400 ft). Cross the col and contour northwesterly across talus, then descend westerly to the creek at approximately 6,200 feet. Keep left (west) and ascend to gain the gentle base of Monument Peak's long southeast ridge at approximately 6,400 feet. Scramble (class 2 and 3), on or left (west) of the crest, to reach open talus slopes. Above is Monument's summit area consisting of two small summits; the left (west) one is the true summit. Ascend the talus slopes to the base of the left (west) summit, then scramble up a short, steep slope (class 2–3) to the summit (8,592 ft).

Descent: Descend the route.

33 Lake Mountain

8,371 ft; 79th highest

Lake Mountain is a prominent peak with a steep north face. The eastern flank of Lake's south ridge drops quickly into scree and talus slopes above Lake of the Woods. The western and southwestern flanks are similarly debris covered.

SOUTH ROUTE

Become one with the talus and scree on this ascent that takes you off the beaten track into some seldom-visited areas.

APPROACH

Time to camp	6–7 hours
Mileage	12 miles
Elevation change	+4,700 ft; -500 ft
GT 15-minute	Billy Goat Mountain (No. 19), Washington Pass (No. 50), Mazama (No. 51)
Contact	Okanogan/Wenatchee NF, Methow Valley Ranger District

ROUTE

Difficulty	▲ Grade I+; class 2–3 rock
Time to summit	2–3 hours
Elevation change	+1,800 ft; -0 ft
USGS 7.5-minute	Mount Lago
Season	June–October

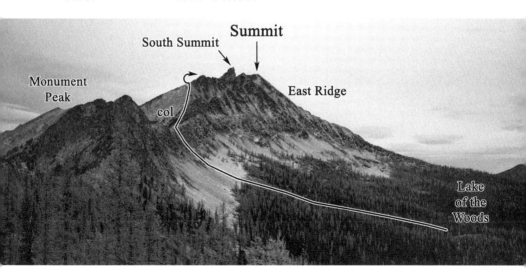

Lake Mountain from the south (Pistol Pass) Photo by Brian Bongiovanni

Lake Mountain from the west-northwest (Monument Peak) Photo by Paul Klenke

Approach: Follow the approach for Monument Peak to Lake of the Woods and good camping (approx. 6,600 ft).

Route: From Lake of the Woods, ascend talus and scree slopes westerly to a col in Lake Mountain's south ridge (approx. 7,400 ft). Cross the col and contour northwesterly across talus, then make an ascending traverse northwesterly to gain Lake's west slopes at approximately 7,700 feet. Contour northerly at 7,700 feet across talus, slabs, ribs, and gullies, past the south summit, to reach a broad gully west of the summit. Ascend the slabby, surprisingly debris-free gully (class 2–3) easterly, then hop boulders and talus to the summit (8,371 ft).

Descent: Descend the route.

Ptarmigan Slam

Peaks & routes	Ptarmigan Peak (Lease–Dot Creek Divide Traverse), Lost Peak (West Route), Blackcap Mountain (Northeast Ridge)
Max difficulty	▲▲ Grade II; class 3 rock
Duration	6 days
Roundtrip to camp	33 miles
Elevation gain	+16,700 ft
USGS 7.5-minute	Lost Peak, Mount Lago
GT 15-minute	Pasayten Peak (No. 18), Washington Pass (No. 50)
Trailhead	Buckskin Ridge Trail
Season	June–October

This classic, physically demanding Slam is all about time up high in the sky. All the recommended routes feature fantastic ridge runs and, from the remote summits of Ptarmigan and Lost peaks, you'll feel a long way from the hustle and bustle of civilization. If all the fresh air awakens your inner beast, consider mixing and matching peaks from the nearby Lago Slam. This is truly beautiful country.

ITINERARY

Day	Elevation change	Instructions
1	+ 2,100 ft; -2,100 ft	Follow the approach for Ptarmigan Peak to Lake Doris and camp (6,975 ft).
2	+ 2,600 ft; -3,200 ft	Continue the approach for Ptarmigan Peak to camp just west of Shellrock Pass (6,400 ft). Climb Blackcap Mountain and return to camp.
3	+ 4,500 ft; -4,500 ft	Climb Lost Peak and return to camp.
4	+ 4,400 ft; -4,400 ft	Climb Ptarmigan Peak and return to camp.
5	+ 1,400 ft; -2,700 ft	Start hiking out. Camp somewhere in the Middle Fork Pasayten River valley (approx. 5,100 ft).
6	+ 1,800 ft; -0 ft	Finish hiking out.

34 Ptarmigan Peak

8,614 ft; 39th highest

Ptarmigan Peak is a remote and large summit with a rugged, steep northeastern flank. The mountain's other aspects are comparatively gentle, composed largely of extensive scree and talus slopes.

LEASE–DOT CREEK DIVIDE TRAVERSE

This is a great, long scramble mostly above 7,800 feet along a moderate ridge with fantastic views. It's a fun way to spend a day and rejuvenate your soul with so much time up high.

APPROACH

Time to camp	2 days
Mileage	17 miles
Elevation change	+ 2,700 ft; -3,200 ft
GT 15-minute	Pasayten Peak (No. 18), Washington Pass (No. 50)
Contact	Okanogan/Wenatchee NF, Methow Valley Ranger District

Ptarmigan Peak from the south (Mount Lago) Photo by Paul Klenke

ROUTE

Difficulty   ▲▲ Grade II; class 3 rock
Time to summit 5–7 hours
Elevation change +3,300 ft; -1,100 ft
USGS 7.5-minute Mount Lago
Season   June–October

Approach: Backcountry self-registration permits are required for the Pasayten Wilderness and may be obtained at the trailhead. A Northwest Forest Pass is required to park at the trailhead.

From Winthrop, drive west on Highway 20 (North Cascades Highway) to Mazama and turn north onto the Mazama Cutoff Road. Cross the river, turn left (west) onto Harts Pass Road (County Road 1163), and continue approximately 9.8 miles (road becomes Forest Road 5400) to the junction with the River Bend Access Road. Turn right to continue on Forest Road 5400 to Harts Pass and the junction with Forest Road 200. Turn right onto Forest Road 200 and follow it for 2 miles to Slate Pass and the trailhead for the Buckskin Ridge Trail (approx. 6,900 ft). The trail starts at a road switchback.

Hike the Buckskin Ridge Trail 1.3 miles, past the junction with the Slate Pass Trail, to the junction with the Whistler Trail (approx. 6,500 ft). Turn right (east) onto the Whistler Trail and hike 2.7 miles, descending into the Middle Fork Pasayten River valley, to the junction with the Robinson Creek Trail (approx. 5,200 ft). Turn left (north) onto the Robinson Creek Trail and

Ptarmigan Peak from the south (Dot Mountain) Photo by Paul Klenke

hike 5.1 miles to the junction with the Eureka Creek Trail (approx. 5,000 ft), just before the trail crosses Berk Creek. There's ample camping all along the Middle Fork Pasayten River valley and at Berk Creek.

Turn right (east) onto the Eureka Creek Trail (becomes the Shellrock Trail) and hike approximately 7 miles past Freds Lake (6,507 ft), over a pass (approx. 7,100 ft), past Lake Doris (6,975 ft, good camping), and across the head of the Eureka Creek valley to a meadow at the western base of Shellrock Pass and good camping (approx. 6,400 ft).

Route: From the base of Shellrock Pass, hike the Shellrock Trail westerly to approximately 6,200 feet at the base of a gully. Ascend the gully (class 2) to 6,600 feet, then exit the gully and pick up a climber's path that traverses the cliffy slopes and ascends northwesterly through the forest to 7,000 feet. Bear northerly and ascend to the Carru-Lago col (approx. 7,600 ft).

Cross the col and contour east-northeasterly across the basin beneath Lago's steep north face, staying below cliff bands, until able to ascend to a saddle (approx. 7,720 ft) in the Lease–Dot Creek divide. (This saddle can also be reached by descending Mount Lago's north ridge from its summit.) Turn left (north) and scramble along the ridge crest until approximately 75 feet below the summit of Point 8165. Locate and traverse a loose ledge (class 3) northerly around the left (west) side of Point 8165 and regain the ridge crest. Continue northerly along the ridge crest, scramble over the summit of Dot Mountain (8,220 ft), and descend to a saddle at the base of Ptarmigan Peak's broad south ridge (7,840 ft). Walk northerly up the ridge to the summit (8,614 ft).

Descent: Descend the route.

35 Lost Peak

8,464 ft; 59th highest

Lost Peak is a remote, gentle eminence apart from a steep north face. The northeast summit (8,327 ft) marks the start of the rugged, craggy Rampart Ridge, while the southwest slopes are predominantly talus and scree.

WEST ROUTE

This is an enjoyable, but long, ridge run and traverse to the summit of this seldom-climbed peak.

APPROACH

	Primary	Alternate
Time to camp	2 days	2 days
Mileage	17 miles	18 miles
Elevation change	+2,700 ft; -3,200 ft	+6,700 ft; -2,500 ft
GT 15-minute	Pasayten Peak (No. 18), Washington Pass (No. 50)	Pasayten Peak (No. 18), Billy Goat Mountain (No. 19), Washington Pass (No. 50), Mazama (No. 51)
Contact	Okanogan/Wenatchee NF, Methow Valley Ranger District	Okanogan/Wenatchee NF, Methow Valley Ranger District

ROUTE

Difficulty	▲ Grade I+; class 3 rock
Time to summit	5 hours (primary approach); 4 hours (alternate approach)
Elevation change	+3,300 ft, -1,200 ft (primary approach); +2,200 ft, -300 ft (alternate approach)
USGS 7.5-minute	Lost Peak
Season	June–October

Primary Approach: Follow the approach for Ptarmigan Peak to the meadow at the western base of Shellrock Pass and good camping (approx. 6,400 ft).

Alternate Approach: Permits are the same as those required for the primary approach: trailhead self-registration and a Northwest Forest Pass for parking. From Winthrop, drive west on Highway 20 (North Cascades Highway) to Mazama and turn north onto the Mazama Cutoff Road. Cross the river and turn left (west) onto Harts Pass Road (County Road 1163) and continue

Lost Peak from the northwest (Pass Butte) Photo by Brian Bongiovanni

7 miles to the trailhead for the Lost River Trail/Monument Creek Trail (approx. 2,400 ft), just beyond the Lost River Airstrip.

Hike the Monument Creek Trail north along the Lost River. At 3.6 miles the trail crosses Eureka Creek, the last source of water in summer until Monument Creek, approximately 9 miles farther on. From Eureka Creek the trail climbs steeply up the slopes of Pistol Peaks to Pistol Pass (approx. 7,100 ft), 10.7 miles from the trailhead. Cross the pass and follow the trail 7.2 miles north along Monument Creek, past plenty of campsites, to the junction with the Shellrock Trail and good camping (approx. 6,600 ft).

Route: If coming via the primary approach, ascend the trail east to Shellrock Pass (7,500 ft). Cross the pass and descend the trail approximately 1.3 miles to the junction with the Monument Creek Trail (approx. 6,600 ft).

From the junction of the Shellrock and Monument Creek trails, follow the Monument Creek Trail 0.8 mile to Butte Pass (approx. 6,800 ft). Leave the trail and ascend easterly up and over Point 7275 and descend to a saddle on its east side (approx. 7,000 ft). From the saddle, ascend a west-trending spur ridge easterly to just below the ridge crest at 7,700 feet. Turn right and contour southeasterly, then easterly, until able to ascend directly to a col between Pass Butte and Point 8107 (approx. 7,800 ft). Contour at 7,800 feet southeasterly beneath Point 8107 to the base of Lost Peak's northwest ridge. Follow the ridgeline southeasterly over slabby rocks and talus to the summit (8,464 ft).

Descent: Descend the route.

36 Blackcap Mountain

8,397 ft; 75th highest

Blackcap Mountain is an interesting black-topped summit with steep northern and western flanks. It's topographically connected to Monument Peak by a rugged, mile-long south ridge that is almost entirely above 8,000 feet.

NORTHEAST RIDGE
This route offers a short and enjoyable scrambling ridge run to the summit.

APPROACH

Time to camp	2 days
Mileage	17 miles
Elevation change	+2,700 ft; -3,200 ft
GT 15-minute	Pasayten Peak (No. 18), Washington Pass (No. 50)
Contact	Okanogan/Wenatchee NF, Methow Valley Ranger District

ROUTE

Difficulty	▲ Grade I+; class 3 rock
Time to summit	3 hours
Elevation change	+2,000; -0 ft
USGS 7.5-minute	Mount Lago
Season	June–October

Blackcap Mountain from the northeast (near Shellrock Pass) Photo by Paul Klenke

Approach: Follow the approach for Ptarmigan Peak to the meadow at the western base of Shellrock Pass and good camping (approx. 6,400 ft).

Route: From the base of Shellrock Pass, ascend the trail easterly toward the pass until approximately 7,100 feet, just below where the trail bears east up a section of tight, steep switchbacks. Leave the trail and make a gradual rising traverse south-southwesterly across a grassy, rocky basin and a talus boulder field, staying beneath cliff bands. Aim for the base of a talus slope between the steep cliffs at the head of the basin on the left (south) and a short north-trending spur ridge on the right (north). Ascend the left (east) edge of this talus slope southerly (class 2) to a saddle in the ridge crest just right (west) of the end of the cliff bands. Turn right (west) and scramble rock (class 2–3) along the ridge, staying on or left (south) of the crest, to the northeast corner of Blackcap Mountain's black summit pyramid. Scramble the flakey, lichen-covered rock (very slippery when wet) of the summit pyramid (class 3) to the summit (8,397 ft).

Descent: Descend the route.

● Free Agents

37 Jack Mountain

9,066 ft; 14th highest

Jack Mountain is a massive peak with a precipitous north face rising above the impressive Nohokomeen Glacier. The glacier occupies a large cirque on the peak's northern flank. On the west, the mountain rises more than 7,000 feet above Ross Lake in less than 3 miles. Finally, on the east, just below the summit, is another impressive glacier with a narrow head that drops sharply, descending more than 1,400 feet in a quarter mile. It's rugged country and a great place to spend a few days of your life.

SOUTHEAST ROUTE

This is a challenging scramble. A low trailhead elevation and a lot of ups and downs make for a physically demanding approach. Add to that, glacier travel and an exposed completion along the edge of the precipitous north face and you've got a classic Cascade scramble ahead of you.

APPROACH

Time to camp	6–7 hours
Mileage	7 or 9 miles
Elevation change	+5,200 ft; -1,200 ft

| GT 15-minute | Mount Logan (No. 49) |
| Contact | North Cascades NP, Headquarters; or Okanogan/ Wenatchee NF, Methow Valley Ranger District |

ROUTE

Difficulty	▲▲ Grade II; glacier travel; class 3–4 rock
Time to summit	4–5 hours
Elevation change	+3,800 ft; -600 ft
USGS 7.5-minute	Crater Mountain, Jack Mountain
Season	June–September

Approach: Backcountry self-registration permits are required for the Pasayten Wilderness and may be obtained at the trailhead. A Northwest Forest Pass is required to park at the trailhead.

From Interstate 5 north of Mount Vernon, take exit 230 (Anacortes/ Burlington). Drive 85 miles east on Highway 20 (North Cascades Highway) to the parking area on the left at the Canyon Creek Trailhead (1,900 ft).

Descend the trail a short distance, cross Granite Creek and turn left at the first fork. Continue a short distance and cross Canyon Creek to reach a T junction with the Ruby Creek Trail on the left and the Jackita Ridge Trail on the right. Turn right onto the Jackita Ridge Trail and ascend 3.9 miles steeply

Jack Mountain from the southeast Photo by Lowell Skoog

to the junction with the Crater Mountain Trail (5,300 ft). Turn left onto the Crater Mountain Trail and ascend approximately 1 mile to a flat area with a tarn on the left side of the trail (5,800 ft). From here, there are two options. The first option is to leave the trail and ascend northwesterly to a notch (approx. 7,200 ft) east of Crater Mountain and access the Jerry Glacier (possible moat problems in late season). The second option is to continue another 1.4 miles on the trail to its end (7,100 ft), then descend gravel slopes westerly to the east end of the Jerry Glacier.

Once on the Jerry Glacier, traverse westerly, then northwesterly across the glacier to a ridgeline at 6,500 feet. Descend to Jerry Lakes and good camping (5,900 ft).

Route: From between the Jerry Lakes, ascend westerly to a notch in the ridgeline at 6,600 feet. Descend north-northwesterly into a meadow (approx. 6,000 ft) near the head of the northeast branch of Crater Creek. From the meadow, ascend alp slopes westerly, over the southeast ridge of Jack Mountain (approx. 7,000 ft), to where the snow patches meet the rock (approx. 7,500 ft). Between the two main snow patches, ascend a gully (class 3–4) to reach the slabby rock scarp at about the midpoint of Jack's southeast face. Scramble (class 3) northwesterly to the summit ridge. Turn right (north) and scramble a short distance along the exposed ridge crest (class 3) to the summit (9,066 ft).

Descent: Descend the route.

38 Robinson Mountain

8,726 ft; 32nd highest

Robinson Mountain is one of the easiest peaks to access in the Pasayten Wilderness. The mountain features a broad, steep northwest face and a long, defined southeast ridge. The southwestern flank is scree and talus corrugated by numerous ribs and gullies.

SOUTHEAST RIDGE

This ascent is a classic, fun scramble up a defined ridge with a pleasant base camp.

APPROACH

Time to camp	5–6 hours
Mileage	5 miles
Elevation change	+4,100 ft; -0 ft
GT 15-minute	Washington Pass (No. 50)
Contact	Okanogan/Wenatchee NF, Methow Valley Ranger District

ROUTE

Difficulty   ▲ Grade I+; class 3 rock
Time to summit 3 hours
Elevation change +2,100 ft; -0 ft
USGS 7.5-minute Robinson Mountain
Season   June–October

Approach: Backcountry self-registration permits are required for the Pasayten Wilderness and may be obtained at the trailhead. A Northwest Forest Pass is required to park at the trailhead.

From Winthrop, drive west on Highway 20 (North Cascades Highway) to Mazama and turn north onto the Mazama Cutoff Road. Cross the river, turn left (west) onto Harts Pass Road (County Road 1163), and continue 9 miles (road becomes Forest Road 5400) to the trailhead for the Robinson Creek Trail on the right (approx. 2,600 ft).

Hike the Robinson Creek Trail approximately 2.25 miles and cross the bridge over Beauty Creek (approx. 3,600 ft). Approximately 25 yards beyond the crossing, turn right (north-northeast) onto a reasonably defined climber's path that follows the west side of Beauty Creek. Hike approximately 1.5 miles to where a brush-enveloped stream enters Beauty Creek from the left (approx. 5,200 ft). Cross the stream, turn left (northwest), and ascend open slopes and forest along the north side of the stream into a basin and good camping at a pond (approx. 6,700 ft).

Route: Ascend scree/snow slopes on the north side of the basin to gain Robinson Mountain's southeast ridge. Scramble northwesterly approximately 1 mile along the obvious ridge crest (class 3), past several subsummits, to the east end of Robinson's high summit ridge (approx. 8,480 ft). Turn left (north-northwest), scramble past another subsummit, and continue to a narrow, exposed section of the ridge near the summit. Carefully scramble along the exposed crest (class 3) for approximately 75 feet, then continue up easier terrain to the summit (8,726 ft).

Descent: Descend the route.

39 Remmel Mountain

8,685 ft; 35th highest

Remmel Mountain is a massive peak whose northern-southeastern aspects contain numerous high basins. Nestled into the northernmost basin is Cornwell Lake (6,955 ft) and in the easternmost is Four Point Lake (6,850 ft). This is wild, gorgeous country, less than 6 miles from the U.S.-Canadian border.

SOUTHEAST ROUTE

This is a straightforward hike up easy talus slopes with a base camp at a beautiful high lake.

APPROACH

Time to camp	6–7 hours
Mileage	13 miles
Elevation change	+2,600 ft; -1,300 ft
GT 15-minute	Coleman Peak (No. 20)
Contact	Okanogan/Wenatchee NF, Tonasket Ranger District

ROUTE

Difficulty	▲ Grade I; hiking
Time to summit	2 hours
Elevation change	+2,000 ft; -100 ft
USGS 7.5-minute	Remmel Mountain
Season	June–October

Remmel Mountain from the southeast; trail ascends left-hand slopes
Photo by Scott Stephenson

Approach: Backcountry self-registration permits are required for the Pasayten Wilderness and may be obtained at the trailhead. A Northwest Forest Pass is required to park at the trailhead.

From Loomis, drive 2.2 miles north on Sinlahekin Valley Road (County Route 9425) to the junction with Toats Coulee Road (Forest Road 39). Turn left (west) onto Toats Coulee Road (Forest Road 39) and continue approximately 20.5 miles to the junction with Forest Road 300 near the Long Swamp Campground. Bear right onto Forest Road 300 and drive approximately 3 miles to the trailhead for the Cathedral Driveway Trail (5,600 ft).

Hike the Cathedral Driveway Trail 2.2 miles west to the junction with the Chewuch Trail (4,300 ft). Turn right (north) onto the Chewuch Trail and hike approximately 7.9 miles to the junction with the Coleman Ridge Trail (5,240 ft). Turn left (west) onto the Coleman Ridge Trail, hike 2.4 miles and turn right (north) onto a short spur trail leading to Four Point Lake and good camping (6,850 ft).

Route: From Four Point Lake, backtrack to the Coleman Ridge Trail and follow it westerly, then southwesterly across the basin. At the top of the tight switchbacks immediately before the trail crosses the stream, turn right onto an old trail. Follow the old trail northwesterly up Remmel's talus covered southeast slopes to the summit (8,685 ft).

Descent: Descend the route.

40 Windy Peak

8,333 ft; 89th highest

Windy Peak is a gentle eminence and has the distinction of being the only high point in this guide with a hiking trail to its summit. It rises out of wide-open, rolling countryside not far from the U.S.-Canadian border.

WINDY CREEK TRAIL
This is a hike presenting no technical difficulties.

APPROACH

Time to camp	n/a (done as a day trip)
Mileage	n/a
Elevation change	n/a
GT 15-minute	Horseshoe Basin (No. 21)
Contact	Okanogan/Wenatchee NF, Tonasket Ranger District

Windy Peak summit pyramid from the plateau Photo by Paul Klenke

ROUTE

Difficulty	▲ Grade I; hiking
Time to summit	3–4 hours (5.2 miles on trails)
Elevation change	+3,000 ft; -200 ft
USGS 7.5-minute	Horseshoe Basin
Season	June–October

Approach: Backcountry self-registration permits are required for the Pasayten Wilderness and may be obtained at the trailhead. A Northwest Forest Pass is required to park at the trailhead.

From Loomis, drive 2.2 miles north on Sinlahekin Valley Road (County Route 9425) to the junction with Toats Coulee Road (Forest Road 39). Turn left (west) onto Toats Coulee Road and continue approximately 20.5 miles to the junction with Forest Road 300 near the Long Swamp Campground. Bear right onto Forest Road 300 and drive approximately 3 miles to the trailhead for the Cathedral Driveway Trail (5,600 ft).

Route: Hike the Cathedral Driveway Trail 0.4 mile west to the junction with the Windy Creek Trail (approx. 5,400 ft). Turn right (north) onto the Windy Creek Trail and hike 4.8 miles to a signed trail junction beneath Windy's Summit pyramid (approx. 7,800 ft). The last few hundred yards switchback up sandy and rocky terrain to the summit (8,333 ft).

Descent: Descend the route.

41 Castle Peak

8,306 ft; 98th highest

Castle Peak has a 1.5-mile-wide north face punctuated by seven steep buttresses interspersed with glacier remnants. The face rises precipitously for more than 1,300 feet, indeed appearing as formidable battlements when viewed from below. The southern slopes of the mountain are comparatively gentle and composed primarily of talus and scree.

WEST RIDGE

The crux of this route might just be following the abandoned Freezeout Creek Trail. It's not too bad, really, and the creek provides a helpful landmark. The route along the west ridge is a moderate scramble.

APPROACH

Time to camp	2 days
Mileage	15 miles
Elevation change	+2,500 ft; -0 ft
GT 15-minute	Ross Lake (No. 16), Jack Mountain (No. 17)
Contact	North Cascades NP, Headquarters; or Okanogan/ Wenatchee NF, Methow Valley Ranger District

ROUTE

Difficulty	▲▲ Grade II; class 3 rock
Time to summit	5–7 hours
Elevation change	+4,200 ft; -0 ft
USGS 7.5-minute	Castle Peak, Skagit Peak
Season	June–September

Approach: Access to Castle Peak via Silver-Skagit Road and the East Bank Trail requires crossing the U.S.-Canadian border. There is a U.S.-Canada immigration/customs office on the way to Hozomeen Campground, so bring along your passport and any other required proof of identity and citizenship.

Backcountry self-registration permits are required for the Pasayten Wilderness and may be obtained at the trailhead. A Northwest Forest Pass is required to park at the trailhead.

From Interstate 5 near Bellingham, take exit 255 (Mount Baker). Drive 10 miles east on Highway 542 to Nugents Crossing and the junction with Highway 9. Turn left (north) onto Highway 9 and drive 14 miles to Sumas. Cross into Canada and proceed toward Abbotsford and the junction with Trans-Canada Highway 1. Turn right (east) onto Highway 1 toward Hope and proceed approximately 46 miles to exit 165 (Flood Hope Road). Continue on Flood Hope Road to the junction with the Silver-Skagit Road. Turn onto Silver-Skagit Road and drive approximately 37 miles south to Hozomeen Campground and the trailhead for the Willow Lake Trail (1,700 ft) on the shores of Ross Lake.

Hike the Willow Lake Trail 7.8 miles to Nightmare Camp (good camping, believe it or not) and the junction with the abandoned Freezeout Creek Trail (2,200 ft). Turn left onto the Freezeout Creek Trail and hike until you reach a large earth slide several hundred yards wide that has obliterated the trail. Take the path of least resistance through the brush, then sidehill through the forest until you rejoin the trail. From here on there's significant windfall along the trail, so take care not to lose the tread. The trail is reasonably easy to follow until about 4,200 feet (approx. 7 miles from Nightmare Camp), at which point it turns north and climbs into the Freezeout Creek basin west of Castle Peak. Rather than bushwhacking with a full backpack, bivi/camp here at any reasonable flat spot you can find along the creek (approx. 4,200 ft).

Route: From camp along Freezeout Creek at approximately 4,200 feet, ascend northerly along the creek, following the trail wherever possible, until the end of the trail at approximately 5,000 feet. Continue easterly along the south side of Freezeout Creek for approximately 1 mile to about 5,600 feet. Ascend slopes southeasterly, staying right (west) of cliff bands, to reach a notch in Castle Peak's west ridge at the head of the Castle Creek drainage (approx. 6,800 ft). Turn left (east) and scramble the south side of Castle's west ridge easterly (class 3), then northeasterly to the summit (8,306 ft).

Descent: Descend the route.

42 Andrews Peak

8,301 ft; 99th highest

Andrews Peak, incorrectly called Andrew Peak on some maps, is a summit of moderate size with gentle west and south slopes.

SOUTH ROUTE

This is an easy scramble with few, if any, technical difficulties.

APPROACH

Time to camp	6–7 hours
Mileage	13 miles
Elevation change	+ 4,200 ft; -0 ft
GT 15-minute	Coleman Peak (No. 20)
Contact	Okanogan/Wenatchee NF, Methow Valley Ranger District

ROUTE

Difficulty   ▲ Grade I+; class 2 rock
Time to summit 2 hours
Elevation change +1,200 ft; -0 ft
USGS 7.5-minute Remmel Mountain
Season   June–October

Approach: Backcountry self-registration permits are required for the Pasayten Wilderness and may be obtained at the trailhead. A Northwest Forest Pass is required to park at the trailhead.

From Winthrop, drive 23 miles north on West Chewuch Road (Forest Road 51) to the trailhead for the Andrews Creek Trail on the left (3,050 ft). (This trail has been closed since summer 2003 due to fire damage; call ahead.)

Hike the Andrews Creek Trail 11.5 miles northerly, past several turnoffs, to approximately 1 mile south of Andrews Pass (approx. 6,400 ft). Leave the trail and bear westerly, crossing Andrews Creek, for approximately a quarter mile to intersect with the Peepsight Trail (approx. 6,600 ft). Turn left onto the Peepsight Trail and hike approximately 1 mile to Rock Lake and good camping (approx. 7,160 ft).

Andrews Peak from the east (Remmel Mountain) Photo by Scott Stephenson

Route: From Rock Lake, head northerly to reach the base of a gully that originates left (west) of Point 8003. Ascend the right side of the gully to 7,500 feet, then exit right onto a forested ridge. Ascend the ridge to reach a broad, rocky shoulder beneath Point 8003. Cross the shoulder and ascend a loose, dirty gully (class 2) to below and left of Point 8003. Pass Point 8003 on the left and ascend to gain the crest of Andrews's gentle south ridge. Hike northerly along the ridge, past false summits, then scramble through large boulders (class 2) to the summit (8,301 ft).

Descent: Descend the route.

WASHINGTON PASS/ RAINY PASS

•

THE PEAKS IN THIS SECTION ARE ALL ACCESSED from Highway 20 (North Cascades Highway), and many of them lie within the immense Okanogan National Forest. However, none of the summits reside in North Cascades National Park, which greatly simplifies the permit situation. Because the highway grants easy access to both sides of the Cascade Crest, the routes presented here are varied, ranging from a classic Cascade glacier ascent to high and dry vistas with scrambling on superb granite. Ascend this area's peaks and you'll get a great sampling of the scenery and terrain in the Washington Cascades.

This section contains seven of this guide's high points. Of the seven, four of them can be climbed in two distinct Slam itineraries, leaving three Free Agent peaks to be climbed individually.

● Azurite Slam

Peaks & routes	Azurite Peak (South Route), Mount Ballard (West Route)
Max difficulty	▲ Grade I+; class 3 rock
Duration	4 days
Roundtrip to camp	22 miles
Elevation gain	+10,500 ft
USGS 7.5-minute	Azurite Peak, Slate Peak
GT 15-minute	Mount Logan (No. 49)
Trailhead	Canyon Creek
Season	May–October

Follow in the footsteps of nineteenth-century gold miners on this fantastically scenic journey up the rarely visited Mill Creek Valley. Keep an eye on your map and compass, as the trail is rough and poorly maintained in sections. Your camp at the abandoned Azurite Mine at the base of Mount Ballard will get you thinking about just how tough these miners must have been to make it in here long before the days of the North Cascades Highway. Absorb a little of this toughness—it'll help you with the physically challenging scrambling that awaits you.

Azurite Slam peaks from the south-southeast (Tower Mountain)
Photo by Paul Klenke

ITINERARY

Day	Elevation change	Instructions
1	+ 2,500 ft; -0 ft	Hike to Azurite Mine and camp (4,400 ft).
2	+ 4,000 ft; -4,000 ft	Climb Azurite Peak and return to camp.
3	+ 4,000 ft; -4,000 ft	Climb Mount Ballard and return to camp.
4	+ 0 ft; -2,500 ft	Hike out.

43 Azurite Peak

8,400 ft; 72nd highest

Azurite Peak has a steep eastern flank and pinkish, golden-colored rock characteristic of Golden Horn granite. The mountain is located immediately north of Azurite Pass between Mill Creek, South Fork Slate Creek, and West Fork Methow River.

SOUTH ROUTE

This moderate scramble gets you up close and personal with the golden rock that dominates the southern flank of the peak.

APPROACH

Time to camp	6 hours
Mileage	11 miles
Elevation change	+ 2,500 ft; -0 ft
GT 15-minute	Mount Logan (No. 49)
Contact	North Cascades NP, Headquarters; or Okanogan/ Wenatchee NF, Methow Valley Ranger District

ROUTE

Difficulty	▲ Grade I + ; class 3 rock
Time to summit	4 hours
Elevation change	+ 4,000 ft; -0 ft
USGS 7.5-minute	Azurite Peak, Slate Peak
Season	May–October

Approach: Permits are not required to camp or climb in the Okanogan National Forest. A Northwest Forest Pass is required to park at the trailhead.

From Interstate 5 north of Mount Vernon, take exit 230 (Anacortes/ Burlington). Drive 85 miles east on Highway 20 (North Cascades Highway) to the parking area on the left at the Canyon Creek Trailhead (1,900 ft).

Descend the trail a short distance, cross Granite Creek, and turn right at the first fork onto the Chancellor Trail. Hike the Chancellor Trail 5.9 miles east to the junction with the Mill Creek Trail (2,800 ft). Turn right (southeast) onto the Mill Creek Trail and hike 3.3 miles to the junction with the Cady Pass Trail (4,000 ft). Continue on the Mill Creek Trail for approximately 1 mile to the abandoned Azurite Mine and good camping along the creek (4,400 ft).

Route: Hike approximately 4 miles farther south on the Mill Creek Trail to Azurite Pass (approx. 6,680 ft). Leave the trail and ascend talus northeasterly to reach the base of Azurite Peak's south ridge at approximately 7,400 feet. Scramble northerly along the ridge crest, keeping to easier terrain on the left (west) side above 8,000 feet, to reach a gully that leads to the summit area. Scramble up the loose gully, then up rock to reach the summit ridge south of the summit (class 3). Turn left (north) and finish with a short scramble to the summit (8,400 ft).

Descent: Descend the route.

44 Mount Ballard

8,340 ft; 87th highest

Mount Ballard is a large, complex peak with two summits separated by approximately a quarter mile. The north (false) summit measures 8,301 feet and is incorrectly marked as the true summit on the USGS quad. The true summit is, in fact, the south summit. It measures 8,340 feet based on analysis of contour lines. The mountain has steep northern and northwestern flanks and a complex eastern flank corrugated by numerous gullies and ribs. The western flank, in comparison, slopes moderately down to Mill Creek and is composed primarily of talus and scree.

WEST ROUTE

This long ascent is largely a hike up talus and scree slopes with a few minor scrambling sections.

APPROACH

Time to camp	6 hours
Mileage	11 miles
Elevation change	+2,500 ft; -0 ft
GT 15-minute	Mount Logan (No. 49)
Contact	North Cascades NP, Headquarters; or Okanogan/ Wenatchee NF, Methow Valley Ranger District

ROUTE

Difficulty   ▲ Grade I +; class 3 rock
Time to summit 4 hours
Elevation change +4,000 ft; -0 ft
USGS 7.5-minute Azurite Peak, Slate Peak
Season   June–October

Approach: Follow the approach for Azurite Peak to the abandoned Azurite Mine (4,400 ft) and good camping along Mill Creek beneath Mount Ballard.

Route: From Azurite Mine, continue approximately 0.4 mile farther south on the Mill Creek Trail, crossing a small stream that drains Mount Ballard's west slopes, to 4,600 feet. Leave the trail and ascend Ballard's mostly talus and scree west slopes east-northeasterly, staying south of the stream, to a shoulder just south of the main summit (approx. 8,000 ft). Turn left (north) and scramble a short distance (class 3) to the summit (8,340 ft).

Descent: Descend the route.

Golden Slam

Peaks & routes Tower Mountain (West Route), Golden Horn (Southwest Route)
Max difficulty ▲▲ Grade II; class 3–4 rock with a short section of low-fifth class
Duration 3 days
Roundtrip to camp 20 miles
Elevation gain +6,400 ft
USGS 7.5-minute Washington Pass
GT 15-minute Washington Pass (No. 50)
Trailhead Pacific Crest Trail (Rainy Pass)
Season May–October

Rugged peaks, green meadows, groves of larch, and crystal-clear alpine lakes sum up this enjoyable outing. It's so beautiful here you'll wonder why it's not part of the North Cascades National Park just a short distance away. Mysteries aside, come and see the unique Golden Horn granite for yourself, up close and personal.

ITINERARY

Day	Elevation change	Instructions
1	+2,700 ft; -600 ft	Hike to upper Snowy Lake and camp (6,839 ft).
2	+1,700 ft; -1,700 ft	Climb Tower Mountain and return to camp.
3	+2,200 ft; -4,200 ft	Climb Golden Horn and hike out.

45 Tower Mountain

8,444 ft; 63rd highest

Tower Mountain is an imposing rock edifice, particularly its impressive sheer northeast face. It's located southeast of Golden Horn between Swamp Creek, Pine Creek, and West Fork Methow River.

WEST ROUTE

This is a challenging scramble with a lot of loose rock and some challenging routefinding.

APPROACH

Time to camp	5–6 hours
Mileage	10 miles
Elevation change	+2,700 ft; -600 ft
GT 15-minute	Washington Pass (No. 50)
Contact	North Cascades NP, Headquarters; or Okanogan/ Wenatchee NF, Methow Valley Ranger District

ROUTE

Difficulty	▲▲ Grade II; class 3–4 rock
Time to summit	3 hours
Elevation change	+1,700 ft; -0 ft
USGS 7.5-minute	Washington Pass
Season	May–October

Approach: Permits are not required to camp or climb in the Okanogan National Forest. A Northwest Forest Pass is required to park at the trailhead.

From Interstate 5 north of Mount Vernon, take exit 230 (Anacortes/ Burlington). Drive 97 miles east on Highway 20 (North Cascades Highway) to Rainy Pass and park at the trailhead for the Pacific Crest Trail on the left (east) side of the road (4,800 ft).

Hike the Pacific Crest Trail (PCT) 5 miles to Cutthroat Pass (6,860 ft). From the pass, turn left onto the PCT (the right fork leads to Cutthroat Lake) and proceed 2.5 miles to Granite Pass (6,280 ft). Contour westerly around the large Swamp Creek drainage on the PCT (passing beneath the south face of Tower Mountain) for approximately 2.5 miles to the near (east) side of Methow Pass (approx. 6,300 ft); there's camping here. Turn right (north) onto a side trail and climb to lower Snowy Lake and good camping (6,735 ft). Camping is also available at the upper lake, a short distance farther on (6,839 ft).

Tower Mountain from the west Photo by Brian Bongiovanni

Route: From lower Snowy Lake, make a rising traverse easterly over easy terrain into the talus basin at the base of Tower Mountain's west face. Ascend the basin to its head at the base of a broad gully. Scramble up the very loose gully (class 3), past a chockstone, to reach a sharp notch in a southwest-trending spur ridge. From here on, keep a sharp eye out for strategically placed cairns that help mark the way. Scramble up the spur ridge, staying on or right of the crest, to reach the base of cliffs beneath the summit area. Locate a gully that leads up and left through the cliffs. The correct gully has an obvious rock spire with a capstone just left of its entrance (see Beckey 1995, p. 366). Scramble up this gully to reach a small notch. Cross the notch and descend slightly until able to traverse beneath cliff bands to reach yet another steep gully. Scramble up the gully (class 3) to the base of a rock step and pass it by traversing right until able to climb up and back into the gully. Continue up the gully to the base of a steep, white rock wall just below the ridgeline. Traverse right on a series of exposed ledges for several hundred feet until able to climb (class 3) to the crest of the ridge above. Scramble a short distance along the exposed crest to the summit (8,444 ft).

Descent: Descend the route.

46 Golden Horn

8,366 ft; 80th highest

Golden Horn has a striking appearance, both its sheer north and east faces and its pinkish, golden rock, termed Golden Horn granite. The peak is northwest of Tower Mountain between Tower Creek and West Fork Methow River.

SOUTHWEST ROUTE

This is primarily a scree and talus hike until the last two committing and exposed moves to the top of the flat summit block.

APPROACH

Time to camp	5–6 hours
Mileage	10 miles
Elevation change	+ 2,700 ft; -600 ft
GT 15-minute	Washington Pass (No. 50)
Contact	North Cascades NP, Headquarters; or Okanogan/ Wenatchee NF, Methow Valley Ranger District

Golden Horn final summit scramble Photo by Brian Bongiovanni

ROUTE

Difficulty   ▲▲ Grade II; class 3 rock with two moves of low-fifth class on the summit block

Time to summit 2–3 hours

Elevation change +1,600 ft; -0 ft

USGS 7.5-minute Washington Pass

Season   May–October

Approach: Follow the approach for Tower Mountain to either lower Snowy Lake (6,735 ft) or upper Snowy Lake (6,839 ft) and camp.

Route: From upper Snowy Lake, take a compass bearing on the summit rocks and follow it, roughly northwesterly, up loose scree and talus to beneath the summit horn; from close below, it's apparent that the horn is actually split by a wide cleft. Ascend talus and a loose gully (class 3) aiming for the cleft. Scramble (class 2) along an exposed, blocky ledge that passes through the cleft and around to the rear of the left-hand horn to reach a sandy bench approximately 20 feet below the summit. From the bench, make an exposed move right and mantel (low-fifth class) to the top of the flat (slightly downsloping) summit block and the summit (8,366 ft).

Descent: Descend the route.

⟩ Free Agents

47 Black Peak

8,970 ft; 17th highest

Black Peak is a massive, imposing mountain and one of the easiest of the state's high points to reach. Apart from the south side, all flanks of the peak harbor glacier remnants, the northernmost of which is bordered by the impressive west summit (8,820 ft). The mountain rises immediately above Wing Lake in a classically scenic alpine setting.

SOUTH FACE

This popular route makes for an enjoyable outing in a superb alpine environment. Watch for loose rock in the gullies and take special care when climbing beneath other parties. There are great views of Mount Goode, Storm King Mountain, and Mount Logan from the summit that'll have you dreaming of the Thunder Slam.

Black Peak from the east Photo by Scott Stephenson

APPROACH

Time to camp	4 hours
Mileage	5 miles
Elevation change	+2,500 ft; -400 ft
GT 15-minute	Mount Logan (No. 49), Washington Pass (No. 50)
Contact	North Cascades NP, Headquarters; or Okanogan/ Wenatchee NF, Methow Valley Ranger District

ROUTE

Difficulty	▲▲ Grade II; moderate snow; class 4 rock
Time to summit	2–3 hours
Elevation change	+2,100 ft; -0 ft
USGS 7.5-minute	Mount Arriva
Season	April–October

Approach: The approach and base camp at Wing Lake are not within North Cascades National Park, so permits are not required for camping or climbing. A Northwest Forest Pass is required to park at the trailhead.

From Interstate 5 north of Mount Vernon, take exit 230 (Anacortes/ Burlington). Drive 97 miles east on Highway 20 (North Cascades Highway) to Rainy Pass and park at the picnic area and trailhead for the Maple Pass Loop Trail on the right (west) side of the road (4,800 ft).

Hike the Maple Pass Loop Trail 1.5 miles to the junction with the Lake Ann Trail. Stay right and continue on the Maple Pass Loop Trail to Heather Pass (6,100 ft), which is accessed by a short side trail. Please adhere to the camping ban within a quarter mile of either side of the pass to give the heavily impacted area a chance to recover. From the pass, leave the trail and follow a climber's path to the north side of the pass. Descend west on the path to the edge of a talus/boulder field and cross it, following cairns. Rejoin the path on the opposite side and continue to Lewis Lake and good camping (5,700 ft). Follow the trail around the right (north) side of the lake and ascend westerly through a series of larch meadows to Wing Lake and good camping (6,900 ft).

Route: From the outlet stream on the east shore of Wing Lake, follow the climber's path around the right (north) shore of the lake into a gentle stream gully. Ascend the gully (snow-filled to late summer), then travel on scree along the rim of the lateral moraine. Ascend moderately steep scree/talus/snow slopes westerly to a saddle on the crest of the south ridge (8,000 ft). Starting just west of the crest, climb a gully (class 2) northerly (climber's path when snow cover has melted) to its head. Traverse left (west) into a neighboring gully (class 3) and continue to its head. Traverse left (west) once more and continue climbing (class 3) to reach a broad, flat shoulder west of the summit (approx. 8,800 ft). From the shoulder, follow cairns right (east) along an easy, somewhat loose, ledge system (exposed class 2) to the base of the summit block. Finish with a short, exposed scramble (class 4) up the summit block to the summit (8,970 ft).

Descent: Descend the route.

48 Silver Star Mountain

8,876 ft; 24th highest

Silver Star Mountain is a big, craggy peak located just east of Washington Pass. When you straddle the exposed sharp summit, it's hard to suppress the urge to shout "Hi Ho Silver!" Views from the summit include the Early Winters Spires, Liberty Bell, and the Wine Spires.

SILVER STAR GLACIER

This popular scramble is a perfect introduction to the combined elements of glacier travel and scrambling found on many of the peaks in this guide. The gentle, forgiving Silver Star Glacier has few crevasses so routefinding is simple. Rock quality on the final scramble is good and the exposed summit provides an exciting finish to this enjoyable route.

APPROACH

Time to camp	3–4 hours
Mileage	3 miles
Elevation change	+2,500 ft; -300 ft
GT 15-minute	Washington Pass (No. 50)
Contact	North Cascades NP, Headquarters; or Okanogan/ Wenatchee NF, Methow Valley Ranger District

ROUTE

Difficulty	▲▲ Grade II; moderate snow; glacier travel; class 3 rock
Time to summit	3–4 hours
Elevation change	+2,800 ft; -300 ft
USGS 7.5-minute	Silver Star Mountain
Season	May–September

Approach: Permits are not required to camp or climb in the Okanogan National Forest. A Northwest Forest Pass is required to park at the trailhead.

From Interstate 5 north of Mount Vernon, take exit 230 (Anacortes/

Silver Star Mountain from the west in spring Photo by Scott Stephenson

Silver Star Mountain from the north in spring Photo by Lowell Skoog

Burlington). Drive Highway 20 (North Cascades Highway) to 4 miles east of Washington Pass and park at the wide shoulder (approx. 4,300 ft). From here, much of the approach can be seen, including Burgundy Spire and Burgundy Col.

From the road, drop down 300 feet over boulders, enter the forest and cross Early Winters Creek (ford or log); this crossing can be tricky in spring with heavy runoff. Look for the climber's trail that can be found just north of Burgundy Creek. The trail climbs steeply well left (north) of the creek to reach a flat bench (6,400 ft) and good camping (no water in late season).

Route: From the flat bench, continue on the climber's path to below the west face of Burgundy Spire. Turn left (north) and ascend a very loose gully to Burgundy Col and decent bivi sites (approx. 7,900 ft). Watch for rockfall from climbers above. From Burgundy Col, descend approximately 250 feet until able to traverse right (east) below Burgundy Spire and ascend to the Silver Star Glacier. Ascend the glacier southeasterly beneath the east faces of the Wine Spires, then bear southerly and ascend to a broad col (8,600 ft). Stay on the right (west) side of the final snowslope to avoid a small bergschrund. From the col, turn left (east) and scramble rock (class 3) to the exposed summit (8,876 ft). The summit consists of large blocks propped on top of one another. The highest block (the summit) has a sizable air space beneath it. For a heart-thumping thrill, dare to sit atop it.

Descent: Descend the route.

49 Big Snagtooth

8,330 ft; 91st highest

Big Snagtooth is the southernmost and highest "tooth" on Snagtooth Ridge, the serrated crest located just south of Silver Star Mountain. A short but steep summit crag gives way on the south to extensive scree slopes descending into the Cedar Creek valley.

SOUTHWEST FACE

This challenging scramble has an exposed, airy finish. Fred Beckey used a "shoulder" to surmount the smooth summit block on the first ascent (Beckey 1995, p. 286), so you've got a bit of fun in store for you too.

APPROACH

Time to camp	n/a (done as a day trip)
Mileage	n/a
Elevation change	n/a
GT 15-minute	Washington Pass (No. 50)
Contact	North Cascades NP, Headquarters; or Okanogan/ Wenatchee NF, Methow Valley Ranger District

ROUTE

Difficulty	▲▲ Grade II; class 3–4 rock with a short section of unprotectable low-fifth class on the summit block
Time to summit	6–7 hours
Elevation change	+ 4,400 ft; -300 ft
USGS 7.5-minute	Silver Star Mountain
Season	May–September

Approach: Permits are not required to camp or climb in the Okanogan National Forest. A Northwest Forest Pass is required to park at the trailhead.

From Interstate 5 north of Mount Vernon, take exit 230 (Anacortes/ Burlington). Drive Highway 20 (North Cascades Highway) to 4 miles east of Washington Pass and park at the wide shoulder (approx. 4,300 ft). From here, much of the route can be seen.

Route: This is a pure cross-country route requiring map and compass work as well as some bushwhacking through a moderately dense forest. From the road, drop down 300 feet over boulders, enter the forest, and cross Early Winters Creek (ford or log); this crossing can be tricky in spring with heavy runoff. Once across the creek, ascend and traverse slopes southeasterly toward upper Willow Creek, through occasionally brushy forest and

Big Snagtooth and Snagtooth Ridge from the west in spring Photo by Scott Stephenson

Big Snagtooth from the southwest Photo by Paul Klenke

across two small gullies with easy creek crossings. At 5,600 feet, ascend easterly up the drainage into a basin below Snagtooth Ridge and above tree line (approx. 7,200 ft). Ascend southeasterly up loose talus and scree (class 2–3) to the crest of the ridge above (approx. 7,800 ft). Cross the ridge and make a contouring traverse southwesterly, past a minor rock rib, to reach the entrance to a hidden gully leading up and left to the summit. Ascend the gully, initially up slabby terrain and then, as it narrows, a series of short rock steps (class 3–4) to reach the first of two very large chockstones. Scramble under the chockstones over moderately steep and exposed terrain, then hop boulders to reach a sandy notch below the summit block. Utilizing your partner's shoulders for assistance, ascend the smooth summit block (unprotectable low-fifth class) with small hand and footholds to gain the summit (8,330 ft). It's helpful if the leader trails a rope for use in belaying his partner to the top.

Descent: Rappel off an existing makeshift horn (slightly wobbly) from the summit back to the notch below the summit rock. From the notch, scramble immediately west down to rappel anchors. Rappel (single rope) to the Big Snagtooth–Willow Tooth col. From the col, descend westerly to 8,000 feet to join the ascent route and descend the remainder of the route.

LAKE CHELAN–SAWTOOTH WILDERNESS

•

THE LAKE CHELAN–SAWTOOTH WILDERNESS was designated in 1984. It's managed by the Okanogan and Wenatchee national forests and today encompasses more than 150,000 acres. The wilderness includes the sublime Lake Chelan, which is more than 1,500 feet deep (the third deepest lake in the United States) and more than 55 miles long. A journey up the lake is one of Washington's most unique experiences, passing from the condo-ridden southern shore into the wild, undeveloped splendor of its remote northern reaches. Along the lake's northeastern shore, the terrain rises abruptly to the crest of the Sawtooth Range before dropping again into the Twisp River valley. The wilderness is bordered by North Cascades National Park and Lake Chelan National Recreation area to the west and the rest of the Okanogan National Forest's vast expanse to the north and east, creating a secluded ecosystem in which wildlife, including bears and deer, thrive in the forested lowlands. The wilderness is a hiker's dream. There are countless gorgeous alpine lakes, many of them nestled in steep-walled cirques. Groves of larch trees often line their shores, particularly impressive in fall when their needles turn a remarkable shade of gold. This is high and dry scenery at its best.

Twelve of this guide's high points lie within the wilderness boundaries. All twelve of these high points can be climbed in five distinct Slam itineraries, leaving no Free Agent peaks to be climbed individually.

● Gardner Slam

Peaks & routes North Gardner Mountain (South Route), Gardner Mountain (South Route)

Max difficulty ▲ Grade I+; class 3 rock

Duration 3 days

Roundtrip to camp 21 miles

Elevation gain +6,700 ft

USGS 7.5-minute Gilbert, Mazama, Midnight Mountain, Silver Star Mountain

GT 15-minute Buttermilk Butte (No. 83)

Trailhead Wolf Creek Trail

Season June–October

Make a trip up this deep wilderness valley and you'll see ancient forest, green meadows, and a swift, cold creek teeming with trout. And if you're really lucky you'll hear howling timber wolves. Add to that the enjoyable scrambling to the summit of two peaks and you've got it all. What more could you ask for?

ITINERARY

Day	Elevation change	Instructions
1	+ 2,900 ft; -0 ft	Follow the approach for North Gardner Mountain to Gardner Meadows and camp (5,700 ft).
2	+ 3,800 ft; -3,800 ft	Climb Gardner Mountain and North Gardner Mountain and return to camp.
3	+0 ft; -2,900 ft	Hike out.

Notes: For day 2, to traverse from Gardner to North Gardner, scramble (class 2–3) the connecting ridge westerly from Gardner to reach Point 8487 (South Peak of North Gardner), at times staying on the left (south) side of the ridge for easier going. At Point 8487 join the route for North Gardner Mountain for both the ascent and descent. To save a day, you could hike out on day 2 since it's mostly downhill.

---

50 North Gardner Mountain

8,956 ft; 20th highest

North Gardner Mountain and nearby Gardner Mountain, less than 1 mile southeast, form a large, desolate mountain massif. North Gardner is between Cedar, Wolf, and North creeks and southeast of Silver Star Mountain, just outside of the Lake Chelan–Sawtooth Wilderness boundary.

SOUTH ROUTE

This is a long but reasonably straightforward scramble to the highest point of the Gardner massif.

APPROACH

Time to camp	6 hours
Mileage	11 miles
Elevation change	+2,900 ft; -0 ft
GT 15-minute	Buttermilk Butte (No. 83)
Contact	Okanogan/Wenatchee NF, Methow Valley Ranger District

ROUTE

Difficulty	▲ Grade I+; class 3 rock
Time to summit	4 hours
Elevation change	+3,300 ft; -0 ft
USGS 7.5-minute	Gilbert, Mazama, Midnight Mountain, Silver Star Mountain
Season	June–October

North Gardner and Gardner mountains from the southwest (Abernathy Peak)
Photo by Scott Stephenson

Approach: Permits are not required to camp or climb in the Lake Chelan–Sawtooth Wilderness. A Northwest Forest Pass is required to park at the trailhead.

From Winthrop, drive south on Highway 20 (North Cascades Highway) across the Methow River and turn right (west) onto Twin Lakes Road (County Road 9120). Continue 1.3 miles and turn right onto Wolf Creek Road (County Road 1131). Drive 2.9 miles and turn left onto Left Fork Wolf Creek Road (the sign says "L." for "Left") and continue 4.5 miles, following signs at forks, to the trailhead for Wolf Creek Trail (2,800 ft).

Hike the Wolf Creek Trail 10.5 miles through timber, an old burn, and meadows to Gardner Meadows beneath Gardner Mountain and good camping (5,700 ft).

Route: From Gardner Meadows, ascend westerly along the right (north) side of Wolf Creek up the meadows to a flat area (approx. 6,300 ft) beneath the southwest slopes of Gardner Mountain. Climb almost due north up the steep slopes, staying left (west) of a southeast-trending spur ridge above 6,800 feet, to Point 8487 (South Peak of North Gardner). Climb over Point 8487 (class 2–3) and scramble rock (class 3) 1 mile northerly along a ridge to the summit (8,956 ft).

Descent: Descend the route.

51 Gardner Mountain

8,898 ft; 22nd highest

Gardner Mountain is a sprawling massif with a steep northeastern flank. Extensive talus and scree slopes, particularly on the south, give the mountain a desolate, weathered appearance. It's connected to North Gardner Mountain by a long, moderate ridge.

SOUTH ROUTE

This is a straightforward scramble but be prepared for plenty of scree and talus. Snow cover simplifies the ascent, but complicates the already long approach.

APPROACH

Time to camp	6 hours
Mileage	11 miles
Elevation change	+2,900 ft; -0 ft
GT 15-minute	Buttermilk Butte (No. 83)
Contact	Okanogan/Wenatchee NF, Methow Valley Ranger District

Summit

Gardner Mountain from the south (Gardner Meadows) in spring
Photo by Scott Stephenson

ROUTE

Difficulty ▲ Grade I+; class 2–3 rock
Time to summit 3–4 hours
Elevation change +3,200 ft; -0 ft
USGS 7.5-minute Mazama, Midnight Mountain
Season June–October

Approach: Follow the approach for North Gardner Mountain to Gardner Meadows and good camping (5,700 ft).

Route: From Gardner Meadows, start left (west) of a small brushy stream and ascend northerly up gradual open slopes to gain a forested south-trending ridge to the left (west) of a broad gully. As a point of reference, this gully passes just west of an unmistakable gigantic rock spur in the middle of Gardner's south face. Ascend the forested ridge until it ends at a rocky outcrop (approx. 7,500 ft). Pass the outcrop on the left (west) and ascend a loose gully (class 2–3), then continue up open scree and talus slopes northerly to the summit (8,898 ft).

Descent: Descend the route.

● Sawtooth Slam

Peaks & routes	Mount Bigelow (Southeast Route), Martin Peak (South Route), Switchback Peak (South Route)
Max difficulty	▲ Grade I+; class 3 rock
Duration	3 days
Roundtrip to camp	23 miles
Elevation gain	+7,100 ft
USGS 7.5-minute	Martin Peak
GT 15-minute	Prince Creek (No. 115)
Trailhead	Eagle Lakes Trail
Season	June–October

This Slam is at its best in fall, particularly late September and early October, when the larches are ablaze with gold, the nights crisp and clear, and the people absent. It's a great way to wrap up your scrambling season. It's also one of the few Slams that can be done as a loop hike, providing new scenery at every step of your journey. Perhaps the only drawback to this otherwise perfect Slam is that motorcycles may be present in large numbers. If this will bother you, do this trip in early season when snow patches make the trails impassable to wheels.

ITINERARY

Day	Elevation change	Instructions
1	+2,300 ft; -0 ft	Hike to upper Eagle Lake and camp (7,110 ft).
2	+3,700 ft; -3,600 ft	Climb Mount Bigelow. Break camp and climb Switchback Peak on the way to Cooney Lake and camp (7,241 ft).
3	+1,200 ft; -3,600 ft	Climb Martin Peak and hike out via the Martin Creek Trail to complete the loop.

Notes: For day 2, to climb Switchback Peak, break camp at upper Eagle Lake and backtrack 0.5 mile to the junction with the Eagle Lakes Trail. Turn right (west) onto the Eagle Lakes Trail and hike 1 mile, past the turnoff to Eagle Lake, to Horsehead Pass (7,600 ft). Cross the pass and descend 2 miles (now called the Prince Creek Trail) to the junction with the Summit Trail (6,600 ft). Turn left (south) onto the Summit Trail and hike 2.2 miles to the junction with the Angel Staircase Trail (7,000 ft). Turn left (east) onto the Angel Staircase Trail and climb 1.4 miles to a pass at the crest of Sawtooth Ridge (8,000 ft) and join the route for Switchback Peak. Switchback and Martin peaks are connected by an easy north-south talus ridge.

52 Mount Bigelow

8,440 ft; 64th highest

Mount Bigelow is a craggy peak with extensive talus slopes and a large northern cirque. It's located east of Hoodoo Pass and northwest of upper Eagle Lake.

SOUTHEAST ROUTE

This moderate scramble, with its exposed completion, is a remarkably quick ascent from upper Eagle Lake.

APPROACH

Time to camp	3 hours
Mileage	6 miles
Elevation change	+2,300 ft; -0 ft
GT 15-minute	Prince Creek (No. 115)
Contact	Okanogan/Wenatchee NF, Methow Valley Ranger District

ROUTE

Difficulty	▲ Grade I+; class 3 rock
Time to summit	2 hours
Elevation change	+1,400 ft; -0 ft
USGS 7.5-minute	Martin Peak
Season	June–October

Approach: Permits are not required to camp or climb in the Lake Chelan–Sawtooth Wilderness. A Northwest Forest Pass is required to park at the trailhead.

From Twisp, drive south on Highway 153 to the junction with North Fork Gold Creek Road (County Road 1029) and turn right (west). Stay right at the junction near the forest boundary onto Forest Road 4340. Continue 5.6 miles to Forest Road 300, a narrow dirt road leading to the left. Drive 5 miles to the end of the road and the trailhead for the Eagle Lakes Trail (approx. 4,800 ft).

Hike the Eagle Lakes Trail 1.9 miles, staying left at the turnoff to Crater Creek Trail at 0.1 mile, to the junction with the Martin Creek Trail (approx. 5,700 ft). Stay right and continue on the Eagle Lakes Trail 3.3 miles to the junction with the upper Eagle Lake Trail (approx. 7,000 ft). Turn right onto the upper Eagle Lake Trail and hike 0.5 mile to upper Eagle Lake and good camping (7,110 ft).

Route: From the northwest end of upper Eagle Lake, ascend northwest-erly up easy talus slopes and through minor cliff bands to reach the upper talus/boulder slope. Scramble northerly up blocky and sandy terrain to reach

Mount Bigelow summit tower from the east Photo by Paul Klenke

the crest of the upper east ridge at the base of the steep summit tower. Scramble rock up and right (exposed class 3) to reach the northeast face of the summit tower below and right of the summit. Scramble up along the edge of a small face (often holds a snow patch) to reach a small notch (exposed class 3). Cross the notch to the left (south) and enter a shallow gully below and left of the summit. Scramble up the gully (class 3) to the summit (8,440 ft).

Descent: Descend the route.

53 Martin Peak

8,375 ft; 78th highest

Martin Peak (not to be confused with a peak of the same name in the Glacier Peak Wilderness) is a pronounced but mostly moderate peak apart from a cliffy north face. It's located on the crest of Sawtooth Ridge north of Switchback Peak and immediately southwest of the Martin Lakes.

SOUTH ROUTE

This is an easy scramble presenting few technical difficulties. From the summit, you can easily traverse southerly along the talus-covered ridge crest to the summit of Switchback Peak.

APPROACH

Time to camp	4–5 hours
Mileage	9 miles
Elevation change	+2,500 ft; -0 ft
GT 15-minute	Prince Creek (No. 115)
Contact	Okanogan/Wenatchee NF, Methow Valley Ranger District

ROUTE

Difficulty	▲ Grade I+; class 2–3 rock
Time to summit	2 hours
Elevation change	+1,200 ft; -0 ft
USGS 7.5-minute	Martin Peak
Season	June–October

Approach: Follow the approach for Mount Bigelow to the junction with the Martin Creek Trail (approx. 5,700 ft). Turn left onto the Martin Creek Trail and hike 4 miles to the junction with the Martin Lakes Trail (approx. 6,400 ft). Stay left and continue on the Martin Creek Trail another 2.2 miles to Cooney Lake and good camping (7,241 ft).

Route: From the flat area on the west end of Cooney Lake (approx. 7,300 ft), ascend easy, open slopes and then talus northerly to reach a small col in Martin Peak's upper south ridge (approx. 8,200 ft). Scramble rock (class 2–3) northerly along the ridge to the summit (8,375 ft).

Descent: Descend the route.

54 Switchback Peak

8,321 ft; 93rd highest

Switchback Peak, also known unofficially as Cooney Peak, is a minor, rounded eminence not labeled on the USGS quad. It's located on Sawtooth Ridge south of Martin Peak and immediately southwest of Cooney Lake.

SOUTH ROUTE

There's a trail to within several hundred vertical feet of the summit and the remainder is easy walking. From the summit, it's mostly an easy talus hop northerly along the ridge to the summit of Martin Peak.

APPROACH

Time to camp	4–5 hours
Mileage	9 miles
Elevation change	+2,500 ft; -0 ft
GT 15-minute	Prince Creek (No. 115)
Contact	Okanogan/Wenatchee NF, Methow Valley Ranger District

ROUTE

Difficulty	▲ Grade I; hiking
Time to summit	1–2 hours
Elevation change	+1,100 ft; -0 ft
USGS 7.5-minute	Martin Peak
Season	June–October

Approach: Follow the approach for Mount Bigelow to the junction with the Martin Creek Trail (approx. 5,700 ft). Turn left onto the Martin Creek Trail and hike 4 miles to the junction with the Martin Lakes Trail (approx. 6,400 ft). Stay left and continue on the Martin Creek Trail another 2.2 miles to Cooney Lake and good camping (7,241 ft).

Route: From Cooney Lake, pick up a trail that heads south along the east side of the lake. After approximately 0.5 mile, the trail switchbacks steeply up the open slope until the gradient eases and the trail forks (approx. 7,950 ft).

Switchback Peak from the north (Martin Peak) Photo by Paul Klenke

Take the right fork and ascend gradually to a pass at the crest of Sawtooth Ridge (8,000 ft), 1.2 miles from the lake. From the pass, leave the trail and walk northeasterly up the easy, broad ridge to the summit (8,321 ft).

Descent: Descend the route.

Spirit Slam

Peaks & routes	Raven Ridge (North Route), Hoodoo Peak (South Ridge)
Max difficulty	▲ Grade I+; class 3 rock
Duration	2 days
Roundtrip to camp	10 miles
Elevation gain	+5,700 ft
USGS 7.5-minute	Hoodoo Peak, Martin Peak
GT 15-minute	Buttermilk Butte (No. 83), Prince Creek (No. 115)
Trailhead	Libby Creek Trail
Season	June–October

Get your spirits soaring on this great scramble outing. The moderately rough approach, especially the final boulder field, keeps most of the horse packers out for a change. The starkly beautiful Libby Lake, with its rocky and barren shores and impressive views, will make you glad you came.

ITINERARY

Day	Elevation change	Instructions
1	+ 2,800 ft; -0 ft	Hike to the cabin site in the forest clearing and camp (7,200 ft).
2	+ 2,900 ft; -5,700 ft	Climb Raven Ridge and Hoodoo Peak. Hike out.

Notes: For day 1, if you've still got energy when you arrive at camp, Hoodoo Peak makes a nice afternoon ascent. For day 2, both routes share a common point at the cabin site in the forest clearing at 7,200 feet.

55 Raven Ridge

8,572 ft; 48th highest

Raven Ridge is a craggy east-west crest rising southeast of Hoodoo Peak and north of Crater Creek. The true summit is generally accepted to be the surveyed Point 8572 at the east end of the ridge despite the USGS quad showing an elevation of 8,580 feet at the ridge's west end. The west summit is sometimes referred to as Libby Mountain, while the east summit is known as Corax Peak.

NORTH ROUTE

This is an exciting scramble to the high point of the craggy ridge with great views of Libby Lake and Hoodoo Peak along the way. For a bit more scrambling, you can easily run the ridge west to the false (west) summit.

APPROACH

Time to camp	3–4 hours
Mileage	5 miles
Elevation change	+2,800 ft; -0 ft
GT 15-minute	Buttermilk Butte (No. 83), Prince Creek (No. 115)
Contact	Okanogan/Wenatchee NF, Methow Valley Ranger District

ROUTE

Difficulty	▲ Grade I+; class 3 rock
Time to summit	3 hours
Elevation change	+1,500 ft; -200 ft
USGS 7.5-minute	Martin Peak
Season	June–October

Approach: Permits are not required to camp or climb in the Lake Chelan–Sawtooth Wilderness. A Northwest Forest Pass is required to park at the trailhead.

Raven Ridge from the north (Hoodoo Peak) Photo by Scott Stephenson

From Twisp, drive aproximately 12 miles south on Highway 153 to the junction with Libby Creek Road (Forest Road 43). Turn right (west) onto Libby Creek Road and continue 7.5 miles to the junction with Gold Creek Road (Forest Road 4340). Turn left (southwest) onto Gold Creek Road and drive 1.2 miles before turning right onto Forest Road 700. Continue 1.5 miles and turn left onto Forest Road 750. Drive 1 mile to the end of the road and the trailhead for the Libby Creek Trail (approx. 4,400 ft).

Hike approximately 4.8 miles on the Libby Creek Trail to a cabin site in a clearing in the forest and good camping (7,200 ft), just before where the trail begins a final steep ascent to Libby Lake.

Route: Ascend the trail approximately 0.5 mile to Libby Lake (7,618 ft). Cross the outlet stream at the southeast corner of the lake and proceed around the south shore to its southwest corner. From the lake, it's apparent that the slopes above are cut by multiple gullies (and they often hold snow into midsummer). Ascend the wide, loose gully (almost a low-angle face) located immediately between two prominent rock buttresses (class 3). The gully/face bears southwest from the lake to reach the crest of Raven Ridge (approx. 8,480 ft) immediately left (east) of the false (west) summit. (The west summit can be reached by a short 300-yard scramble up boulders and talus.) The true summit is approximately 0.5 mile to the east. Hop boulders and talus, either on the crest or on the south slope, to the summit (8,572 ft).

Descent: Descend the route.

56 Hoodoo Peak

8,464 ft; 59th highest

Hoodoo Peak is a rocky, dome-shaped prominence located between East Fork Buttermilk Creek and North Fork Libby Creek, north of Raven Ridge.

SOUTH RIDGE

This moderate scramble is a quick and enjoyable ascent. There are good views of Raven Ridge from the summit.

APPROACH

Time to camp	3–4 hours
Mileage	5 miles
Elevation change	+2,800 ft; -0 ft
GT 15-minute	Buttermilk Butte (No. 83), Prince Creek (No. 115)
Contact	Okanogan/Wenatchee NF, Methow Valley Ranger District

Hoodoo Peak from the south-southeast (Raven Ridge) Photo by Scott Stephenson

ROUTE

Difficulty	▲ Grade I+; class 2 rock
Time to summit	2 hours
Elevation change	+1,300 ft; -0 ft
USGS 7.5-minute	Hoodoo Peak, Martin Peak
Season	June–October

Approach: Follow the approach for Raven Ridge to the cabin site in a clearing in the forest and good camping (7,200 ft).

Route: From camp, ascend rocky slopes westerly to reach a col in Hoodoo Peak's south ridge right (north) of Point 8071 (approx. 8,000 ft). Turn right (north) and hop boulders (class 2) along the blocky ridge crest to the summit (8,464 ft).

Descent: Descend the route.

Twisp Slam

Peaks & routes	Reynolds Peak (Southeast Route), Abernathy Peak (Southeast Route)
Max difficulty	▲▲ Grade II; class 3 rock
Duration	2 days
Roundtrip to camp	n/a (the peaks are done as day trips)
Elevation gain	+10,600 ft
USGS 7.5-minute	Gilbert, Sun Mountain
GT 15-minute	Stehekin (No. 82), Buttermilk Butte (No. 83)
Trailhead	Reynolds Creek Trail (Reynolds Peak), Scatter Lake Trail (Abernathy Peak)
Season	June–October

This is the only Slam that features a base camp in a car-accessible campground. It's a great opportunity to get in some enjoyable scrambling in gorgeous country encumbered with only a daypack and then spoil yourself at night with all the comforts of home. Save this "reward" for when you just can't face loading up your pack and humping it in to yet another remote base camp. The campground among the large ponderosa pines along the banks of the Twisp River is a great place to spend a night or two of your life.

ITINERARY

Day	Elevation change	Instructions
1	+5,500 ft; -5,500 ft	Get an early start and climb Reynolds Peak. Car camp at Mystery Campground or Poplar Flat Campground (3,200 ft).
2	+5,200 ft; -5,200 ft	Climb Abernathy Peak.

Notes: For a less strenuous outing, consider adding a rest day in between the ascents. Day 2 is a steep, hot, and dry ascent up the Scatter Lake Trail, so it's best to get an early start.

57 Reynolds Peak

8,512 ft; 52nd highest

Reynolds Peak is an isolated, seldom-climbed mountain with two very distinct summits, the south being higher, and a small glacier beneath its east face. The peak is between War and Reynolds creeks northeast of Stehekin.

SOUTHEAST ROUTE

The crux of this moderate scramble is the routefinding and bushwhacking through dense slide-alder thickets.

APPROACH

Time to camp	n/a (done as a day trip)
Mileage	n/a
Elevation change	n/a
GT 15-minute	Stehekin (No. 82), Buttermilk Butte (No. 83)
Contact	Okanogan/Wenatchee NF, Methow Valley Ranger District

ROUTE

Difficulty	▲▲ Grade II; class 3 rock
Time to summit	6–7 hours
Elevation change	+5,400 ft; -100 ft
USGS 7.5-minute	Gilbert, Sun Mountain
Season	June–October

Approach: Permits are not required to camp or climb in the Lake Chelan–Sawtooth Wilderness. A Northwest Forest Pass is required to park at the trailhead.

From Twisp, drive 18.8 miles west on Twisp River Road (Forest Road 44) to Mystery Campground (camp here if you're doing the Slam). Cross the river, turn right (northwest) onto Forest Road 4435 and continue approximately 1 mile to the junction with Forest Road 4435-015. Turn left onto Forest Road

Reynolds Peak from the south Photo by Paul Klenke

4435-015 and drive to the end of the road and the trailhead for the Reynolds Creek Trail (approx. 3,200 ft).

Route: Hike the Reynolds Creek Trail approximately 2.5 miles west, past a clearing with a steep grass slope, to reach a flat area of ancient forest with minimal understory (approx. 4,700 ft). From here, the entrance to the broad South Fork Reynolds Creek valley lies directly south. Continue another 500 yards to 4,850 feet, then leave the trail and descend a short distance south to cross Reynolds Creek (ford or log).

Bushwhack southerly up the South Fork Reynolds Creek valley through a nasty section of dense slide alder, staying on the left (east) side of the creek; use game trails to make the going easier. Continue ascending to reach the head of the valley and open terrain (approx. 5,600 ft). Ascend slopes westerly, easily bypassing minor cliff bands along the way, to reach the base of the south side of Reynolds Peak's summit pyramid. Scramble (class 3) to a high notch, then turn left and climb to the summit (8,512 ft).

Descent: Descend the route.

58 Abernathy Peak

8,321 ft; 93rd highest

Abernathy Peak is the high point of Abernathy Ridge. The peak lies between North Creek, Wolf Creek, and North Fork Twisp River southwest of the Gardner–North Gardner massif.

SOUTHEAST ROUTE

This route is primarily a hike with a steep approach trail and a final short but steep scree and talus slope.

APPROACH

Time to camp	n/a (done as a day trip)
Mileage	n/a
Elevation change	n/a
GT 15-minute	Stehekin (No. 82)
Contact	Okanogan/Wenatchee NF, Methow Valley Ranger District

ROUTE

Difficulty	▲ Grade I+; class 2 rock
Time to summit	6 hours
Elevation change	+5,200 ft; -0 ft
USGS 7.5-minute	Gilbert
Season	June–October

Abernathy Peak from the southeast (Scatter Lake) Photo by Scott Stephenson

Approach: Permits are not required to camp or climb in the Lake Chelan–Sawtooth Wilderness. A Northwest Forest Pass is required to park at the trailhead.

From Twisp, drive 22 miles west on Twisp River Road (Forest Road 44) to the trailhead for the Scatter Creek Trail (3,200 ft) on the right, shortly after the Poplar Flat Campground.

Route: Hike the steep trail 4.2 miles to Scatter Lake (7,047 ft, good camping if you'd rather not car camp). Follow the trail northwesterly around the right (east) side of the lake to the base of Abernathy Peak's southeast slopes. Ascend the moderate, mostly scree slopes (class 2) northwesterly to the summit (8,321 ft).

Descent: Descend the route.

Wish Slam

Peaks & routes Oval Peak (South Ridge), Star Peak (South Route), Courtney Peak (Southeast Ridge)

Max difficulty ▲ Grade I+; class 2 rock

Duration 3 days

Roundtrip to camp 21 miles

Elevation gain +9,200 ft

USGS 7.5-minute Oval Peak, Prince Creek

GT 15-minute Buttermilk Butte (No. 83)

Trailhead West Fork Buttermilk Trail

Season June–October

Here's a grouping of three technically easy scrambles/hikes with a great campsite on the shores of Star Lake. The high and dry scenery will help you forget the dusty, buggy approach, as will a swim in the lake's invigorating waters. Go ahead, make a wish upon a Star—it might even come true.

ITINERARY

Day	Elevation change	Instructions
1	+3,500 ft; -300 ft	Follow the approach for Star Peak to Star Lake and camp (7,173 ft).
2	+2,800 ft; -2,800 ft	Climb Star Peak and Courtney Peak and return to camp.
3	+2,900 ft; -6,100 ft	Break camp and follow the West Fork Buttermilk Trail back to the junction with the Buttermilk Ridge Trail (7,000 ft) and join the approach to Oval Peak. Climb Oval Peak, leaving your packs at the pond. Hike out.

Notes: Optionally, for the hike out on day 3, consider descending cross-country from the pond through semi-open forest with a moderately brushy understory, maintaining a southeast bearing, to intersect the West Fork Buttermilk Trail at 6,000 feet; finish hiking out.

59 Oval Peak

8,795 ft; 28th highest

Oval Peak is a gentle, egg-shaped mountain with a steep northeast face and extensive scree and talus slopes. It's located northeast of Oval Lakes, between Oval Creek and West Fork Fish Creek and north of Sawtooth Ridge.

SOUTH RIDGE

This route offers an easy way to the summit, avoiding the worst of the extensive talus and scree. It's all about boulder hopping—watch out for the loose ones!

APPROACH

Time to camp	5–6 hours
Mileage	10 miles
Elevation change	+3,400 ft; -400 ft
GT 15-minute	Buttermilk Butte (No. 83)
Contact	Okanogan/Wenatchee NF, Methow Valley Ranger District

ROUTE

Difficulty	▲ Grade I +; class 2 rock
Time to summit	2–3 hours
Elevation change	+1,900 ft; -0 ft
USGS 7.5-minute	Oval Peak
Season	June–October

Approach: Permits are not required to camp or climb in the Lake Chelan–Sawtooth Wilderness. A Northwest Forest Pass is required to park at the trailhead.

Oval Peak from the southwest (Courtney Peak) Photo by Scott Stephenson

From Twisp, drive 11 miles west on Twisp River Road (Forest Road 44) to the junction with the Buttermilk Creek Road (Forest Road 43). Turn left (south) onto Buttermilk Creek Road and continue 4.2 miles (stay left at the junction at 0.2 mile) to the junction with Forest Road 4300-500 (signposted "West Fork Buttermilk Road"). Turn right (west) onto Forest Road 4300-500 and drive 3 miles to its end at the trailhead for the West Fork Buttermilk Trail (4,000 ft).

Hike the West Fork Buttermilk Trail 7.7 miles to the junction with the faint, abandoned Buttermilk Ridge Trail marked by a small cairn (7,000 ft). (Note that the Green Trails map incorrectly shows this junction at 6,800 ft.) Turn right (north) and follow the trail (some windfalls but generally easy going) approximately 1.5 miles as it descends gradually, passing beneath boulder fields, to approximately 6,600 feet before climbing to reach a pond south of Oval Peak and good camping (6,936 ft).

Route: From the pond, ascend north-northwesterly through forest, alp, and talus/scree to a col in Oval's south ridge (7,600 ft). Turn right (north) and scramble/boulder hop (class 2) along the long, gentle ridge to the summit (8,795 ft). Even the large boulders are unstable, so be extra careful not to get a leg or foot pinned.

Descent: Descend the route. Alternatively, scramble down the east ridge to 8,000 feet. Locate and descend a sandy gully southerly back into the basin to 7,200 feet, then hike back to the pond.

60 Star Peak

8,690 ft; 34th highest

Star Peak is steep on all flanks except the southwest, which is composed primarily of extensive fields of scree and talus. The mountain is on Sawtooth Ridge at the head of West Fork Buttermilk Creek, immediately southeast of Courtney Peak and Fish Creek Pass.

SOUTH ROUTE

This route is a scree and talus hike interspersed with sections of boulder hopping.

APPROACH

Time to camp	5–6 hours
Mileage	9 miles
Elevation change	+3,500 ft; -300 ft
GT 15-minute	Buttermilk Butte (No. 83)
Contact	Okanogan/Wenatchee NF, Methow Valley Ranger District

Star Peak from the northwest (Courtney Peak) Photo by Scott Stephenson

ROUTE

Difficulty	▲ Grade I + ; class 2 rock
Time to summit	2–3 hours
Elevation change	+ 1,600 ft; -0 ft
USGS 7.5-minute	Oval Peak, Prince Creek
Season	June–October

Approach: Follow the approach for Oval Peak to the junction with the Buttermilk Ridge Trail (7,000 ft). Continue on the West Fork Buttermilk Trail 1 mile to Fish Creek Pass (7,480 ft). Cross the pass and descend to Star Lake and good camping (7,173 ft).

Route: From Star Lake, ascend southerly to a basin above the lake. Pick up an obvious climber's path that ascends the steep scree slope southerly to a col in a spur ridge just north of Point 7912 (approx. 7,830 ft). Turn left and make a rising traverse below and right of the ridgeline up scree, talus and boulder slopes to the summit (8,690 ft).

Descent: Descend the route.

61 Courtney Peak

8,392 ft; 76th highest

Courtney Peak has a precipitous north face and extensive scree and talus slopes. It's located on Sawtooth Ridge immediately northwest of Star Peak and Fish Creek Pass.

SOUTHEAST RIDGE

This route provides an easy scramble to the summit where you are treated to great views of Star Peak, Oval Peak, and sparkling Middle Oval Lake straight down the sheer north face.

APPROACH

Time to camp	5–6 hours
Mileage	9 miles
Elevation change	+3,500 ft; -300 ft
GT 15-minute	Buttermilk Butte (No. 83)
Contact	Okanogan/Wenatchee NF, Methow Valley Ranger District

Courtney Peak from the southeast (Fish Creek Pass) Photo by Scott Stephenson

ROUTE

Difficulty   ▲ Grade I+; class 2 rock
Time to summit 2 hours
Elevation change +1,300 ft; -0 ft
USGS 7.5-minute Oval Peak
Season   June–October

Approach: Follow the approach for Oval Peak to the junction with the Buttermilk Ridge Trail (7,000 ft). Continue on the West Fork Buttermilk Trail 1 mile to Fish Creek Pass (7,480 ft). Cross the pass and descend to Star Lake and good camping (7,173 ft).

Route: From Fish Creek Pass, scramble (class 2) northwesterly up Courtney Peak's easy southeast ridge to the summit (8,392 ft).

Descent: Descend the route.

GLACIER PEAK WILDERNESS

•

THE U.S. CONGRESS DESIGNATED GLACIER PEAK WILDERNESS as part of the original Wilderness Act of 1964. Today the wilderness encompasses more than 572,000 acres and is managed by both the Mount Baker–Snoqualmie and Wenatchee national forests. Glacier Peak, called "DaKobed" or "Great Parent" by some Native Americans, is the crown jewel of the wilderness and the most remote of Washington's volcanoes. Glacier's symmetrical beauty and pristine white glaciers provide a picture-perfect backdrop for some of the state's most spectacular alpine scenery. Lovely meadows, nestled between rugged ridges, explode with wildflowers in the summer and ice-cold creeks flow from more than 200 lakes. Deer, wolverines, black bears, gray wolves, and grizzly bears call the wilderness home.

All this spectacular alpine terrain provides seemingly endless opportunities for scrambling and climbing. The Ptarmigan Traverse, arguably the most famous off-trail route in Washington, crosses 15 miles of glaciers and rugged terrain through the northern section. Within its boundaries, the wilderness contains twenty-four of this guide's high points, more than any other wilderness area in this guide. Of the twenty-four high points found within Glacier Peak Wilderness, twenty-two of them can be climbed in nine distinct Slam itineraries, leaving only two Free Agent peaks to be climbed individually.

● Bonanza Slam

Peaks & routes	Bonanza Peak (Mary Green Glacier), Martin Peak (West Ridge)
Max difficulty	▲▲▲ Grade III; steep snow; glacier travel; class 4 rock
Duration	3 days
Roundtrip to camp	10 miles
Elevation gain	+8,400 ft
USGS 7.5-minute	Holden
GT 15-minute	Holden (No. 113)
Trailhead	Railroad Creek Trail
Season	June–August

This Slam takes you to the summit of Bonanza Peak, the highest nonvolcanic peak in the entire Cascade Range. Climbing Bonanza is a serious endeavor, inviting comparisons with large peaks in the Canadian Rockies. It has all the elements of a classic Cascade climb. We can't say you'll always enjoy it, but we're certain you'll get the complete climbing experience. You'll also be treated to a scenic boat ride up Lake Chelan and a visit to the remote village of Holden.

ITINERARY

Day	Elevation change	Instructions
1	+3,100 ft; -0 ft	Hike to Holden Pass and camp (6,400 ft).
2	+3,200 ft; -3,200 ft	Get a very early start and climb Bonanza Peak. Return to camp.
3	+2,200 ft; -5,300 ft	Climb Martin Peak and hike out.

Notes: For day 3, remember to arrive back in Holden in time to catch the bus back to Lucerne and, subsequently, the ferry back down the lake. If you miss the bus, you may have to arrange for private transportation to Lucerne (if available), so bring along some extra money just in case.

62 Bonanza Peak

9,511 ft; 6th highest

Climb Bonanza Peak and strike your claim to a motherlode of classic Cascade climbing challenges: big glaciers, hidden crevasses, loose rock, challenging routefinding, waterfalls...It's a demanding but fantastic climb. Bonanza is an immense alpine massif with three large glaciers and a mile-long jagged summit ridge that lies entirely above 9,000 feet. The peak lies immediately west-northwest of Holden Lake and west of Martin Peak at the head of the Railroad and Company Creek valleys.

MARY GREEN GLACIER

Bonanza Peak is a demanding ascent by any route. The Mary Green Glacier, the least technical route, has challenging routefinding, a lot of loose rock, rock and icefall hazards, and hidden crevasses. Don't climb below another party once on the rock above the glacier, and definitely only attempt this ascent in stable weather.

APPROACH

Time to camp	3 hours
Mileage	5 miles
Elevation change	+3,100 ft; -0 ft
GT 15-minute	Holden (No. 113)
Contact	Okanogan/Wenatchee NF, Chelan Ranger District

ROUTE

Difficulty	▲▲▲ Grade III; steep snow; glacier travel; class 3 and 4 rock
Time to summit	5–6 hours
Elevation change	+3,200 ft; -0 ft
USGS 7.5-minute	Holden
Season	June–August

Approach: Permits are not required to camp or climb in the Glacier Peak Wilderness.

This approach requires use of commercial transportation to reach Lucerne on the west shore of Lake Chelan. The *Lady of the Lake* ferry (or a high-speed catamaran run by the same company) departs from Fields Point Landing on the west shore or from the town of Chelan at the lake's southern tip. Contact the Lake Chelan Boat Company in Chelan for the current boat schedule (see Appendix E for all company contact information). Or, if you've got less time and a lot more money, a floatplane to Chelan or Stehekin might be an option worth considering. In the Seattle area, try Kenmore Air or Seattle Seaplanes, and in Chelan, contact Chelan Airways.

If catching the ferry at Fields Point Landing, drive US 2 east to Alternate US 97 at Wenatchee. Continue north on Alternate US 97 to the town of Entiat. Drive another 9 miles on Alternate US 97, turn left (north) onto Highway 971 (Navarre Coulee Road) and continue to Lake Chelan State Park. Bear left (north) onto South Lakeshore Road and drive 8 miles to Fields Point Landing. If catching the ferry at Chelan, drive US 2 east to Alternate US 97 at Wenatchee. Continue on Alternate US 97 to Chelan at the southern tip of the lake. Take the *Lady of the Lake* ferry to Lucerne on the west shore of the lake. For the 13-mile journey to Holden (3,262 ft), take the school bus shuttle

Bonanza Peak from the northeast Photo by Paul McClellan

that is synchronized with boat arrivals ($5 per person one-way; bring exact change). Camping is available at the Holden Campground (3,300 ft) at the end of the Railroad Creek Road approximately a mile west of the village.

From Holden Campground, follow Railroad Creek Trail 0.9 mile west to the junction with Holden Lake Trail (3,600 ft). Turn right and follow Holden Lake Trail 4 miles to Holden Lake (5,278 ft) and good camping on its east side (bring insect repellent). Alternatively, from the head of the lake, ascend the slopes above bearing north-northwesterly to Holden Pass (6,400 ft) and additional good camping.

Route: From Holden Pass, ascend and traverse westerly along the ridge to reach a snowfield at the base of slabs (snow-covered in early season) that have been exposed by the retreat of the glacier. Scramble up the slabs, which are often wet due to meltwater runoff from the glacier, to reach the northern edge of the Mary Green Glacier. Move quickly in this section to minimize exposure to icefall off the glacier.

Rope up and ascend the glacier westerly along its right (north) edge and then make a gradual southwesterly traverse along the base of Bonanza Peak's northeast ridge to the glacier's upper (southwest) corner. Don't cut straight across the glacier—its central section has numerous crevasses and is difficult to navigate. From the upper (southwest) corner of the glacier, climb the steep upper snow thumb rightward to its highest corner below the hanging snowslope. Cross a moat to gain rock on the right side. This section can be difficult by August due to a bergschrund and/or lack of a bridge across the moat.

Climb rock (class 3–4) just right of a gully for about four rope lengths. Traverse left into another gully system and scramble (class 4) to reach a prominent notch in the crest of the upper northeast ridge right (north) of the summit. A rope is of limited use in these sections as there are few opportunities for placing protection, plus it could trigger rockfall. Scramble rock southerly along the loose ridge crest (class 4) past a series of large blocks; the horn at the south end is the summit (9,511 ft).

Descent: Descend the route back to the glacier. Descend the glacier to its terminus above the slabs. Either carefully downclimb the slabs back to the snowfield, or traverse easterly above the slabs until able to make a short rappel back to the snowfield. Retrace the remainder of the route.

63 Martin Peak

8,511 ft; 53rd highest

Martin Peak (not to be confused with a peak of the same name in the Lake Chelan–Sawtooth Wilderness) is an outstanding bulky mountain with a steep upper east face rising above an unnamed glacier. The peak is immediately east of Bonanza Peak and northeast of Holden Lake.

WEST RIDGE

This challenging scramble has a fair bit of exposure on the often steep west ridge. The views of Bonanza are awesome though. Definitely consider bringing a rope for this ascent.

APPROACH

Time to camp	3 hours
Mileage	5 miles
Elevation change	+3,100 ft; -0 ft
GT 15-minute	Holden (No. 113)
Contact	Okanogan/Wenatchee NF, Chelan Ranger District

Martin Peak from the west in winter Photo by Lowell Skoog

ROUTE

Difficulty	▲▲ Grade II; class 4 rock
Time to summit	3 hours
Elevation change	+ 2,200 ft; -0 ft
USGS 7.5-minute	Holden
Season	June–October

Approach: Follow the approach for Bonanza Peak to Holden Pass and good camping (6,400 ft).

Route: From Holden Pass, ascend easterly to the base of Martin Peak's west ridge. Gain the ridge crest and scramble rock (class 4) easterly, keeping to easier terrain on the right (south) side, to within approximately 100 feet of the summit. Finish with a scramble up a steep, exposed gully (class 4) to the summit (8,511 ft).

Descent: Descend the route.

Chelan Slam

Peaks & routes	Cardinal Peak (West Route), Emerald Peak (West Route), Saska Peak (South Ridge), Pinnacle Mountain (South Route)
Max difficulty	▲ Grade I+; class 3 rock
Duration	5 days
Roundtrip to camp	25 miles
Elevation gain	+13,100 ft
USGS 7.5-minute	Pinnacle Mountain, Pyramid Mountain, Saska Peak
GT 15-minute	Lucerne (No. 114)
Trailhead	North Fork Entiat River Trail
Season	June–October

Here's a Slam combining moderate scrambles to the summits of all of the major peaks in the Chelan Mountains. If you love high and dry country, this is about as scenic as it gets. Bring along your nonclimber friends as there are plenty of great day hikes to keep them busy while you're scrambling. Once they see the peaks, they may even want to join you.

ITINERARY

Day	Elevation change	Instructions
1	+ 2,700 ft; -0 ft	Follow the approach for Cardinal Peak to camp in the meadow (6,600 ft).
2	+ 3,900 ft; -3,900 ft	Climb Cardinal and Emerald peaks and return to camp.
3	+ 2,400 ft; -3,200 ft	Break camp and climb Saska Peak. Continue over Saska Pass and descend to the junction with the Snow Brushy Creek Trail and camp (5,800 ft).
4	+ 2,600 ft; -2,600 ft	Climb Pinnacle Mountain and return to camp.
5	+ 1,700 ft; -3,600 ft	Hike out.

64 Cardinal Peak

8,590 ft; 46th highest

Cardinal Peak is the highest summit in the Chelan Mountains. It has a long, craggy ridge joining three summits, the middle being the highest (by a small margin). Cardinal is not technically within the Glacier Peak Wilderness but lies just outside the wilderness boundary, near the head of the North Fork Entiat River valley southeast of Saska and Emerald peaks.

WEST ROUTE

The crux of this moderate scramble is gaining the ridge via the talus- and scree-filled gully. Be careful, and definitely don't climb in large groups or beneath one another.

APPROACH

Time to camp	4–5 hours
Mileage	9 miles
Elevation change	+2,700 ft; -0 ft
GT 15-minute	Lucerne (No. 114)
Contact	Okanogan/Wenatchee NF, Entiat Ranger District

ROUTE

Difficulty	▲ Grade I+; class 2–3 rock
Time to summit	3 hours
Elevation change	+2,000 ft; -0 ft
USGS 7.5-minute	Pyramid Mountain, Saska Peak
Season	June–October

Approach: Permits are not required to camp or climb in the Glacier Peak Wilderness. A Northwest Forest Pass is required to park at the trailhead.

Drive US 2 east to Alternate US 97 at Wenatchee. Drive north on Alternate US 97 to just before the town of Entiat. Turn left (west) onto Entiat River Road (Forest Road 51) and drive 32.5 miles to the junction with North Fork Entiat River Road (Forest Road 5606). Turn right (east) and continue 2 miles

North Summit   Summit   South Summit

Cardinal Peak from the west (Saska Peak) Photo by Paul Klenke to the end of the road and the trailhead for the North Fork Entiat River Trail (approx. 3,900 ft).

Hike the North Fork Entiat River Trail approximately 8.1 miles to the junction with the Pyramid Mountain Trail (6,600 ft). Turn left (north) onto the Pyramid Mountain Trail and hike approximately a mile to reach an open meadow beneath Cardinal Peak and good camping (approx. 6,600 ft).

Route: From camp, head east until below and west of the large basin beneath Cardinal Peak's middle peak (approx. 6,640 ft). Leave the trail and ascend easterly through forest, then up open talus slopes and a loose talus- and scree-filled gully to reach a saddle (approx. 8,360 ft) between Cardinal's north and middle (true) summits. Turn right (south) and scramble up slabs and shallow gullies (class 2–3) along the ridge to reach the crest just left (east) of the summit rocks. Circle around to the back (south) side of summit rocks and scramble ledges (class 2–3) to the summit (8,590 ft).

Descent: Descend the route.

65 Emerald Peak

8,422 ft; 67th highest

Emerald Peak is a rocky, eroded mountain with a steep north face. It's located at the head of the North Fork Entiat River valley immediately east of Saska Peak and northwest of Cardinal Peak, just outside the Glacier Peak Wilderness boundary.

WEST ROUTE
This moderate scramble presents few technical difficulties. There's some exposure when scrambling around the summit.

APPROACH

Time to camp	4–5 hours
Mileage	9 miles
Elevation change	+2,700 ft; -0 ft
GT 15-minute	Lucerne (No. 114)
Contact	Okanogan/Wenatchee NF, Entiat Ranger District

ROUTE

Difficulty	▲ Grade I+; class 2–3 rock
Time to summit	3 hours
Elevation change	+1,900 ft; -0 ft
USGS 7.5-minute	Saska Peak
Season	June–October

Emerald Peak from the southwest Photo by Paul Klenke

Approach: Follow the approach for Cardinal Peak to camp in the meadow beneath Cardinal Peak (approx. 6,600 ft).

Route: From camp, continue approximately 0.75 mile farther north on the Pyramid Mountain Trail to where the trail curves sharply left (west) in a small meadow at the head of the valley (approx. 6,900 ft). Leave the trail and ascend easy dirt, rock, and pumice slopes northerly into an upper basin (approx. 7,700 ft) below a gentle saddle located at the base of Emerald Peak's west ridge. Scramble easterly up a broad, loose gully about halfway until it is possible to traverse right (south) into the next gully over. Ascend this gully (also loose) all the way to the blocky notch between the two summits; the left (north) one is the true summit (8,422 ft). There's exposure at both summits but the climbing is not difficult (class 2–3).

Descent: Descend the route.

66 Saska Peak

8,404 ft; 71st highest

Saska Peak is a rocky, weathered summit with a steep upper northwestern flank. It's located on the Snow Brushy Creek–North Fork Entiat River divide west of Emerald Peak, just outside the Glacier Peak Wilderness boundary.

SOUTH RIDGE

This is a relatively straightforward scramble with few technical difficulties up mostly scree, talus, and rocky ribs.

APPROACH

	Primary	Alternate
Time to camp	4–5 hours	5 hours
Mileage	9 miles	10 miles
Elevation change	+2,700 ft; -0 ft	+2,700 ft; -0 ft
GT 15-minute	Lucerne (No. 114)	Lucerne (No. 114)
Contact	Okanogan/Wenatchee NF, Entiat Ranger District	Okanogan/Wenatchee NF, Entiat Ranger District

ROUTE

Difficulty	▲ Grade I+; class 3 rock
Time to summit	3 hours (primary approach); 4 hours (alternate approach)
Elevation change	+1,900 ft, -0 ft (primary approach); +3,200 ft, -600 ft (alternate approach)
USGS 7.5-minute	Saska Peak
Season	June–October

Primary Approach: Follow the approach for Cardinal Peak to camp in the meadow beneath Cardinal Peak (approx. 6,600 ft).

Alternate Approach: Follow the approach for Cardinal Peak to just before the town of Entiat. Turn left (west) onto Entiat River Road (Forest Road 51) and drive 38 miles to the end of the road at Cottonwood Campground and the trailhead for the Entiat River Trail (3,140 ft).

Saska Peak from the southeast Photo by Paul Klenke

Hike the Entiat River Trail 6.4 miles northerly, past numerous turnoffs, to the junction with the Snow Brushy Creek Trail (incorrectly labeled the Emerald Park Trail on the Green Trails map) at 4,000 feet. Turn right onto the Snow Brushy Creek Trail and hike approximately 3.5 miles to the junction with the Pyramid Mountain Trail and good camping (5,800 ft).

Route: If coming via the primary approach, continue approximately 1.7 miles farther north and west on the Pyramid Mountain Trail until several hundred yards before Saska Pass (approx. 6,900 ft).

If coming via the alternate approach, follow the Pyramid Mountain Trail 2.2 miles east to Saska Pass (approx. 7,440 ft). Cross the pass and continue for several hundred yards to approximately 6,900 feet.

From east of Saska Pass at 6,900 feet, leave the trail and ascend northerly up slopes into the basin beneath Saska Peak's south face (it's also possible to keep to the semi-timbered ridge to the right of the basin). Scramble a broad gully (class 2) up and left to gain the crest of Saska Peak's south ridge. Scramble northerly along the loose ridge crest (class 3) to beneath the summit rocks. Scramble up the summit rocks (class 2–3) to the summit (8,404 ft).

Descent: Descend the route.

67 Pinnacle Mountain

8,400 ft; 72nd highest

Pinnacle Mountain is a long, twisted, and impressive granite crest. The peak is immediately north of Borealis Pass and northwest of Saska and Emerald peaks.

SOUTH ROUTE

This is a moderate scramble to the highest "pinnacle" on the mountain's crest.

APPROACH

Time to camp	6 hours
Mileage	11 miles
Elevation change	+2,700 ft; -0 ft
GT 15-minute	Lucerne (No. 114)
Contact	Okanogan/Wenatchee NF, Entiat Ranger District

ROUTE

Difficulty	▲ Grade I+; class 2–3 rock
Time to summit	4 hours
Elevation change	+2,600 ft; -0 ft
USGS 7.5-minute	Pinnacle Mountain, Saska Peak
Season	June–October

Approach: Follow the approach for Cardinal Peak to just before the town of Entiat. Turn left (west) onto Entiat River Road (Forest Road 51) and drive 38 miles to the end of the road at Cottonwood Campground and the trailhead for the Entiat River Trail (3,140 ft).

Hike the Entiat River Trail 6.4 miles northwesterly, past numerous turnoffs, to the junction with the Snow Brushy Creek Trail (incorrectly labeled as the Emerald Park Trail on the Green Trails map) at 4,000 feet. Turn right onto the Snow Brushy Creek Trail and hike approximately 3.5 miles to the junction with the Pyramid Mountain Trail and good camping (5,800 ft).

Route: From the junction of the Snow Brushy Creek and Pyramid Mountain trails, continue northeasterly on the Snow Brushy Creek Trail another 0.6 mile to the junction with the 45-Mile Drive Trail. Turn left (northwest) onto the 45-Mile Drive Trail and ascend to Borealis Pass (7,680 ft). The trail is faint in places, so keep a close eye out for cairns. From the pass, follow the ridge northerly to the head of the basin southwest of Pinnacle Mountain. Ascend northeasterly up a gully and talus to a notch in the crest south of Pinnacle's summit (7,840 ft). From the notch, scramble northerly on or left (west) of the crest (class 2–3) to the summit (8,400 ft).

Descent: Descend the route.

Pinnacle Mountain from the south-southwest (Borealis Pass) Photo by Paul Klenke

● Chickamin Slam

Peaks & routes	Dome Peak (Dome Glacier), Sinister Peak (Northwest Face)
Max difficulty	▲▲ Grade II+; moderate snow; glacier travel; class 3–4 rock
Duration	3 days
Roundtrip to camp	28 miles
Elevation gain	+11,400 ft
USGS 7.5-minute	Dome Peak, Downey Mountain
GT 15-minute	Cascade Pass (No. 80)
Trailhead	Downey Creek Trail
Season	June–September

This physically demanding Slam has some of the best alpine ambience in the Cascades. It's a long, tough and rough approach to make it in here due to significant elevation gain and loss along the military obstacle course that is the Bachelor Creek Trail. So, give yourself some extra time and you'll truly love this incredible place.

ITINERARY

Day	Elevation change	Instructions
1	+ 5,700 ft; -700 ft	Hike to Itswoot Ridge and camp (6,400 ft).
2	+ 5,100 ft; -5,100 ft	Climb Sinister Peak and Dome Peak and return to camp.
3	+ 700 ft; -5,700 ft	Hike out.

Notes: This is a strenuous Slam no matter how you break it up. To make the outing more enjoyable, consider adding a day on the approach and camping at Sixmile Camp or in the open side valley (11 miles from the trailhead) on the first night. Climbing Sinister and Dome in a single day is definitely a grunt, so get an early start.

---

68 Dome Peak

8,920 ft; 21st highest

Dome Peak is a high, remote, and heavily glaciated summit that makes for a fantastic climb. The Dome and Chickamin glaciers cover its southwestern and northeastern flanks, respectively. Dome Peak is on the West Fork Agnes–Sulphur Creek divide immediately west of Sinister Peak. From Dome's summit, there are stupendous views of the Ptarmigan Traverse peaks stretching north to Cascade Pass.

DOME GLACIER

This route has a long, challenging approach on a rough and brush-encroached trail offset by enjoyable climbing in a stunning alpine setting.

APPROACH

Time to camp	1–2 days
Mileage	14 miles
Elevation change	+5,700 ft; -700 ft
GT 15-minute	Cascade Pass (No. 80)
Contact	Mount Baker–Snoqualmie NF, Darrington Ranger District

ROUTE

Difficulty	▲▲ Grade II +; moderate snow; glacier travel; class 3–4 rock
Time to summit	4 hours
Elevation change	+2,600 ft; -0 ft
USGS 7.5-minute	Dome Peak, Downey Mountain
Season	June–September

Approach: Permits are not required to camp or climb in the Glacier Peak Wilderness. A Northwest Forest Pass is required to park at the trailhead.

From Interstate 5 take exit 208 (Arlington) and drive approximately 32 miles east on Highway 530 to Darrington. Continue 7 miles north on Highway 530 to the junction with Suiattle River Road (Forest Road 26), just after crossing the Sauk River Bridge. Turn right (east) onto Suiattle River Road and drive approximately 21 miles to the Downey Creek Campground and the trailhead for the Downey Creek Trail (1,450 ft). (The automobile bridge over Downey Creek, just before the trailhead, and the campground were severely damaged in the October 2003 floods and may take some time to repair or replace. If the bridge is not passable to pedestrians, a difficult and potentially dangerous ford of the creek would be required; call ahead.)

Follow the Downey Creek Trail 6.5 miles through lush old-growth forest along Downey Creek to Sixmile Camp on the north side of Bachelor Creek (crossing can be difficult in early season) and good camping (approx. 2,400 ft). Locate and follow an abandoned trail easterly along the left (north) side of Bachelor Creek (the trail is rough and prone to windfall) to where it crosses Bachelor Creek (approx. 3,700 ft) at 9.5 miles. After crossing the creek, follow the trail into a dense, brushy thicket where it turns sharply left (east) and ascends the valley near the creek (see Nelson and Potterfield 2000, p. 117). Continue on the trail through timber and up steep switchbacks, through an open side valley at 11 miles (good camping), and up to Cub Lake Pass (6,000 ft)

Dome Peak from the west Photo by Paul McClellan

at 12.5 miles. (Avalanche debris has eradicated a portion of the trail below the pass. Don't attempt to follow the trail through the debris. Instead, from the point where the trail enters the debris, ascend the semi-open steep forested hillside to the right of the avalanche swathe to rejoin the trail at a flat area above and right of the devastated area.) From the pass, follow the trail down steep switchbacks to Cub Lake (5,338 ft) and good camping at approximately 13 miles. For a shorter summit day, ascend the steep trail northeasterly for approximately 1 mile to Itswoot Ridge and additional camping (at both 6,400 ft and 6,900 ft) with good views of Dome Peak.

Route: From Itswoot Ridge at 6,900 feet, make a long traverse easterly across heather, snow, talus, minor rock ribs, and snowmelt streams to enter the first of a sequence of three gullies (probably snow-filled) that lead to the upper left (west) side of the Dome Glacier. Ascend the gullies, then bear right (east) over varied terrain beneath Snow Dome and onto the glacier. Cross the glacier to a flat area (8,000 ft), then climb a moderate snowslope easterly to the base of a scree/snow-filled gully. Ascend the gully to the Dome Glacier–Chickamin Glacier col (approx. 8,500 ft). Follow a snow ridge southeasterly to sandy benches and good camping (approx. 8,700 ft). Finish with a scramble (class 3–4) up an exposed rock arête to the summit (8,920 ft).

Descent: Descend the route.

69 Sinister Peak

8,440 ft; 64th highest

Sinister Peak is a remote summit overshadowed by Dome Peak. It has a steep, icy north face rising above the Chickamin Glacier and a short but precipitous south face. It's located on the West Fork Agnes–Sulphur Creek divide immediately east of Dome Peak.

NORTHWEST FACE

This is a great climb in a spectacular alpine environment. There are a lot of crevasses in the Chickamin Glacier, so don't forget proper glacier travel equipment and crampons, as the route can be icy.

APPROACH

Time to camp	1–2 days
Mileage	14 miles
Elevation change	+5,700 ft; -700 ft
GT 15-minute	Cascade Pass (No. 80)
Contact	Mount Baker–Snoqualmie NF, Darrington Ranger District

ROUTE

Difficulty	▲▲ Grade II +; moderate snow; glacier travel; class 2 rock
Time to summit	5–6 hours
Elevation change	+3,400 ft; -1,300 ft
USGS 7.5-minute	Dome Peak, Downey Mountain
Season	June–September

Approach: Follow the approach for Dome Peak to camping (at 6,400 ft or 6,900 ft) on Itswoot Ridge.

Route: From Itswoot Ridge at 6,900 feet, make a long traverse easterly across heather, snow, talus, minor rock ribs, and snowmelt streams to enter the first of a sequence of three gullies (probably snow-filled) that lead to the upper left (west) side of the Dome Glacier. Ascend the gullies, then bear right (east) over varied terrain beneath Snow Dome and onto the glacier. Cross the glacier to a flat area (8,000 ft), then climb a moderate snowslope easterly to the base of a scree/snow-filled gully. Ascend the gully to the Dome Glacier–Chickamin Glacier col (approx. 8,500 ft). (Good camping can be found by following a snow ridge southeasterly from the col to reach sandy benches at approximately 8,700 ft.)

From the col, descend the Chickamin Glacier northeasterly, weaving

Sinister Peak from the northeast (Gunsight Peak) Photo by Lowell Skoog

around large crevasses, to approximately 7,200 feet. Turn right and contour southeasterly across the glacier until able to ascend southerly to the Dome-Sinister col situated on the upper west ridge of Sinister Peak (approx. 7,640 ft). From the col, climb the 30-degree snowslopes of the northwest face to just below the summit. Make a short rock scramble (class 2) to the summit (8,440 ft).

Descent: Descend the route.

● Copper Slam

Peaks & routes	Mount Fernow (East Ridge), Copper Peak (East Face)
Max difficulty	▲▲ Grade II; steep snow; class 3 rock
Duration	3 days
Roundtrip to camp	8 miles
Elevation gain	+9,400 ft
USGS 7.5-minute	Holden
GT 15-minute	Holden (No. 113)
Trailhead	Railroad Creek Trail
Season	June–October

This Slam combines enjoyable climbing with a scenic journey up Lake Chelan and a visit to the village of Holden. On the way out, treat yourself to an ice-cream cone with two scoops, one for each summit. Go ahead, you deserve it.

ITINERARY

Day	Elevation change	Instructions
1	+2,300 ft; -0 ft	Follow the approach to Copper Creek basin and camp (5,600 ft).
2	+3,700 ft; -3,700 ft	Climb Mount Fernow and return to camp.
3	+3,400 ft; -5,700 ft	Climb Copper Peak and hike out.

Notes: For day 3, remember to arrive back in Holden in time to catch the bus back to Lucerne and, subsequently, the ferry back down the lake. If you miss the bus, you may have to arrange for private transportation to Lucerne (if available), so bring along some extra money just in case.

70 Mount Fernow

9,249 ft; 8th highest

Mount Fernow is the highest peak in the Entiat Mountains and has steep northern and northwestern flanks. Fernow is north of Seven Fingered Jack and south of Copper Peak at the head of the Entiat River valley.

EAST RIDGE

This challenging and often exposed scramble is an exciting route to the summit.

APPROACH

Time to camp	3 hours
Mileage	4 miles
Elevation change	+2,300 ft; -0 ft
GT 15-minute	Holden (No. 113)
Contact	Okanogan/Wenatchee NF, Chelan Ranger District

ROUTE

Difficulty	▲▲ Grade II; class 3 rock
Time to summit	4 hours
Elevation change	+3,700 ft; -0 ft
USGS 7.5-minute	Holden
Season	June–October

Mount Fernow from the south (Mount Maude) Photo by Scott Stephenson

Approach: Permits are not required to camp or climb in the Glacier Peak Wilderness.

This approach requires use of commercial transportation to reach Lucerne on the west shore of Lake Chelan. The *Lady of the Lake* ferry (or a high-speed catamaran run by the same company) departs from Fields Point Landing on the west shore or from the town of Chelan at the lake's southern tip. Contact the Lake Chelan Boat Company in Chelan for the current boat schedule (see Appendix E for all company contact information). Or, if you've got less time and a lot more money, a floatplane to Chelan or Stehekin might be an option worth considering. In the Seattle area, try Kenmore Air or Seattle Seaplanes, and in Chelan, contact Chelan Airways.

If catching the ferry at Fields Point Landing, drive US 2 east to Alternate US 97 at Wenatchee. Continue north on Alternate US 97 to the town of Entiat. Drive another 9 miles on Alternate US 97, turn left (north) onto Highway 971 (Navarre Coulee Road) and continue to Lake Chelan State Park. Bear left (north) onto South Lakeshore Road and drive 8 miles to Fields Point Landing. If catching the ferry at Chelan, drive US 2 east to Alternate US 97 at Wenatchee. Continue on Alternate US 97 to Chelan at the southern tip of the lake. Take the *Lady of the Lake* ferry to Lucerne on the west shore of the lake. For the 13-mile journey to Holden (3,262 ft), take the school bus shuttle that is synchronized with boat arrivals ($5 per person one-way; bring exact change). Camping is available at the Holden Campground (3,300 ft) at the end of the Railroad Creek Road approximately a mile west of the village.

From the campground, hike approximately 0.5 mile east on the Railroad Creek Road to a spur road. Turn right (south) onto the spur road, cross Railroad Creek and continue to a fork in the road. Turn left (east) and hike approximately 0.3 mile, past mine tailings and across Copper Creek, to the junction with the Copper Creek Trail. This junction is on top of the tailings pile at the edge of the woods. Turn right (north) onto the Copper Creek Trail and continue approximately 3 miles to Copper Creek basin and good camping (5,600 ft).

Route: From camp, head southwesterly and ascend open slopes and a steep, loose gully through cliff bands aiming for the westernmost (right-hand) of two adjacent cols in Mount Fernow's long east ridge (approx. 7,200 ft). Once at the col, turn right (west) and scramble (class 3) along the ridge, keeping always to easier terrain on the left (south) side, past two subsummits. Stay well below the ridge crest when passing both subsummits, particularly for the second where the easiest route passes beneath cliff bands. When the ridge ends in a step (approx. 8,800 ft), scramble along a ledge system on the left (south) side of the crest to reach a gully. Climb the gully, then move leftward on rock (class 3) to gain the ridge crest just below the summit. Finish with a short scramble (class 3) to the summit (9,249 ft).

Descent: Descend the route.

71 Copper Peak

8,964 ft; 19th highest

Copper Peak is a pyramidal mountain that is rugged on all flanks. It's located southwest of Holden at the northern terminus of the Entiat Mountains between Big, Railroad, and Copper creeks. Rumor has it that the center of Copper is hollow from all the mining that took place here, so be sure to make your ascent a quick one just in case it collapses. More seriously, it's an enjoyable outing in a beautiful setting.

EAST FACE

This moderate scramble has a little bit of everything: snow, loose rock, and steep (often slippery) heather.

APPROACH

Time to camp	3 hours
Mileage	4 miles
Elevation change	+2,300 ft; -0 ft
GT 15-minute	Holden (No. 113)
Contact	Okanogan/Wenatchee NF, Chelan Ranger District

Copper Peak from the south-southeast (South Spectacle Butte) Photo by Paul Klenke

ROUTE

Difficulty	▲ Grade I +; steep snow; class 3 rock
Time to summit	4 hours
Elevation change	+3,400 ft; -0 ft
USGS 7.5-minute	Holden
Season	June–October

Approach: Follow the approach for Mount Fernow up into the Copper Creek basin and good camping (5,600 ft).

Route: From camp, contour and traverse slopes northerly at 5,600 feet for approximately 1 mile, rounding the base of an east-trending spur ridge, to gain the center of Copper Peak's east face at approximately 5,600 feet. From this vantage, the east face is a complex system of heather slopes, rock bands, gullies, and snow requiring good routefinding skills to navigate. Scramble (class 3) straight up (west), deviating only to bypass obstacles, to the base of the final snowfield directly below the summit. Ascend the steep snowfield to its upper right corner, then scramble up (exposed class 3) to the blocky crest of the upper northeast ridge. Turn left and climb through blocks to the summit (8,964 ft).

Descent: Descend the route.

DaKobed Slam

Peaks & routes	Clark Mountain (Walrus Glacier), Luahna Peak (Walrus-Richardson Glacier)
Max difficulty	▲▲ Grade II; glacier travel; class 3 rock
Duration	3 days
Roundtrip to camp	19 miles
Elevation gain	+7,800 ft
USGS 7.5-minute	Clark Mountain
GT 15-minute	Holden (No. 113), Wenatchee Lake (No. 145)
Trailhead	White River Trail
Season	June–August

This Slam is a fantastic journey across two large, remote glaciers deep in the heart of the wild and scenic DaKobed Range. Superb alpine ambience is your constant companion, and from the top of seldom-climbed Luahna Peak you'll feel a long way from civilization. If you just can't get enough of this beautiful country, consider including an ascent of Buck Mountain by descending the Boulder Pass Trail into the incredible Napeequa Valley. Regardless of your choice, you won't be disappointed.

DaKobed Slam peaks from the north Photo by Scott Stephenson

ITINERARY

Day	Elevation change	Instructions
1	+2,700 ft; -0 ft	Hike the Boulder Pass Trail to the meadow at 5,000 feet and camp.
2	+5,100 ft; -5,100 ft	Get an early start, climb Luahna Peak and Clark Mountain and return to camp.
3	+0 ft; -2,700 ft	Hike out.

Notes: The routes on Clark Mountain and Luahna Peak share a common point at 8,000 feet on the Walrus Glacier just below the col at the base of Clark's east ridge.

72 Clark Mountain

8,602 ft; 41st highest

Clark Mountain, the highest point in the DaKobed Range, is an imposing, glaciated peak with a steep north face. Its northern and eastern flanks are clad by the Richardson and Walrus glaciers. (The Walrus Glacier is labeled the Clark Glacier on the USGS quad.) Clark Mountain is on the White–Napeequa River divide.

WALRUS GLACIER

This is a straightforward, but long, glacier route finishing with a technically easy summit scramble. Beware of loose rock, though.

APPROACH

Time to camp	5 hours
Mileage	10 miles
Elevation change	+2,700 ft; -0 ft
GT 15-minute	Holden (No. 113), Wenatchee Lake (No. 145)
Contact	Okanogan/Wenatchee NF, Lake Wenatchee Ranger District

ROUTE

Difficulty	▲▲ Grade II; glacier travel; class 2–3 rock
Time to summit	4–5 hours
Elevation change	+3,700 ft; -0 ft
USGS 7.5-minute	Clark Mountain
Season	June–August

Approach: Permits are not required to camp or climb in the Glacier Peak Wilderness. A Northwest Forest Pass is required to park at the trailhead.

Drive US 2 to Coles Corner 19 miles east of Stevens Pass. Turn north onto Highway 207 (Lake Wenatchee Road) and follow it for 4.4 miles, past the turnoff to Plain/Leavenworth and over the Wenatchee River Bridge, to a fork. Stay left at the fork and continue another 6.2 miles, past Lake Wenatchee State Park, to the junction with White River Road (Forest Road 6400) on the right. Turn right onto White River Road and continue 10.2 miles to its end at the trailhead for the White River Trail (2,300 ft).

Hike the White River Trail north for 4.1 miles to the junction with the Boulder Pass Trail (approx. 2,540 ft). Turn right (northeast) onto the Boulder Pass Trail and follow the initially steep trail for approximately 5 miles, fording Boulder Creek midway (difficult in early season), to a meadow area and good camping at 5,000 feet.

Route: From the meadow at 5,000 feet, ascend the trail approximately 1 mile northeasterly to Boulder Pass (6,300 ft). Ascend and traverse northwesterly up slopes to reach the edge of the Walrus Glacier (labeled as the Clark Glacier on the USGS quad) at approximately 6,900 feet. Rope up and ascend the glacier westerly to reach a col approximately a quarter mile east of Clark Mountain's summit (approx. 8,100 ft). Leave the glacier and scramble westerly up Clark's east ridge (class 2–3), staying on and sometimes left (south) of the crest, to the summit (8,602 ft).

Descent: Descend the route.

Clark Mountain from the east Photo by Brian Bongiovanni

SOUTHEAST ROUTE

This moderate scramble has a few interesting routefinding problems.

APPROACH

Time to camp	5 hours
Mileage	10 miles
Elevation change	+2,700 ft; -0 ft
GT 15-minute	Holden (No. 113), Wenatchee Lake (No. 145)
Contact	Okanogan/Wenatchee NF, Lake Wenatchee Ranger District

ROUTE

Difficulty	▲▲ Grade II; class 2–3 rock
Time to summit	4–5 hours
Elevation change	+3,900 ft; -200 ft
USGS 7.5-minute	Clark Mountain
Season	June–October

Approach: Follow the approach for the Walrus Glacier route to the meadow area below Boulder Pass and good camping (5,000 ft).

Route: Walk northerly up the meadow to approximately 5,100 feet. Pick up a sheepherder's path and follow it west-southwesterly up the brushy

Clark Mountain from the southeast Photo by Scott Stephenson

Summit

slopes to reach an open upper basin at approximately 5,800 feet. Leave the path and bear northwesterly up heather and grass slopes to approximately 6,900 feet. Locate a notch in the south spur ridge of Clark Mountain's southeast peak (Point 8373), which is a couple of hundred yards right (north) of the obvious double notches; ascend steep scree slopes westerly to the notch (7,400 ft). From this vantage point Clark's summit is visible to the northwest. From the notch, downclimb a steep, loose gully (class 2–3) for approximately 200 feet to reach Clark's easy southeast slopes. Ascend the rocky slopes northwesterly (there's a convenient snow ramp that often lingers into late summer) to 7,700 feet, then scramble (class 2) up and left to reach the crest of Clark's south ridge at approximately 8,000 feet. Walk the easy ridge northerly, then scramble the final rocks (class 2–3) to the summit (8,602 ft).

   Descent: Descend the route.

73 Luahna Peak

8,400 ft; 72nd highest

Luahna Peak is a remote, seldom-visited summit whose northeastern flank is occupied by the Pilz Glacier. The peak is in the DaKobed Range on the White–Napeequa River divide. Luahna is not labeled on the USGS quad, but it's the summit 1.1 miles northwest of Clark Mountain.

WALRUS–RICHARDSON GLACIER

This route has it all: extensive glacier travel, enjoyable routefinding challenges, and plentiful moderate rock scrambling. Get an early start and try to keep moving, as it's a long journey.

APPROACH

Time to camp	5 hours
Mileage	10 miles
Elevation change	+2,700 ft; -0 ft
GT 15-minute	Holden (No. 113), Wenatchee Lake (No. 145)
Contact	Okanogan/Wenatchee NF, Lake Wenatchee Ranger District

ROUTE

Difficulty	▲▲ Grade II; glacier travel; class 3 rock
Time to summit	5–6 hours
Elevation change	+3,900 ft; -500 ft
USGS 7.5-minute	Clark Mountain
Season	June–August

Approach: Follow the approach for Clark Mountain's Walrus Glacier route to the meadow area below Boulder Pass and good camping (5,000 ft).

Route: From the meadow at 5,000 feet, ascend the trail approximately 1 mile northeasterly to Boulder Pass (6,300 ft). Ascend and traverse northwesterly up slopes to reach the edge of the Walrus Glacier (labeled as the Clark Glacier on the USGS quad) at approximately 6,900 feet. Rope up and ascend the glacier westerly to 8,000 feet. Contour westerly at 8,000 feet beneath the north face of Clark Mountain to reach a col approximately a quarter mile northwest of Clark's summit (7,800 ft). This col is located just before (southeast) of where a prominent buttress drops sharply north into the Richardson Glacier. Leave the glacier (potential moat problems in late season) and descend southerly to approximately 7,500 feet, then turn right (west) and traverse steep talus and scree slopes until able to scramble over the southwest ridge of Point 7970. Bear northerly and ascend to a col just north of Point 7970 at the base of Luahna Peak's south ridge (approx. 7,840 ft).

From the col, downclimb a short slab (class 3) to a snow platform and access the Richardson Glacier. In late season a moat may form, potentially requiring a very short rappel (consider leaving a fixed rope to simplify the return journey). Continue northerly on a rising traverse across the glacier to reach the base of Luahna's east ridge (approx. 8,000 ft). Cross to the back (north) side of the ridge to reach an obvious fault. Scramble westerly up the fault (loose class 3) until approximately 20 feet below the summit, then climb out of the fault and scramble (class 3) to the summit (8,400 ft).

If conditions won't allow access to the Richardson Glacier or if a scrambling

Luahna Peak from the southeast (Clark Mountain) Photo by Paul Klenke

completion is preferred, consider the following option. From the col north of Point 7970 or the slopes below, contour northerly along the west side of Luahna's south ridge, descending if required (stay above 7,600 ft). Scramble over a south-trending rock rib and enter a gully that slants up and left across Luahna's western flank, ending at the summit. Scramble up the loose gully (class 3) directly to the summit.

Descent: Descend the route.

Devore Slam

Peaks & routes	Devore Peak (Southeast Ridge), Flora Mountain (Southwest Route), Tupshin Peak (Southeast Face)
Max difficulty	▲▲ Grade II; low-fifth class rock
Duration	5 days
Roundtrip to camp	17 miles
Elevation gain	+14,200 ft
USGS 7.5-minute	Mount Lyall, Pinnacle Mountain, Stehekin
GT 15-minute	Stehekin (No. 82), Lucerne (No. 114)
Trailhead	Devore Creek Trail
Season	June–October

Don't fret if you step off the boat to hordes of summer tourists in Stehekin. You'll quickly leave them all behind as you head into the remote wilderness of the Devore Creek drainage. The peaks in this Slam are seldom climbed, so don't expect a worn path to show you the way. Do expect bushwhacking, enjoyable scrambling, interesting routefinding problems, and a healthy dose of peace and solitude. This Slam is for those who really want to get away from it all and explore some wild country.

ITINERARY

Day	Elevation change	Instructions
1	+ 4,200 ft; -0 ft	Follow the approach for Devore Peak to the basin at 5,400 feet near Bird Creek and camp.
2	+ 3,000 ft; -3,000 ft	Climb Tupshin Peak and return to camp.
3	+ 3,000 ft; -4,200 ft	Climb Devore Peak and move camp down to Bird Creek Campground (4,200 ft).
4	+ 4,200 ft; -4,200 ft	Climb Flora Mountain and return to camp.
5	+ 0 ft; -3,000 ft	Hike out.

Notes: For day 5, remember to arrive back at the trailhead for the Stehekin River Trail in time to catch the shuttle bus back to Stehekin and, subsequently, the ferry back down the lake.

74 Devore Peak

8,360 ft; 84th highest

Devore Peak is a bulky mountain with a steep northeast face. It rises out of an isolated basin with several lakes. The peak is on the Devore–Hilgard Creek divide southwest of Stehekin and south of Tupshin Peak.

SOUTHEAST RIDGE

Nasty brush and an exposed rock step make this a tough scramble. Definitely consider bringing a rope to make for an easier and safer climb.

APPROACH

Time to camp	5–6 hours
Mileage	9 miles
Elevation change	+4,200 ft; -0 ft
GT 15-minute	Stehekin (No. 82)
Contact	North Cascades NP, Golden West Visitor Center; or Okanogan/Wenatchee NF, Chelan Ranger District

ROUTE

Difficulty	▲▲ Grade II; class 4 rock
Time to summit	4–5 hours
Elevation change	+3,000 ft; -0 ft
USGS 7.5-minute	Mount Lyall, Stehekin
Season	June–October

Approach: Permits are not required to camp or climb in the Glacier Peak Wilderness.

This approach requires use of commercial transportation to reach Stehekin at the northern tip of Lake Chelan. The *Lady of the Lake* ferry (or a high-speed catamaran run by the same company) departs from Fields Point Landing on the west shore or from the town of Chelan at the lake's southern tip. Contact the Lake Chelan Boat Company in Chelan for the current boat schedule (see Appendix E for all company contact information). Or, if you've got less time and a lot more money, a floatplane to Chelan or Stehekin might be an option worth considering. In the Seattle area, try Kenmore Air or Seattle Seaplanes, and in Chelan, contact Chelan Airways. From Stehekin, with luck you might be able to hitch a ride on a motorboat from Purple Point Campground across the lake to Weaver Point Campground. Otherwise, there's a shuttle bus that goes to High Bridge that can drop you off at the trailhead for the Stehekin River Trail ($6 per person one-way; bring exact change). Contact the Chelan Ranger District for the current bus schedule. Make sure you synchronize your transport options so that you don't get stuck in Stehekin overnight.

If catching the ferry at Fields Point Landing, drive US 2 east to Alternate US 97 at Wenatchee. Continue north on Alternate US 97 to the town of Entiat. Drive another 9 miles on Alternate US 97, turn left (north) onto Highway 971 (Navarre Coulee Road) and continue to Lake Chelan State Park. Bear left (north) onto South Lakeshore Road and drive 8 miles to Fields Point Landing. If catching the ferry at Chelan, drive US 2 east to Alternate US 97 at Wenatchee. Continue on Alternate US 97 to Chelan at the southern tip of the lake. Take the *Lady of the Lake* ferry to Stehekin on the northern tip of the lake. If you can't hitch a ride on a motorboat to Weaver Point Campground, take the shuttle bus to the trailhead for the Stehekin River Trail near the Harlequin Campground and Stehekin airstrip. Hike 3.5 miles southeast on the Stehekin River Trail to the trailhead for the Devore Creek Trail near the Weaver Point Campground (1,200 ft).

From Weaver Point Campground, hike the Devore Creek Trail southeast approximately 4 miles to the Bird Creek Campground and good camping (4,200 ft). Alternatively, leave the trail at Bird Creek Campground and follow the right (north) side of Bird Creek (some bushwhacking) approximately 1 mile west into a brushy, flat basin and additional good camping (approx. 5,400 ft).

Route: From the basin at 5,400 feet, continue upstream along Bird Creek and cross another brushy basin (approx. 5,600 ft). Ascend into forest at the head of the basin and climb steeply, near and north of the creek, into a large, open basin near lakes and beneath Devore Peak (approx. 7,000 ft). There's some nasty and unavoidable bushwhacking through slide alder and vine maple in these sections (one climber warned to "bring a machete"). Cross Bird Creek at its source at the northernmost lake and hike south-southeasterly, staying left (east) of the lakes. Aim for a broad col (approx. 7,500 ft) in Devore's southeast ridge at the south end of the basin, just right (west) of Point 7657. From the col, turn right (west) and scramble along the ridge to the base of a short (approx. 30 ft) rock step several hundred yards from the summit. Ascend the rock step or pass it on the left via an exposed ledge (both class 4) and climb back to the crest. Continue along the ridge crest to the summit block and ascend a series of loose, dirty gullies to the summit (8,360 ft).

Descent: Descend the route using a combination of rappels and downclimbing.

75 Flora Mountain

8,320 ft; 95th highest

Flora Mountain is a gentle, desolate peak with extensive scree and talus slopes. The attraction of this seldom-climbed summit is remote wilderness. Flora lies between Castle, Riddle, and Bridal Veil creeks, southwest of Stehekin and west of Lake Chelan.

SOUTHWEST ROUTE

The challenge of this scramble is primarily routefinding, which really isn't all that bad. That aside, it's largely a scree and talus hike punctuated by sections of rock scrambling.

APPROACH

Time to camp	5–6 hours
Mileage	10 miles
Elevation change	+3,900 ft; -0 ft
GT 15-minute	Stehekin (No. 82), Lucerne (No. 114)
Contact	North Cascades NP, Golden West Visitor Center; or Okanogan/Wenatchee NF, Chelan Ranger District

ROUTE

Difficulty	▲ Grade I +; class 3 rock
Time to summit	5–6 hours
Elevation change	+3,300 ft; -0 ft
USGS 7.5-minute	Pinnacle Mountain
Season	June–October

Approach: Follow the approach for Devore Peak to Bird Creek Campground (4,200 ft). Continue to upper Devore Creek and the entrance to Fourth of July Basin, 6 miles from the Devore Creek Trailhead and good camping (approx. 5,100 ft).

Route: From the entrance to Fourth of July Basin, leave the trail and cross Devore Creek. Ascend due southeast up a narrow valley between two prominent northwest-trending spur ridges to a col overlooking the Riddle Creek valley (approx. 7,040 ft). Scramble northerly, then easterly along the divide to reach a broad col overlooking the Castle Creek valley (approx. 7,360 ft). From here, the goal is to reach the plateau at the base of Flora Mountain's southwest slopes across the valley to the east. There are two ways to achieve this. The first option is to contour benches easterly (class 3) around the head of Castle Creek valley, staying north of Point 7734, to the plateau. The second option, which is technically easier, is to descend northeasterly into the Castle Creek valley to approximately 6,600 feet. Contour northerly along the right (east) side of the valley, then ascend to reach the base of a north-northwest-trending spur ridge at 6,800 feet. Ascend the easy spur ridge south-southeasterly to the plateau. Once at the plateau, ascend loose talus and scree slopes northeasterly, then make a final short scramble (class 3) to the summit (8,320 ft).

Descent: Descend the route.

76 Tupshin Peak

8,320 ft; 95th highest

Tupshin Peak is a towering mountain with a serrated summit crest and a broad, precipitous north face. It's located on the Devore–Hilgard Creek divide west of Stehekin and north of Devore Peak.

SOUTHEAST FACE

This is a challenging climb due to routefinding and sections of exposed, technical rock. Definitely bring a rope and rock protection for this ascent.

APPROACH

Time to camp	5–6 hours
Mileage	9 miles
Elevation change	+4,200 ft; -0 ft
GT 15-minute	Stehekin (No. 82)
Contact	North Cascades NP, Golden West Visitor Center; or Okanogan/Wenatchee NF, Chelan Ranger District

ROUTE

Difficulty	▲▲ Grade II; low-fifth class rock
Time to summit	5–6 hours
Elevation change	+3,000 ft; -0 ft
USGS 7.5-minute	Mount Lyall, Stehekin
Season	June–October

Approach: Follow the approach for Devore Peak to the brushy, flat basin and good camping (approx. 5,400 ft).

Route: From the basin at 5,400 feet, make a rising traverse northeasterly through semi-open forest (some bushwhacking) approximately 0.75 mile into the neighboring drainage (approx. 5,800 ft). Ascend this drainage northwest-erly (more bushwhacking) onto talus slopes and continue to its head beneath Tupshin Peak's southeast face (7,600 ft). Climb rightward up the face, using a series of ramps and ledges, then scramble up a chimney to just below the crest of the upper east ridge. Careful and methodical routefinding will make the climbing in this section no harder than class 4; some exploratory climbing may be required. Traverse leftward along exposed, broken ledges (low-fifth class) to directly beneath the summit rocks, then scramble up (class 3) to the summit (8,320 ft).

Descent: Descend the route using a combination of rappels and down-climbing.

● Dumbell Slam

Peaks & routes	Dumbell Mountain (Southwest Route), Greenwood Mountain (Southwest Route)
Max difficulty	▲▲ Grade II; class 3 rock
Duration	2 days
Roundtrip to camp	14 miles
Elevation gain	+5,900 ft
USGS 7.5-minute	Holden
GT 15-minute	Holden (No. 113)
Trailhead	Phelps Creek Trail
Season	July–October

Dumbell Slam peaks from the southeast (Mount Fernow) Photo by Lowell Skoog

This Slam provides an opportunity to summit two of the highest peaks in the state. Their easy approach allows for a reasonable weekend outing. You'll hike through bucolic Spider Meadow and spend a night tucked away in a quiet valley off the main trail. If you've got more time and energy, consider incorporating one or more of the summits from the nearby Entiat Slam.

ITINERARY

Day	Elevation change	Instructions
1	+1,900 ft; -0 ft	Follow the approach for Dumbell Mountain to upper Phelps Basin and camp (5,800 ft).
2	+4,000 ft; -5,900 ft	Climb Dumbell and Greenwood mountains and hike out.

Notes: The prominent notch in Dumbell Mountain's right (south) shoulder leads to the summit of Greenwood Mountain.

77 Dumbell Mountain

8,421 ft; 68th highest

Dumbell Mountain's double summits, when viewed from the north, might just resemble its namesake. Perhaps more obvious are the peak's long west and south spur ridges that form the head of Spider Meadow and upper Phelps Basin. The peak lies at the converging divides of Phelps, Big, and Railroad creeks.

SOUTHWEST ROUTE

This is an enjoyable route with a beautiful base camp in the upper Phelps Basin.

APPROACH

Time to camp	3-4 hours
Mileage	7 miles
Elevation change	+1,900 ft; -0 ft
GT 15-minute	Holden (No. 113)
Contact	Okanogan/Wenatchee NF, Lake Wenatchee Ranger District

ROUTE

Difficulty	▲ Grade I+; class 3 rock
Time to summit	3-4 hours
Elevation change	+3,100 ft; -0 ft
USGS 7.5-minute	Holden
Season	June–October

Approach: Permits are not required to camp or climb in the Glacier Peak Wilderness. A Northwest Forest Pass is required to park at the trailhead.

Drive US 2 to Coles Corner 19 miles east of Stevens Pass. Turn north onto Highway 207 (Lake Wenatchee Road) and follow it for 4.4 miles, past the turnoff to Plain/Leavenworth and over the Wenatchee River Bridge, to a fork. Bear right at the fork and continue 1.3 miles, past the Lake Wenatchee State Airport, then turn left onto Chiwawa River Road (Forest Road 62) at the sign for Fish Lake/Chiwawa Valley. Follow Chiwawa River Road approximately 23 miles to the turnoff for Forest Road 6211 on the right. Turn right onto Forest Road 6211 and continue to its end at the trailhead for Phelps Creek Trail (3,500 ft).

Hike the Phelps Creek Trail through Douglas-fir forest. After 5.3 miles, the trail opens into beautiful Spider Meadow; there's good camping here at both ends of the large meadow. The trail forks at 6.5 miles (5,300 ft): the left fork goes sharply left up switchbacks to Spider Pass and the right fork goes into upper Phelps Basin. Take the right fork and continue to the upper basin and decent camping at various spots along Phelps Creek (approx. 5,400 ft).

Route: From upper Phelps Basin, ascend the meadow to its upper-right corner to where the gradient steepens considerably (approx. 6,200 ft). Locate and climb a broad gully (waterfall in early season) easterly through cliffs to gain the base of a large talus boulder field. (The entrance to the correct gully can be challenging to find, so some scouting is required. The correct gully bears east toward the basin below Dumbell Mountain's southwest side.) Ascend the boulder field northeasterly aiming for a prominent notch right

Dumbell Mountain from the south Photo by Paul Klenke

Scrambling high on Dumbell Mountain Photo by Lowell Skoog

(south) of Dumbell's right (south) shoulder. About 200 feet below the notch (approx. 7,700 ft), locate and climb a steep, narrow fault (at first a ledge then later a cleft) that ascends diagonally leftward (north-northwesterly) to a saddle between the false summit (on the left) and the true summit (on the right). Turn right (east) and scramble along the ridge, mostly on its left (north) side, to the true summit (8,421 ft).

   Descent: Descend the route.

78 Greenwood Mountain

8,415 ft; 69th highest

Greenwood Mountain, also known as Northeast Dumbell Mountain, is a bulky, impressive peak with two high summits, 0.2 mile apart, situated on an arcing summit crest. There's some debate as to which summit is higher. The south summit, the most often climbed, has been triangulated at 8,415 feet. The north summit has not been triangulated, but some climbers estimate its elevation to be 8,420 feet. There's a small glacier in a cirque east of the summit crest. The steep and complex northeastern flank features a series of rugged subsummits and numerous spur ridges. The peak is not labeled on the USGS quad, but it's the summit 0.5 mile northeast of Dumbell Mountain on the Big–Railroad Creek divide.

SOUTHWEST ROUTE

This is a challenging scramble due to travel along an exposed ledge that traverses the eastern flank of Dumbell Mountain. Don't attempt this route if the ledge is snow-covered or wet. If you choose to go to the north summit, there's additional exposed scrambling and some routefinding challenges.

APPROACH

Time to camp	3–4 hours
Mileage	7 miles
Elevation change	+1,900 ft; -0 ft
GT 15-minute	Holden (No. 113)
Contact	Okanogan/Wenatchee NF, Lake Wenatchee Ranger District

ROUTE

Difficulty	▲▲ Grade II; class 3 rock
Time to summit	4–5 hours (to south summit); 5–6 hours (to north summit)
Elevation change	+3,100 ft; -0 ft
USGS 7.5-minute	Holden
Season	July–October

Greenwood Mountain from the southwest (Dumbell Mountain) Photo by Paul Klenke

Traversing ledge on the way to Greenwood Mountain Photo by Paul Klenke

Approach: Follow the approach for Dumbell Mountain to upper Phelps Basin and decent camping (approx. 5,400 ft).

Route: From upper Phelps Basin, ascend the meadow to its upper-right corner to where the gradient steepens considerably (approx. 6,200 ft). Locate and climb a broad gully (waterfall in early season) easterly through cliffs to gain the base of a large talus boulder field. (The entrance to the correct gully can be challenging to find, so some scouting is required. The correct gully bears east toward the basin below Dumbell Mountain's southwest side.) Ascend the boulder field northeasterly aiming for a prominent notch right (south) of Dumbell's right (south) shoulder. Ascend to the notch (approx. 7,900 ft). Cross the notch and make an exposed traverse left around a corner (class 3) to reach a ledge. Follow the ledge (exposed class 2) as it traverses northerly across Dumbell's east face to the Dumbell-Greenwood col (approx. 7,860 ft). To reach the south summit, ascend the broad ridge northeasterly to its highest point (8,415 ft). (From the south summit, it is possible to down-climb the southeast ridge on class 3 rock to reach the notch mentioned below in the route for the north summit.)

From the col, the route to the north summit is more involved. Descend slightly right (southeast) until beneath cliffs on the south side of the ridge. Turn left (east) and cross two shallow basins (possible snowfields) to the west side of the south summit's southeast ridge. There are a series of notches in the ridge. The correct notch is immediately left (north) of the lowest one and has a light beige scree slope below it. Scramble 40 feet to the notch (class 3). (From here, it is possible to scramble up the southeast ridge on class 3 rock to the south summit.) Cross the notch and follow a north-trending ledge down to the snowfield below. Cross the snowfield, aiming to exit onto rock at the point where it reaches highest onto the north summit's south face. Climb up the face and veer right to gain the crest of the east ridge (class 3). Turn left (west) and scramble up the ridge to its highest point (approx. 8,420 ft).

Descent: Descend the route.

● Entiat Slam

Peaks & routes	Seven Fingered Jack (Southwest Route), Mount Maude (South Ridge), South Spectacle Butte (Southwest Ridge)
Max difficulty	▲▲ Grade II; class 3 rock
Duration	4 days
Roundtrip to camp	14 miles
Elevation gain	+11,900 ft
USGS 7.5-minute	Holden, Trinity
GT 15-minute	Holden (No. 113)
Trailhead	Phelps Creek Trail
Season	June–October

This stupendous, physically demanding Slam visits the summits of two members of the exclusive club of ten nonvolcanic peaks that are more than 9,000 feet. The scenery is great, including the otherworldly Ice Lakes and the spectacular Entiat Cirque. Add to that the enjoyable camping in the Ice Lakes and Leroy basins and you've got a great outing that'll make you more than glad you came. If you're full of youthful vigor and want more summits, the Dumbell Slam is nearby.

ITINERARY

Day	Elevation change	Instructions
1	+4,100 ft; -200 ft	Follow the primary approach and route for Mount Maude to upper Ice Lake basin and camp (7,400 ft).
2	+2,800 ft; -2,800 ft	Climb South Spectacle Butte and return to camp.
3	+1,900 ft; -3,300 ft	Climb Mount Maude and move camp back to Leroy Basin (6,000 ft).
4	+3,100 ft; -5,600 ft	Climb Seven Fingered Jack and hike out.

Notes: For day 2, from camp at 7,400 feet, descend the slopes easterly to reach upper Ice Lake (7,188 ft). Round the south shore of the lake, cross the outlet stream, and pick up a path that continues approximately 0.5 mile down the basin to reach lower Ice Lake (6,822 ft). Continue following the path and descend to 6,500 feet and join the route on South Spectacle Butte. Fit and fast parties can make all three ascents from a single base camp in Leroy Basin.

79 Seven Fingered Jack

9,100 ft; 12th highest

Seven Fingered Jack, in the Entiat Mountains, is aptly named for a row of craggy needles along its summit ridge. Its precipitous east face forms the head of the spectacular Entiat Cirque. The peak is north of Mount Maude and south of Mount Fernow.

SOUTHWEST ROUTE

This relatively straightforward scramble has plenty of loose rock, so watch your step. Don't climb in large groups or beneath one another.

APPROACH

Time to camp	3–4 hours
Mileage	5 miles
Elevation change	+2,500 ft; -0 ft
GT 15-minute	Holden (No. 113)
Contact	Okanogan/Wenatchee NF, Lake Wenatchee Ranger District

ROUTE

Difficulty	▲ Grade I+; class 2 rock
Time to summit	3–4 hours
Elevation change	+3,100 ft; -0 ft
USGS 7.5-minute	Holden
Season	June–October

Approach: Permits are not required to camp or climb in the Glacier Peak Wilderness. A Northwest Forest Pass is required to park at the trailhead.

Drive US 2 to Coles Corner 19 miles east of Stevens Pass. Turn north onto Highway 207 (Lake Wenatchee Road) and follow it for 4.4 miles, past the turnoff to Plain/Leavenworth and over the Wenatchee River Bridge, to a fork. Bear right at the fork and continue 1.3 miles, past the Lake Wenatchee State Airport, then turn left onto Chiwawa River Road (Forest Road 62) at the sign for Fish Lake/Chiwawa Valley. Follow Chiwawa River Road approximately 23 miles to the turnoff for Forest Road 6211 on the right. Turn right onto Forest Road 6211 and continue to its end at the trailhead for Phelps Creek Trail (3,500 ft).

Follow the Phelps Creek Trail 3.2 miles through Douglas-fir forest to where the trail crosses Leroy Creek (4,200 ft). Turn right onto an unmaintained trail that closely follows the left (north) side of the creek and ascends

Seven Fingered Jack from the southwest (Leroy Basin) Photo by Scott Stephenson

steeply to Leroy Basin (5,200 ft). Continue along the stream to the timberline meadows of upper Leroy Basin and good camping (6,000 ft).

Route: From upper Leroy Basin, ascend the broad gully northeasterly toward the Maude-Jack col to a large bench (approx. 7,800 ft). Turn left (north) and traverse up scree and talus toward the summit situated at the far north end of the fingers. Ascend the final scree and talus slopes up and right, then scramble up a gully (loose class 2) to the summit (9,100 ft).

Descent: Descend the route.

80 Mount Maude

9,040 ft; 15th highest

Mount Maude is a massive peak with a dramatic, steep north face clad with the hanging South Entiat Glacier. The peak is south of Seven Fingered Jack and rises immediately northwest of the otherworldly Ice Lakes.

SOUTH RIDGE

This relatively easy scramble presents no technical difficulties and is largely a scree and talus hike with some enjoyable routefinding. There are excellent views of Mount Fernow, Seven Fingered Jack, Glacier Peak, and the peaks of the DaKobed Range from the summit.

APPROACH

	Primary	Alternate
Time to camp	3 hours	7 hours
Mileage	5 miles	13 miles
Elevation change	+2,500 ft; -0 ft	+2,400 ft; -0 ft
GT 15-minute	Holden (No. 113)	Holden (No. 113), Lucerne (No. 114)
Contact	Okanogan/Wenatchee NF, Lake Wenatchee Ranger District	Okanogan/Wenatchee NF, Entiat Ranger District

ROUTE

Difficulty	▲ Grade I+; class 2 rock
Time to summit	4–5 hours (primary approach); 4 hours (alternate approach)
Elevation change	+3,300 ft, -200 ft (primary approach); +3,600 ft, -0 ft (alternate approach)
USGS 7.5-minute	Holden
Season	June–October

Primary Approach: Follow the approach for Seven Fingered Jack to upper Leroy Basin and good camping (6,000 ft).

Alternate Approach: Approaching from the east, permits are still not required to camp or climb in the Glacier Peak Wilderness. A Northwest Forest Pass is still required to park at the trailhead.

Drive US 2 east to Alternate US 97 at Wenatchee. Drive north on Alternate US 97 to just before the town of Entiat. Turn left (west) onto Entiat River Road (Forest Road 51) and drive 38 miles to the end of the road at Cottonwood Campground and the trailhead for the Entiat River Trail (3,140 ft).

Hike the Entiat River Trail northerly past numerous turnoffs for approximately 8.2 miles to the junction with the Ice Creek Trail (4,300 ft) and good camping. Turn left (west) onto the Ice Creek Trail, cross the Entiat River on a log (difficult in early season) and continue to the junction with the Cool Creek Trail. Turn left and continue on the Ice Creek Trail for 0.7 mile as it contours south and then west around the southern flank of South Spectacle Butte to the junction with the Pomas Creek Trail (approx. 4,300 ft). Stay right at the junction and continue on the Ice Creek Trail 3 miles to a meadow and good camping near a waterfall coming down from upper Ice Lake (approx. 5,500 ft).

Route: If coming via the primary approach, from upper Leroy Basin follow the abandoned trail as it contours southeasterly across forested slopes into a boulder and talus basin beneath Mount Maude's west face. Continue

Mount Maude from the south Photo by Scott Stephenson

across the basin (sporadic cairns mark the way) on a gradual rising traverse to reach the edge of an impressive erosion gully (approx. 6,400 ft). Carefully choose a place to cross the dangerously loose gully (changes yearly) and, once on the opposite side, head directly uphill to rejoin the trail at approximately 6,500 feet. Contour on the trail as it skirts below cliff bands at the head of the basin, crosses a forested hillside and emerges into another talus basin below Point 6888. Again contour across the basin (some cairns, but trail is faint) to rejoin the trail as it switchbacks up the slope to reach a notch (6,800 ft) just left (east) of Point 6888. From the notch, continue following the trail for several hundred yards as it contours easterly into an open basin beneath Maude's south ridge before disappearing once again (6,800 ft). From this vantage a notch in Maude's south ridge can be seen above and left at the head of the basin. Ascend the right (south) side of the scree and talus slope easterly to reach the notch overlooking upper Ice Lake (7,600 ft) from where the route up Maude's south slopes can be clearly seen. Turn left (north) and descend into the basin to approximately 7,400 feet.

If coming via the alternate approach, from camp near the waterfall follow a side trail that leads northerly along a fork of Ice Creek, climbing steeply to reach lower Ice Lake (6,822 ft). Continue following the path approximately 0.5 mile westerly, along the south shore of the lake and across the outlet stream, to reach upper Ice Lake (7,188 ft). Round the south shore of the lake, cross the outlet stream and ascend the slopes above trending westerly to approximately 7,400 feet.

From upper Ice Lake basin at 7,400 ft, scramble (class 2) northerly up Mount Maude's mostly scree and talus slopes, staying right (east) of the rugged crest of Maude's lower south ridge, to gain the ridge crest at an obvious shoulder (approx. 8,000 ft). Continue ascending northerly along the broad and gentle crest (class 2) to the summit (9,040 ft).

Descent: Descend the route.

81 South Spectacle Butte

8,392 ft; 77th highest

South Spectacle Butte is a pyramidal peak with four distinct faces. It lies between Ice Creek and the Entiat River immediately southeast of the Ice Lakes.

SOUTHWEST RIDGE

This ascent requires good routefinding skills to successfully navigate around numerous obstacles along the ridge crest.

APPROACH

Time to camp	7 hours
Mileage	13 miles
Elevation change	+2,400 ft; -0 ft
GT 15-minute	Holden (No. 113), Lucerne (No. 114)
Contact	Okanogan/Wenatchee NF, Entiat Ranger District

South Spectacle Butte from the west (Mount Maude) Photo by Scott Stephenson

ROUTE

Difficulty   ▲▲ Grade II; class 3 rock
Time to summit   4 hours
Elevation change +2,900 ft; -0 ft
USGS 7.5-minute Holden, Trinity
Season   June–October

Approach: Follow the alternate approach for Mount Maude to good camping in the meadow near the waterfall (approx. 5,500 ft).

Route: From camp near the waterfall follow a side trail that leads northerly along a fork of Ice Creek and climbs steeply toward lower Ice Lake. Ascend the trail to approximately 6,500 feet, then leave the trail and ascend southerly on a gradual rising traverse to the base of South Spectacle's southwest ridge (6,800 ft). Scramble up rock to gain the ridge and continue along the crest. When gendarmes are encountered along the ridge, pass them on the right (class 3) and climb back to the crest. Continue scrambling along the ridge until 300 feet below the summit, then exit the ridge on the right and enter a system of easy ledges. Follow the ledges to the southeast corner of the summit block, then scramble up loose rock and slabs (class 3) to the summit (8,392 ft). (See also Beckey 2003, p. 192.)

Descent: Descend the route.

● Fortress Slam

Peaks & routes Fortress Mountain (Southeast Route), Chiwawa Mountain (Southwest Route)
Max difficulty ▲▲ Grade II; class 4 rock
Duration 3 days
Roundtrip to camp 13 miles
Elevation gain +8,100 ft
USGS 7.5-minute Suiattle Pass
GT 15-minute Holden (No. 113)
Trailhead Buck Creek Trail
Season June–October

This Slam provides a chance to summit two of the state's highest peaks in a short outing through some striking country. The easy approach will help you save your energy for the physically demanding day of scrambling ahead. Inspiring views of Glacier Peak from the summits and enjoyable climbing will make it all worthwhile.

		ITINERARY
Day	**Elevation change**	**Instructions**
1	+2,200 ft; -200 ft	Hike to Chiwawa Basin and camp (4,800 ft).
2	+5,900 ft; -5,900 ft	Climb Fortress Mountain and Chiwawa Mountain and return to camp.
3	+200 ft; -2,200 ft	Hike out.

Notes: The routes on Fortress and Chiwawa mountains share a common point at 6,600 feet. If you've still got time and energy after the climbs and want to save a day, it's mostly downhill back to the trailhead from camp.

82 Fortress Mountain

8,760 ft; 30th highest

Fortress Mountain is an apt name for this bastion of a peak. It possesses a formidable northwest ridge and northeast face. It's located at the head of the Chiwawa River valley west of Chiwawa Mountain. In early summer, the long southwest slopes are an alpine garden of heather and flowers.

SOUTHEAST ROUTE

This scramble requires good routefinding skills to make your way from Chiwawa Basin through the forest and up onto the open southeast slopes. The summit scramble up an interesting chimney provides an exhilarating finish.

APPROACH

Time to camp	3–4 hours
Mileage	7 miles
Elevation change	+2,200 ft; -200 ft
GT 15-minute	Holden (No. 113)
Contact	Okanogan/Wenatchee NF, Lake Wenatchee Ranger District

ROUTE

Difficulty	▲▲ Grade II; class 3 rock with a short class 4 chimney just below the summit
Time to summit	4–5 hours
Elevation change	+4,000 ft; -0 ft
USGS 7.5-minute	Suiattle Pass
Season	June–October

Approach: Permits are not required to camp or climb in the Glacier Peak Wilderness. A Northwest Forest Pass is required to park at the trailhead.

Drive US 2 to Coles Corner 19 miles east of Stevens Pass. Turn north onto Highway 207 (Lake Wenatchee Road) and drive 4.4 miles, past the Plain/Leavenworth turnoff and over the Wenatchee River Bridge, to a fork. Bear right at the fork and go 1.3 miles, past the Lake Wenatchee State Airport. Turn left onto Chiwawa River Road (Forest Road 62) at the sign for Fish Lake/Chiwawa Valley. Follow Chiwawa River Road 23.5 miles to the parking area at its end at Trinity and the trailhead for Buck Creek Trail (2,770 ft).

Follow the Buck Creek Trail 1.4 miles to a fork (3,100 ft). Bear right at the fork onto the Chiwawa River Trail and hike 3.6 miles to the junction with the unmarked Chiwawa Basin Trail (4,800 ft) just before the sign for the Red Mountain Trail. Turn left onto the Chiwawa Basin Trail and hike 1.4 miles to its end in Chiwawa Basin and good camping (4,800 ft). Camp on the north side of the stream so you don't have to cross it first thing in the morning.

Route: From Chiwawa Basin, walk northerly across the meadow along its right (east) side, past a tongue of brush, and enter the forest and a broad gully. Follow the gully northwesterly along a stream, taking the path of least resistance, to an open slope at the base of Point 5971 at 5,400 feet. Bear up and right back into the forest and enter a large flat basin beneath Chiwawa Mountain. Ascend to the head of the basin (5,600 ft) at the foot of steep rock slabs, talus, and gullies. Avoid the more difficult terrain by ascending the

Fortress Mountain from the southeast (Chiwawa Basin) in spring
Photo by Scott Stephenson

steep slope on the left, which is covered with heather and scrub conifers, to reach the base of an easy gully. Consider marking your course with wands from here onward, as it is imperative that you descend via this route to avoid more difficult terrain. Ascend the gully and slopes above bearing approximately 340 degrees (north-northwesterly) toward the Fortress-Chiwawa col.

From below the col at 6,600 feet, bear left and begin a long rising traverse northwesterly, then westerly (staying above a rock island in the middle of the slopes) to the base of a broad gully leading to Fortress Mountain's east ridge well right (east) of the summit. Ascend the gully to the crest of the east ridge (approx. 8,200 ft). Turn left (west) and scramble toward the summit, being careful not to venture too far left (south) onto the hazardous terrain of the east face. Scramble up a short chimney (class 4) to the summit area and walk to the summit (8,760 ft).

Descent: Descend the route, taking care to follow it exactly to avoid more difficult terrain.

SOUTHWEST ROUTE

This moderate route ascends the long, gentle, and vegetated southwest slopes and finishes with a moderate scramble to the summit. It's an enjoyable ascent in a beautiful alpine environment.

APPROACH

Time to camp	5 hours
Mileage	9 miles
Elevation change	+3,100 ft; -0 ft
GT 15-minute	Holden (No. 113)
Contact	Okanogan/Wenatchee NF, Lake Wenatchee Ranger District

ROUTE

Difficulty	▲ Grade I+; class 3 rock
Time to summit	3–4 hours
Elevation change	+3,000 ft; -0 ft
USGS 7.5-minute	Suiattle Pass
Season	June–October

Approach: Follow the approach for Fortress's Southeast Route to Trinity and the trailhead for Buck Creek Trail (2,770 ft).

Follow the Buck Creek Trail 1.4 miles to a fork (3,100 ft). Bear left at fork and continue approximately 7 miles on the Buck Creek Trail to where the trail finally emerges from the forest into a large meadow beneath the slopes of Fortress Mountain and Helmet Butte. Continue several hundred yards

Fortress Mountain from the south Photo by Scott Stephenson

through the meadow to where the trail crosses Buck Creek (approx. 5,560 ft) and begins a gradual sweeping westerly ascent along the open slopes of Helmet Butte. Leave the trail here to find camping either up a short side trail to the north (room for one tent) or at the entrance to the small valley below Pass No Pass (approx. 5,800 ft).

Route: From the small valley below Pass No Pass, the lower portion of Fortress Mountain's southwest slopes can be clearly seen. The slopes are covered with dense heather and other alpine vegetation that makes for slow going, particularly when wet. The initial slope is more easily ascended if gained from just below the pass. Ascend the long slopes northeasterly into a wide, often snow-filled basin beneath the summit area. Climb the slope above the basin (boulders or snow) to Fortress's south ridge (class 2–3). Turn left and scramble talus and ledges (class 3) to the summit (8,760 ft).

Descent: Descend the route.

83 Chiwawa Mountain

8,459 ft; 61st highest

Chiwawa Mountain is perhaps best known for the Lyman Glacier on its northeastern flank. The glacier periodically calves icebergs into Lyman Lake. The peak lies at the head of the Chiwawa River valley and east of Fortress Mountain.

SOUTHWEST ROUTE

This scramble, while technically easy, requires good routefinding skills to make your way from Chiwawa Basin through the forest and up onto the open southwest slopes.

APPROACH

Time to camp	3–4 hours
Mileage	7 miles
Elevation change	+2,200 ft; -200 ft
GT 15-minute	Holden (No. 113)
Contact	Okanogan/Wenatchee NF, Lake Wenatchee Ranger District

ROUTE

Difficulty	▲▲ Grade II; class 2–3 rock
Time to summit	4–5 hours
Elevation change	+3,700 ft; -0 ft
USGS 7.5-minute	Suiattle Pass
Season	June–October

Approach: Follow the approach for Fortress Mountain's Southeast Route to Chiwawa Basin and good camping (4,800 ft).

Route: From Chiwawa Basin, walk northerly across the meadow along its right (east) side, past a tongue of brush, and enter the forest and a broad

Chiwawa Mountain from the south (Chiwawa Basin) in spring
Photo by Scott Stephenson

gully. Follow the gully northwesterly along a stream, taking the path of least resistance, to the base of Point 5971 at 5,400 feet. Bear up and right back into the forest and enter a large flat basin beneath Chiwawa Mountain. Ascend to the head of the basin (5,600 ft) at the foot of steep rock slabs, talus, and gullies. Avoid the more difficult terrain by ascending the steep slope on the left, which is covered with heather and scrub conifers, to reach the base of an easy gully. Consider marking your course with wands from here onward, as it is imperative that you descend via this route to avoid more difficult terrain. Ascend the gully and slopes above bearing approximately 340 degrees (north-northwesterly) toward the Fortress-Chiwawa col.

From below the col at 7,000 feet, turn right (northeast) and cross a steep-walled gully that descends from the col. Continue climbing northeasterly up rocky slopes (class 2–3), staying well right (south) of Chiwawa Mountain's rugged west ridge and a prominent rock outcrop. Once above the rock outcrop, continue northeasterly up easy talus and scree slopes to the summit ridge. Scramble a short distance along the easy ridge (exposed class 2) to the summit (8,459 ft).

Descent: Descend the route, taking care to follow it exactly to avoid more difficult terrain.

● Free Agents

84 Buck Mountain

8,528 ft; 49th highest

Buck Mountain has a massive north face that drops sharply into the Buck Creek valley. On its eastern flank, the small King Glacier occupies a hanging basin that drains into King Lake. The summit plateau consists of three distinct high points, the middle one being the most prominent (according to Beckey 2003, p. 175; and Goldman 2001, p. 97). Note that the north and middle summits are very close to the same height. The south summit appears to be higher when viewed from the plateau, but it's not. Both the north and middle summits have registers. Buck is on the Napeequa–Chiwawa River divide northeast of Clark Mountain and Luahna Peak.

SOUTHWEST ROUTE

The approach to this route has some heartbreaking elevation gain and loss just to get to base camp in the remote and wild Napeequa Valley. After a stretch of unpleasant, often steep bushwhacking to reach open slopes, the remainder is an enjoyable scramble to the summit.

APPROACH

Time to camp	5–6 hours
Mileage	10 miles
Elevation change	+4,200 ft; -2,100 ft
GT 15-minute	Holden (No. 113)
Contact	Okanogan/Wenatchee NF, Lake Wenatchee Ranger District

ROUTE

Difficulty	▲▲ Grade II; class 3 rock
Time to summit	5 hours
Elevation change	+3,900 ft; -0 ft
USGS 7.5-minute	Clark Mountain
Season	June–October

Approach: Permits are not required to camp or climb in the Glacier Peak Wilderness. A Northwest Forest Pass is required to park at the trailhead.

Drive US 2 to Coles Corner 19 miles east of Stevens Pass. Turn north onto Highway 207 (Lake Wenatchee Road) and follow it for 4.4 miles, past the turnoff to Plain/Leavenworth and over the Wenatchee River Bridge, to a fork. Bear right at the fork and continue 1.3 miles, past the Lake Wenatchee State Airport, then turn left onto Chiwawa River Road (Forest Road 62) at the sign for Fish Lake/Chiwawa Valley. Follow Chiwawa River Road approximately 20

Buck Mountain from the west Photo by Scott Stephenson

miles (1 mile past Nineteenmile Campground) to the trailhead for the Little Giant Trail on the left (2,600 ft).

Cross the Chiwawa River by log or ford (difficult in early season) and ascend the very steep Little Giant Trail 5 miles to Little Giant Pass (6,400 ft). Drop over the pass and descend into the Napeequa Valley and along the north side of the river to the junction with the Boulder Pass Trail, 8.3 miles from the trailhead (4,300 ft). There's good camping along the valley floor. Stay right at the junction onto the Napeequa River Trail and hike approximately 1.7 miles to where the trail crosses Louis Creek (approx. 4,680 ft).

Route: Cross Louis Creek, leave the trail and ascend northeasterly along the left (west) side of the creek through steep brush (unpleasant bushwhacking) and past an impressive waterfall to reach a flat basin above (approx. 6,400 ft). This basin is at the base of Buck Mountain's gentle southwest slopes. Ascend the loose pumice, talus, and snow-covered slopes northeasterly to the summit plateau consisting of three separate high points. Scramble rock and a gully (class 3) up to the middle summit (8,528 ft). The scramble to the north summit is of similar difficulty.

Descent: Descend the route.

85 Mount Formidable

8,325 ft; 92nd highest

Mount Formidable is a remote and glaciated peak. Its name is well deserved, as it possesses impressively rugged north and east ridges, the latter harboring the western flank of the large Middle Cascade Glacier. Several smaller glaciers occupy the northern and western flanks. The peak is between the middle and south forks of the Cascade River, south of Cascade Pass.

SOUTH ROUTE

The approach to this route follows the first portion of the famous Ptarmigan Traverse. It traverses some remote and wild country. This outing will definitely test your navigation, routefinding, and climbing skills, as you'll cross passes, travel over glaciers, and scramble up steep snow and rock. This is a fantastic journey through some of the most spectacular country in the Cascades. (If you plan to complete the Ptarmigan Traverse and exit at Downey Creek Trailhead, take note: the automobile bridge over Downey Creek immediately west of the trailhead was severely damaged in the October 2003 floods and may take some time to repair or replace. If the bridge is not passable to pedestrians, a difficult and potentially dangerous ford of the creek would be required. Contact the Mount Baker–Snoqualmie National Forest's Darrington Ranger District for information.)

APPROACH

Time to camp	5 hours
Mileage	6 miles
Elevation change	+3,300 ft; -800 ft
GT 15-minute	Cascade Pass (No. 80)
Contact	North Cascades NP, Headquarters or Marblemount Ranger Station

ROUTE

Difficulty	▲▲ Grade II +; steep snow; glacier travel; class 3 rock
Time to summit	4–5 hours
Elevation change	+2,800 ft; -600 ft
USGS 7.5-minute	Cascade Pass
Season	June–September

Approach: Permits are not required to camp or climb in the Glacier Peak Wilderness. A Northwest Forest Pass is required to park at the trailhead.

From Interstate 5 north of Mount Vernon, take exit 230 (Anacortes/Burlington). Drive 46 miles east on Highway 20 to Marblemount. Continue a short distance east on Highway 20 to a fork in the road and take the right fork over a bridge onto the Cascade River Road. Drive 22.3 miles on the narrow road to its end at a large parking area and the trailhead for the Cascade Pass Trail (3,600 ft).

Follow the trail for 3.7 miles as it climbs to Cascade Pass (5,400 ft). Leave the trail and pick up a climber's path bearing south-southeasterly on a rising traverse across Mix-up Peak's east slopes. Pass a spur ridge (approx. 6,000 ft) to reach the toe of the Cache Glacier and ascend moderate snowslopes to reach Cache Col (approx. 6,900 ft). A moat forms at the col by late season and can pose a problem. Be careful on the traverse, particularly in early season, as there's no runout due to steep cliff bands below; depending on your comfort level, consider using running belays. Cross the col and make a descending traverse south-southeasterly across snow/talus to Kool-Aid Lake (a pond actually) and good camping (6,120 ft).

Route: From Kool-Aid Lake, head southerly toward a prominent spur ridge descending westerly from Arts Knoll. Cross a steep, narrow snow finger to reach the start of Red Ledge, a broad ledge that leads easily across the spur. Once over the spur, make a gradual descending traverse across meadows, snow/talus, and minor rock ribs aiming for the icefall on the Middle Cascade Glacier (approx. 6,200 ft). Once beside the glacier, ascend snow/talus until able to access the glacier above the icefall (approx. 6,500 ft). Ascend the glacier south-southeasterly to the Spider-Formidable col (7,320 ft), a small col 100 yards left (east) of the most obvious one.

Cross the col and descend southerly to 7,000 feet, then contour westerly aiming for a prominent notch in a southwest-trending spur ridge (approx. 7,000 ft). Cross the notch and scramble down a narrow gully into the basin beneath Mount Formidable's south slopes. From the base of the gully, make a scrambling rising traverse northwesterly across two gullies to reach the main spur ridge descending south-southwesterly from Formidable's summit area. Scramble over the spur ridge to reach a third gully. Don't be tempted to take either of the first two gullies as they lead to difficult terrain high on Formidable's east ridge. Scramble northerly up the gully, rock, and then a small snowfield. From the top of the snowfield, scramble rock (class 3) northerly to the summit (8,325 ft).

Descent: Descend the route.

ALPINE LAKES WILDERNESS

•

ALPINE LAKES WILDERNESS WAS DESIGNATED IN 1976. It lies within both the Mount Baker–Snoqualmie and Wenatchee national forests and today encompasses more than 360,000 acres. Because the wilderness straddles the Cascade Crest, it's a land of stark contrast. On the stormy west side, dense wet forests of Douglas fir, cedar, and western hemlock fill the lowlands. As the terrain rises to the glacier-sculpted crest, open alpine meadows abound, which are often carpeted with flowers in early summer. Lakes and tarns fill seemingly every depression. On the dry east side of the crest, spruce and larch give way to remarkable dry forests of ponderosa and lodgepole pine, which thrive in the sandy soil. This astounding variety of habitat results in a healthy population of wildlife. Deer and black bears roam the woods and mountain goats inhabit the craggy peaks. The indisputable crown jewel of the wilderness is the Stuart Range, whose tremendous granite batholith has been carved by intense alpine glaciation into a superbly rugged, often serrated crest. All this granite provides fantastic climbing in a stunning alpine scene. The range is also a picturesque backdrop for the Enchantments, an incredible high, lake-dotted plateau set among the rugged ridges.

Within the boundaries of the wilderness are found nine of this guide's high points. Six of these peaks can be climbed in three distinct Slam itineraries, leaving three Free Agent peaks to be climbed individually.

● Dragon Slam

Peaks & routes	Dragontail Peak (West Route), Colchuck Peak (Colchuck Glacier)
Max difficulty	▲▲ Grade II; moderate snow; class 3 rock
Duration	2 days
Roundtrip to camp	10 miles
Elevation gain	+6,400 ft
USGS 7.5-minute	Enchantment Lakes
GT 15-minute	The Enchantments (No. 209S)
Trailhead	Stuart Lake–Colchuck Lake Trail
Season	April–August

If you're one of the lucky few to get a permit, this spectacular Slam takes you into the heart of the craggy Stuart Range and the Enchantments. The picture-perfect alpine scenery and your base camp on the shores of Colchuck Lake beneath Dragontail Peak's massive north face will inspire you for the great climbing ahead. The area gets very crowded in summer, so don't expect a wilderness experience. Somehow though, despite the hordes, this place still retains its rugged splendor and remarkable beauty.

ITINERARY

Day	Elevation change	Instructions
1	+2,300 ft; -100 ft	Hike to Colchuck Lake and camp (5,600 ft).
2	+4,100 ft; -6,300 ft	Get an early start and climb Colchuck and Dragontail Peaks. Hike out.

Notes: These ascents are sometimes done in one long day due to the difficulty of obtaining a permit.

86 Dragontail Peak

8,840 ft; 26th highest

Dragontail Peak's massive and precipitous north face rises for more than 3,000 feet above Colchuck Lake and is the subject of numerous photographs. There are several excellent alpine rock routes on the face. The Colchuck Glacier descends from the Dragontail-Colchuck col (aka Colchuck Col).

WEST ROUTE

The crux of this route is getting a permit! The Colchuck Glacier gets icy, particularly in late season, so don't forget the crampons.

Dragontail Peak from the southwest (Argonaut Peak) Photo by Scott Stephenson

APPROACH

Time to camp	3 hours
Mileage	5 miles
Elevation change	+2,300 ft; -100 ft
GT 15-minute	The Enchantments (No. 209S)
Contact	Okanogan/Wenatchee NF, Leavenworth Ranger District

ROUTE

Difficulty	▲▲ Grade II; moderate snow and ice; glacier travel; class 2 rock
Time to summit	4–5 hours
Elevation change	+3,300 ft; -0 ft
USGS 7.5-minute	Enchantment Lakes
Season	April–September

Approach: Permits are required to camp in the Colchuck Zone of the Alpine Lakes Wilderness. Permits can be very difficult (nearly impossible) to obtain during peak season. Either reserve your permit well in advance (months), or take your slim chances with a daily permit lottery where unused permits are handed out on the spot. Permits include a trailhead parking pass. Otherwise, a Northwest Forest Pass is required to park at the trailhead.

During the winter and early spring, Icicle Creek Road is usually gated at Bridge Creek Campground, 3.5 miles from the Stuart Lake–Colchuck Lake trailhead. Mountaineer Creek Road is usually open after early May; contact the ranger district for road-condition reports.

Drive US 2 to Leavenworth. At the western edge of Leavenworth at the gas station, turn south off US 2 onto Icicle Creek Road. Drive 9 miles on Icicle Creek Road to Bridge Creek Campground and turn left (south) across Icicle Creek onto Mountaineer Creek Road. Continue 3.5 miles to the Stuart Lake–Colchuck Lake trailhead at the end of the road (3,400 ft).

Hike the trail along Mountaineer Creek for 2.5 miles to the junction with the Colchuck Lake Trail (4,500 ft). Turn left onto the Colchuck Lake Trail and hike 1.6 miles to reach the northern shore of Colchuck Lake (5,600 ft). There's good camping at several spots along the lakeshore.

Route: Continue following the trail around the right (west) shore of the lake past a small lake and onto the talus field below the Colchuck Glacier moraine. Climb talus and scree to the base of the moraine (approx. 6,300 ft). Ascend snowslopes to the left (east) side of the glacier. Climb the glacier to Colchuck Col (8,100 ft). Cross the col, turn left (east), and ascend snow/talus, then a steep couloir to a notch in Dragontail's summit ridge (approx. 8,700 ft). Descend 50–60 feet leftward down a short, steep slope, then traverse northeasterly to the summit boulders and the summit (8,840 ft).

Descent: Descend the route.

EAST ROUTE

If you're lucky enough to secure a permit, you're in for a tough ascent no matter which way you choose to go. The slopes leading to Aasgard Pass are decidedly unpleasant, with copious scree, talus, and rockfall danger from Dragontail Peak. The ascent via the Snow Lakes is simply long. It's all worth it though, as the Enchantment plateau is gorgeous. So give yourself some extra time to enjoy it. After all, you will have earned it with sweat and toil.

APPROACH

	Primary	Alternate
Time to camp	5–6 hours	4–5 hours
Mileage	7 miles	7 miles
Elevation change	+ 4,500 ft; -200 ft	+ 4,200 ft; -0 ft
GT 15-minute	The Enchantments (No. 209S)	The Enchantments (No. 209S)
Contact	Okanogan/Wenatchee NF, Leavenworth Ranger District	Okanogan/Wenatchee NF, Leavenworth Ranger District

ROUTE

Difficulty	▲▲ Grade II; moderate snow; class 2 rock
Time to summit	2 hours (primary approach); 4–5 hours (alternate approach)
Elevation change	+1,200 ft, -0 ft (primary approach); +3,500 ft, -0 ft (alternate approach)
USGS 7.5-minute	Enchantment Lakes
Season	April–October

Primary Approach: Permits are required to camp in the Enchantment Zone of Alpine Lakes Wilderness. Permits can be very difficult (nearly impossible) to obtain during peak season. Either reserve your permit well in advance (months), or take your slim chances with a daily permit lottery where unused permits are handed out on the spot. Permits include a trailhead parking pass. Otherwise, a Northwest Forest Pass is required to park at the trailhead.

Follow the approach for the Dragontail Peak's West Route to the northern shore of Colchuck Lake (5,600 ft). Continue on the trail around the right (west) shore of the lake past a small lake. Continue along the lakeshore across a large boulder field (cairns mark the way) and around the southwest side of the lake. Ascend east and then south into the broad couloir leading up to Aasgard Pass (incorrectly labeled as Colchuck Pass on the USGS quad), staying well away from the face of Dragontail Peak to avoid rockfall. Climb the snow/scree/talus slope to Aasgard Pass (7,800 ft), approximately 6.1 miles from the trailhead. There's good camping on the south side of the pass (approx. 7,700 ft).

Alternate Approach: Permits are required to camp in the Snow Zone of the Alpine Lakes Wilderness. See the primary approach for information on how to obtain one and for trailhead parking regulations.

Drive US 2 to Leavenworth. At the western edge of town at the gas station, turn south off US 2 onto Icicle Creek Road. Follow the road for 4 miles to the trailhead for the Snow Lakes Trail on the left (approx. 1,300 ft).

Hike the Snow Lakes Trail 6.5 miles to the Snow Lakes and good camping (5,415 ft).

Route: If coming via the alternate approach, continue on the trail past Viviane, Leprechaun, Sprite, Perfection, Inspiration, Isolation, and Tranquil lakes to south of Aasgard Pass (approx. 7,700 ft), 5.2 miles from the narrows between the Snow Lakes. (This gets you to the primary approach base camp, which is south of Aasgard Pass.)

From south of Aasgard Pass, head cross-country southwesterly and climb the moderate snowslopes to the saddle in the crest above (approx. 8,500 ft). From the saddle, turn right and hike/scramble an easy rock spur (class 2) to the summit (8,840 ft).

Descent: Descend the route.

87 Colchuck Peak

8,705 ft; 33rd highest

Colchuck Peak is steep on all flanks except the south. On its northeastern flank is the Colchuck Glacier. It's part of the Stuart Range and lies southwest of Colchuck Lake and west of Dragontail Peak.

COLCHUCK GLACIER

This is a deservedly popular climbing and hiking destination so you may have trouble getting an overnight permit. The ascent is worth the effort though, as it combines many of the elements of a classic Cascade scramble. The glacier gets icy, particularly in late season, so be sure to remember your crampons.

APPROACH

Time to camp	3 hours
Mileage	5 miles
Elevation change	+2,300 ft; -100 ft
GT 15-minute	The Enchantments (No. 209S)
Contact	Okanogan/Wenatchee NF, Leavenworth Ranger District

ROUTE

Difficulty	▲▲ Grade II; moderate snow and ice; glacier travel; class 3 rock
Time to summit	4 hours
Elevation change	+3,200 ft; -0 ft
USGS 7.5-minute	Enchantment Lakes
Season	April–August

Approach: Follow the approach for Dragontail Peak's West Route to Colchuck Lake and good camping (5,600 ft).

Route: Continue following the trail around the right (west) shore of the lake past a small lake and onto the talus field below the Colchuck Glacier moraine. Climb talus and scree to the base of the moraine (approx. 6,300 ft), then ascend snowslopes to reach the left (east) side of the glacier. Ascend the glacier to Colchuck Col (8,100 ft). From the col, turn right (west) and scramble up sandy ledges (class 3) to the summit plateau (8,500 ft). Climb west-northwesterly through large boulders, then up open slopes to the summit (8,705 ft).

Descent: Descend the route.

SOUTH ROUTE

This is a long, moderate scramble up the rocky south slopes. There's some brush to contend with at the base of the route, but it's not too bad.

APPROACH

Time to camp	3–4 hours
Mileage	7 miles
Elevation change	+1,900 ft; -1,300 ft
GT 15-minute	Mount Stuart (No. 209)
Contact	Okanogan/Wenatchee NF, Cle Elum Ranger District

ROUTE

Difficulty	▲ Grade I+; class 3 rock
Time to summit	5–6 hours
Elevation change	+4,600 ft; -0 ft
USGS 7.5-minute	Enchantment Lakes
Season	May–October

Approach: Backcountry self-registration permits are required for the Alpine Lakes Wilderness and may be obtained at the trailhead. A Northwest Forest Pass is required to park at the trailhead.

Drive Interstate 90 to Cle Elum (exit 85) and follow Highway 970, which becomes US 97, for 7 miles to Teanaway Road. Turn left onto Teanaway Road and follow it for 13.2 miles to a fork in the road where the pavement ends. Bear right at the fork onto Forest Road 9737 and drive 3.7 miles to the

Colchuck Peak from the southwest (Argonaut Peak) Photo by Scott Stephenson

junction with Beverly Creek Road just before the bridge over the creek. Turn right onto Beverly Creek Road and follow it for 1.5 miles to its end at the trailhead for the Beverly Turnpike Trail (3,600 ft).

Cross the footbridge and hike the Beverly Turnpike Trail 2.7 miles to the junction with the Fourth Creek Trail (approx. 5,100 ft). Turn right onto the Fourth Creek Trail and hike 0.6 mile to a pass and the junction with the County Line Trail (approx. 5,500 ft). From here there are good views of Colchuck Peak's south slopes. Stay left at the junction and continue on the Fourth Creek Trail for 3.6 miles to Ingalls Creek and good camping on the opposite bank (4,200 ft).

Route: Continue a short distance on the Fourth Creek Trail to the junction with the Ingalls Creek Trail (4,280 ft). Turn right (east) onto the Ingalls Creek Trail and hike approximately 0.5 mile to 4,200 feet. This point is approximately 0.5 mile west of where the trail crosses Porcupine Creek.

Leave the trail and head north-northeasterly up the forested, brushy slopes staying well left (west) of Porcupine Creek to avoid the dense brush. Use of game trails helps to reduce the amount of bushwhacking. Stay right (east) of a spur ridge of Argonaut Peak at 6,000 feet and continue up alp slopes, then open rocky slopes staying on the left (west) side of the drainage. Pass right (east) of an obvious spur ridge knob at 7,400 feet and continue up rocky slopes and slabs (moderate snowslopes in early season) directly to the summit (8,705 ft).

Descent: Descend the route.

● Enchanted Slam

Peaks & routes	Enchantment Peak (South Route), McClellan Peak (North Route)
Max difficulty	▲ Grade I+; steep snow or ice; class 3 rock
Duration	3 days
Roundtrip to camp	13 miles
Elevation gain	+8,200 ft
USGS 7.5-minute	Enchantment Lakes
GT 15-minute	The Enchantments (No. 209S)
Trailhead	Stuart Lake–Colchuck Lake Trail
Season	April–October

This is indeed a magical journey through the heart of the Enchantments. You'll camp on the shores of crystal-clear alpine lakes and be ensorcelled by the rugged granite spires and ridges surrounding you. The solid rock is also a scrambler's dream. It's a long approach no matter how you go about it, but it's definitely worth the sweat—assuming you can get a permit, that is.

ITINERARY

Day	Elevation change	Instructions
1	+ 4,500 ft; -200 ft	Follow the primary approach for Enchantment Peak via Aasgard Pass and camp just below the pass (7,700 ft).
2	+ 3,500 ft; -3,500 ft	Climb McClellan Peak and Enchantment Peak and return to camp.
3	+ 200 ft; -4,500 ft	Hike out.

Notes: The primary approach via Aasgard Pass (incorrectly labeled as Colchuck Pass on the USGS quad) is recommended because it's shorter, despite the unpleasant ascent to the pass. If you've got extra time and energy, Dragontail Peak's East Route shares the same base camp.

88 Enchantment Peak

8,520 ft; 50th highest

Enchantment Peak consists of two short summit crags atop an expansive rocky plateau, the northeast peak being the highest. A long ridge with numerous subsummits protrudes northerly from the summit, disappearing into the high and distinctly alpine terrain of the Druid Plateau. The peak is not labeled on the USGS quad, but it's located approximately 0.6 mile west of Prusik Pass. The high point is shown as the 8,480-foot contour of the northeast peak on the USGS 7.5-minute quad, but was surveyed at 8,520 feet on the older 15-minute quad.

SOUTH ROUTE

This is a moderate scramble with a few enjoyable final moves to the summit and great views of the entire Enchantment plateau.

APPROACH

	Primary	Alternate
Time to camp	5–6 hours	4–5 hours
Mileage	7 miles	7 miles
Elevation change	+ 4,500 ft; -200 ft	+ 4,200 ft; -0 ft
GT 15-minute	The Enchantments (No. 209S)	The Enchantments (No. 209S)
Contact	Okanogan/Wenatchee NF, Leavenworth Ranger District	Okanogan/Wenatchee NF, Leavenworth Ranger District

ROUTE

Difficulty   ▲ Grade I+; class 3 rock
Time to summit 3 hours (primary approach); 4–5 hours (alternate approach)
Elevation change +1,500 ft, -600 ft (primary approach); +3,200 ft, -0 ft (alternate approach)
USGS 7.5-minute Enchantment Lakes
Season   April–October

Primary Approach: Permits are required to camp in the Enchantment Zone of the Alpine Lakes Wilderness. Permits can be very difficult (nearly impossible) to obtain during peak season. Either reserve your permit well in advance (months), or take your slim chances with a daily permit lottery where unused permits are handed out on the spot. Permits include a trailhead parking pass. Otherwise, a Northwest Forest Pass is required to park at the trailhead.

During the winter and early spring, Icicle Creek Road is usually gated at Bridge Creek Campground, 3.5 miles from the Stuart Lake–Colchuck Lake trailhead. Mountaineer Creek Road is usually open after early May; contact the ranger district for road-condition reports.

Drive US 2 to Leavenworth. At the western edge of Leavenworth at the gas station, turn south off US 2 onto Icicle Creek Road. Drive 9 miles on Icicle Creek Road to Bridge Creek Campground and turn left (south) across Icicle Creek onto Mountaineer Creek Road. Continue 3.5 miles to the Stuart Lake–Colchuck Lake trailhead at the end of the road (3,400 ft).

Hike the trail along Mountaineer Creek for 2.5 miles to the junction with the Colchuck Lake Trail (4,500 ft). Turn left onto the Colchuck Lake Trail and hike 1.6 miles to reach the northern shore of Colchuck Lake (5,600 ft). Continue on the trail around the right (west) shore of the lake past a small lake. Continue along the lakeshore across a large boulder field (cairns mark the way) and around the southwest side of the lake. Ascend east and then south into the broad couloir leading up to Aasgard Pass (incorrectly labeled as Colchuck Pass on the USGS quad), staying well away from the face of Dragontail Peak to avoid rockfall. Climb the snow/scree/talus slope to Aasgard Pass (7,800 ft), approximately 6.1 miles from the trailhead. There's good camping on the south side of the pass (approx. 7,700 ft).

Alternate Approach: Permits are required to camp in the Snow Zone of the Alpine Lakes Wilderness. See the primary approach for information on how to obtain one, and for trailhead parking regulations.

Follow the primary approach to Leavenworth. At the western edge of Leavenworth at the gas station, turn south off US 2 onto Icicle Creek Road. Follow the road for 4 miles to the trailhead for the Snow Lakes Trail on the left (1,300 ft).

Hike the Snow Lakes Trail 6.5 miles to the Snow Lakes and good camping (5,415 ft).

Route: If coming via the primary approach, follow the trail 1.7 miles east, past Tranquil, Isolation, and Inspiration lakes, to the north end of Perfection Lake (approx. 7,100 ft).

If coming via the alternate approach, follow the trail 3.5 miles west from the narrows between the Snow Lakes, past Lake Viviane and Leprechaun and Sprite lakes, to the north end of Perfection Lake (approx. 7,100 ft).

From the north end of Perfection Lake, follow a side trail that ascends 0.7 mile north-northeasterly to broad Prusik Pass (approx. 7,400 ft). Turn left (west) and ascend slopes (moderate snow in early season) westerly to the base of the summit rocks of the northeast peak. Scramble rock (class 3) on the south side of the northeast peak for approximately 150 feet to the summit (8,520 ft).

Descent: Descend the route.

Scrambling Enchantment Peak's northeast peak Photo by Scott Stephenson

89 McClellan Peak

8,364 ft; 83rd highest

McClellan Peak, the high point of choppy McClellan Ridge, is a craggy summit with a steep northeastern flank. It's located on the southeast side of the Enchantment plateau, southwest of upper Snow Lake.

NORTH ROUTE

The upper section of this enjoyable scramble features a lofty ridge run along the Ingalls Creek–Snow Lakes divide high above the Enchantment plateau.

APPROACH

	Primary	Alternate
Time to camp	5–6 hours	4–5 hours
Mileage	7 miles	7 miles
Elevation change	+4,500 ft; -200 ft	+4,200 ft; -0 ft
GT 15-minute	The Enchantments (No. 209S)	The Enchantments (No. 209S)
Contact	Okanogan/Wenatchee NF, Leavenworth Ranger District	Okanogan/Wenatchee NF, Leavenworth Ranger District

ROUTE

Difficulty	▲ Grade I+; steep snow or ice; class 3 rock
Time to summit	3 hours (primary approach); 4–5 hours (alternate approach)
Elevation change	+1,400 ft, -700 ft (primary approach); +3,000 ft, -0 ft (alternate approach)
USGS 7.5-minute	Enchantment Lakes
Season	April–October

Primary Approach: Follow the primary approach for Enchantment Peak's South Route to Aasgard Pass and good camping (7,700 ft).

Alternate Approach: Follow the alternate approach for Enchantment Peak's South Route to the Snow Lakes and good camping (5,415 ft).

Route: If coming via the primary approach, follow the trail approximately 2.5 miles east, past Tranquil, Isolation, Inspiration, and Perfection lakes, to the flat area between Sprite and Leprechaun lakes (approx. 7,000 ft).

If coming via the alternate approach, follow the trail approximately 2.7 miles west from the narrows between the Snow Lakes, past Lake Viviane, to the flat area between Sprite and Leprechaun lakes (approx. 7,000 ft).

McClellan Peak and Ridge from the north in spring Photo by Scott Stephenson

From the flat area between Sprite and Leprechaun lakes, leave the trail and head southeasterly and then southerly, ascending toward McClellan Peak's west ridge just right (west) of a prominent rock tower called The Prong (Beckey 2000, p. 265). Ascend steep snow or rock (class 3) to the notch. This section is shaded by the ridge above and can be icy. From the notch, turn left (east) and scramble rock (class 3) along the right (south) side of the ridge to the base of short slabs beneath the summit block. Scramble up the slabs (class 3), then traverse to the right-hand corner of the block and enter a hidden chimney. Scramble up the easy chimney (class 2) to the summit (8,364 ft).

Descent: Descend the route.

Scrambling high on McClellan Ridge
Photo by Scott Stephenson

● Stuart Slam

Peaks & routes	Mount Stuart (Southeast Route), Sherpa Peak (West Ridge)
Max difficulty	▲▲ Grade II; moderate snow; mid-fifth class rock
Duration	3 days
Roundtrip to camp	16 miles
Elevation gain	+8,700 ft
USGS 7.5-minute	Mount Stuart
GT 15-minute	Mount Stuart (No. 209)
Trailhead	Beverly Turnpike Trail
Season	May–October

Undertake these great routes on granite baked by the sun and you'll feel like you've been suddenly transported to California's Sierra Nevada. The high and dry alpine scenery is stunning and the bivi in the high basin between the peaks is a Cascade classic. This Slam is so great that it should be on every Cascade climber's list! If you're loving the sun and the office can wait, consider incorporating an ascent of Colchuck Peak's South Route into your plans.

ITINERARY

Day	Elevation change	Instructions
1	+4,600 ft; -800 ft	Follow the approach for Sherpa Peak to camp on the table rock (7,400 ft).
2	+1,300 ft; -1,300 ft	Climb Sherpa Peak and return to camp.
3	+2,900 ft; -6,700 ft	Climb Mount Stuart and hike out.

Notes: For day 3, from the table rock, ascend the basin to its upper left corner to reach the base of a prominent gully that diagonals up and left between cliff bands and rock outcrops bearing toward Mount Stuart's false summit. Scramble up the loose gully to reach the base of the upper snowfields beneath the false summit and join the route for Mount Stuart.

---

90 Mount Stuart

9,415 ft; 7th highest

Mount Stuart, king of the Stuart Range, is an astounding peak. The huge granite batholith that composes the range has been shaped by intense alpine glaciation into a chiseled visage. The hanging Stuart and Ice Cliff glaciers are continuing this process on Stuart's perfectly alpine north face. The western flank features the long and complex west ridge, while the southern flank is comparatively gentle and is corrugated by numerous ribs and gullies. No matter how you tackle this impressive peak, you're in for a physically demanding and extremely rewarding outing.

SOUTHEAST ROUTE

This moderate scramble is a physically demanding but technically easy way to the summit. It's also a common descent route for climbers ascending other routes on the mountain.

APPROACH

Time to camp	3–4 hours
Mileage	7 miles
Elevation change	+2,000 ft; -800 ft
GT 15-minute	Mount Stuart (No. 209)
Contact	Okanogan/Wenatchee NF, Cle Elum Ranger District

ROUTE

Difficulty	▲▲ Grade II; moderate snow; class 3 rock
Time to summit	4–6 hours
Elevation change	+4,700 ft; -0 ft
USGS 7.5-minute	Mount Stuart
Season	May–October

Mount Stuart and Sherpa Peak from the southeast in winter Photo by Lowell Skoog

Approach: Backcountry self-registration permits are required for the Alpine Lakes Wilderness and may be obtained at the trailhead. A Northwest Forest Pass is required to park at the trailhead.

Drive Interstate 90 to Cle Elum (exit 85) and follow Highway 970, which becomes US 97, for 7 miles to Teanaway Road. Turn left onto Teanaway Road and follow it for 13.2 miles to a fork in the road where the pavement ends. Bear right at the fork onto Forest Road 9737 and drive 3.7 miles to the junction with Beverly Creek Road just before the bridge over the creek. Turn right onto Beverly Creek Road and follow it for 1.5 miles to its end at the trailhead for the Beverly Turnpike Trail (3,600 ft).

Cross the footbridge and hike 3.5 miles on the Beverly Turnpike Trail to reach Beverly Turnpike Pass (5,600 ft) and your first view of Mount Stuart. Cross the pass and follow the trail 3 miles as it descends to the valley floor, crosses Ingalls Creek, and continues to a meadow and the junction with the Ingalls Creek Trail (4,800 ft). Good camping can be found approximately 100 yards left (west) of the junction, where the trail reenters the forest; there's a small stream nearby for water.

Route: From the trail junction in the meadow, ascend north to pick up a climber's path on the left (west) side of the meadow. It's critical to find this path as it provides the easiest route through the forest and brush. It also allows for direct access to the ridge on the left (west) side of the gully. Partway up the ridge the path descends into the gully and disappears. Take the path of least resistance up the gully, negotiating a small cliff band along the way (class 3), until you emerge at a talus basin (approx. 7,000 ft) and decent bivi sites; water can be scarce in late season.

Ascend the talus basin, which becomes a boulder field (approx. 8000 ft), toward the upper snowfields of the false (east) summit. Ascend the moderately steep snow, or scramble rock (class 2) on the left, to approximately 9,000 feet. Cross over a minor rock rib on the left side of the upper snowfields, then scramble diagonally up and left over broken rock (class 3) directly to the true summit.

Descent: Descend the route.

91 Sherpa Peak

8,605 ft; 40th highest

Sherpa Peak is a craggy satellite of Mount Stuart. It's distinguished by a precariously balanced rock near its summit. Its steep north ridge is flanked on the west by the Sherpa Glacier, which originates at the Stuart-Sherpa col. The peak is located immediately east of Mount Stuart.

WEST RIDGE

This is a great alpine rock climb on solid rock in a fantastic alpine setting.

APPROACH

Time to camp	5–7 hours
Mileage	8 miles
Elevation change	+4,600 ft; -800 ft
GT 15-minute	Mount Stuart (No. 209)
Contact	Okanogan/Wenatchee NF, Cle Elum Ranger District

ROUTE

Difficulty	▲▲ Grade II; mid-fifth class rock
Time to summit	5–7 hours
Elevation change	+1,300 ft; -0 ft
USGS 7.5-minute	Mount Stuart
Season	May–October

Approach: Follow the approach for Mount Stuart to the junction of the Beverly Turnpike and Ingalls Creek Trails (4,800 ft). Ascend north to pick up a climber's path on the left (west) side of the meadow (same path as for

Sherpa Peak from the west Photo by Paul Klenke

Mount Stuart's Southeast Route). Ascend the path to approximately 5,800 feet, then traverse right (east) crossing over a ridge and contour into a basin south of Sherpa Peak. Ascend the basin (possible camping at 6,200 ft), staying left of a cliff band and waterfall, to reach an upper basin and additional camping on top of a big, flat table rock in a boulder field (approx. 7,400 ft); water can be scarce in late season.

Route: From camp on the table rock, ascend northerly to the base of a loose gully that leads to the Stuart-Sherpa col. Scramble up the gully toward the notch at the base of Sherpa's west ridge (approx. 8,160 ft). Climb (low-fifth class) easterly along the left (north) side of the ridge to a small notch. Cross the notch (low-fifth class for half a pitch) and traverse along sandy ledges and through rocks on the right (south) side of the ridge to reach the steep southwest face. Climb fractured rock to reach a small cave about a third of the way up the face. Climb a crack on the right (mid-fifth class) to the base of a chimney, then ascend the chimney to the summit ridge. Finish with an exposed scramble along the ridge to the summit (8,605 ft).

Descent: Make three single-rope rappels down the climbing route and a final double-rope rappel back to the Stuart-Sherpa col. Descend the remainder of the route.

● Free Agents

92 Cannon Mountain

8,638 ft; 37th highest

Cannon Mountain is a dominating yet seldom-climbed peak. Its prominent north-face gully is visible from Bridge Creek Campground on Icicle Creek Road. South and east of the summit lies the beautiful high expanse of the Druid Plateau. The peak is located on the Rat–Mountaineer Creek divide southwest of Coney Lake.

NORTH ROUTE
This is a long, challenging scramble featuring steep snow and/or rock.

APPROACH

Time to camp	n/a (done as a day trip)
Mileage	n/a
Elevation change	n/a
GT 15-minute	The Enchantments (No. 209S)
Contact	Okanogan/Wenatchee NF, Leavenworth Ranger District

ROUTE

Difficulty   ▲▲ Grade II; steep snow; class 3 rock
Time to summit 5–7 hours
Elevation change +5,500 ft; -200 ft
USGS 7.5-minute Cashmere Mountain
Season   May–October

Approach: Permits are required to camp in the Colchuck and Enchantment zones (Cannon Mountain is right on the border) of the Alpine Lakes Wilderness. Permits can be very difficult (nearly impossible) to obtain during peak season. Fortunately this ascent is best done as a 1-day outing, so a backcountry self-registration permit obtained at the trailhead is sufficient. A Northwest Forest Pass is required to park at the trailhead.

During the winter and early spring, Icicle Creek Road is usually gated at Bridge Creek Campground, 3.5 miles from the Stuart Lake–Colchuck Lake trailhead. Mountaineer Creek Road is usually open after early May; contact the ranger station for road-condition reports.

Drive US 2 to Leavenworth. At the western edge of Leavenworth at the gas station, turn south off US 2 onto Icicle Creek Road. Drive 9 miles on Icicle Creek Road to Bridge Creek Campground and turn left (south) across Icicle Creek onto Mountaineer Creek Road. Continue 3.5 miles to the Stuart Lake–Colchuck Lake trailhead at the end of the road (3,400 ft).

Route: From the trailhead parking area, hike an abandoned road northeasterly to approximately 4,100 feet at the point where a huge landslide has obliterated the road beyond. From here, the initial goal is to ascend the slopes above for approximately 1.5 miles to gain the crest of the long ridge trending north from Cannon Mountain. Leave the road and ascend south up and across (not directly uphill) the slopes to the base of minor cliff bands at 6,000 feet. Turn right and contour southwesterly beneath the cliffs for several hundred yards to reach a semi-flat area (6,000 ft). The cliffs above this flat area have several timbered breaks that allow access to Cannon's north-trending ridge above. Ascend the slopes southeasterly, passing through one of the breaks, to reach a shallow notch in the ridge crest (approx. 7,880 ft). This notch is immediately northwest of Coney Lake. To bypass a steep ridge step, cross the notch and descend a gully 100–200 feet southeasterly toward the lake (it's not necessary to drop all the way down to the lake), then turn right (south) and contour across the slopes until beyond the step. Ascend up and right (snow, talus, or boulders) back toward the ridge crest. Scramble (exposed class 3) on or just left (east) of the crest to immediately north of the summit. Work up a gully or along the path of least resistance to gain the summit plateau. (The summit plateau can also be reached by ascending one of the gullies, often snow-filled, immediately south of Coney Lake). Circle around the left (east) side of the summit boulders, then make an easy scramble up their southeast side to the base of the huge summit boulder. Finish with 20 feet of friction climbing (class 3) up the boulder to the summit (8,638 ft).

Descent: Descend the route. Alternatively, from the notch northwest of Coney Lake (7,880 ft), descend directly downhill (northwest), easily bypassing steeper sections along the way, back to the trailhead.

93 Cashmere Mountain

8,501 ft; 56th highest

Cashmere Mountain is a solitary peak with a steep north face, numerous radiating ridges, and high subsummits. It's located on the Pioneer–Icicle Creek divide north of the Stuart Range.

SOUTH SLOPES—NORTH FACE

This is a long and exciting scramble in some exquisite country with a base camp at Little Caroline Lake.

APPROACH

Time to camp	3–4 hours
Mileage	6 miles
Elevation change	+3,200 ft; -200 ft
GT 15-minute	The Enchantments (No. 209S)
Contact	Okanogan/Wenatchee NF, Leavenworth Ranger District

ROUTE

Difficulty	▲ Grade I+; class 3–4 rock
Time to summit	3 hours
Elevation change	+2,300 ft; -0 ft
USGS 7.5-minute	Cashmere Mountain
Season	May–October

Approach: Permits are required to camp in the Eightmile/Caroline Zone of the Alpine Lakes Wilderness. Fortunately, Cashmere Mountain is not within the Colchuck, Enchantment or Snow zones, so permits are not nearly as difficult to get. Permits include a trailhead parking pass. Otherwise, a Northwest Forest Pass is required to park at the trailhead.

During the winter and early spring, Icicle Creek Road is usually gated at Bridge Creek Campground, 3 miles from the Eightmile Lake trailhead. Mountaineer Creek Road is usually open after early May; contact the ranger district for road-condition reports.

Drive US 2 to Leavenworth. At the western edge of Leavenworth at the gas station, turn south off US 2 onto Icicle Creek Road. Drive 9 miles on Icicle Creek Road to Bridge Creek Campground and turn left (south) across Icicle Creek onto Mountaineer Creek Road. Continue approximately 3.1 miles to the Eightmile Creek Trail trailhead and the parking area on the left (3,280 ft).

After a short but steep initial stretch, the Eightmile Creek Trail ascends gradually along the stream before reaching Little Eightmile Lake at approximately 2.8 miles (4,404 ft); there's camping here. Turn right onto the initially faint Eightmile–Trout Lake Trail and follow it north-northwesterly as it switchbacks steeply up the slope above the lake, travels through an old burn, and then enters the forest. Continue on the trail to a pronounced col (approx. 6,340 ft) and descend steeply to Lake Caroline (6,190 ft), 5.5 miles from the trailhead. Turn right and follow the trail along the lakeshore (crossing the outlet stream) to a flat area on the shores of Little Caroline Lake (approx. 6,300 ft) and good camping, 6 miles from the trailhead.

Route: From Little Caroline Lake, rejoin the trail toward Windy Pass and ascend to approximately 6,800 feet. Leave the trail and hike northeasterly, across the alp, to gain a south-trending spur ridge that originates near Point 8219 on Cashmere Mountain's west ridge. Ascend the easy ridge northerly to approximately 7,800 feet before traversing right (east-northeasterly) across a boulder field to an obvious notch in Cashmere's upper west ridge (approx. 8,000 ft).

From the notch, ascend approximately 200 feet, then begin an easterly traverse across Cashmere's north face (class 3–4), crossing several rock ribs, to reach a gully on the east side of the north face. The correct gully is located just west of the main north ridge. Ascend the gully (class 3) 100–200 feet to the summit (8,501 ft).

Descent: Descend the route.

94 Argonaut Peak

8,453 ft; 62nd highest

Argonaut Peak is a prominent summit with a steep and alpine northern flank. The short but sheer slabs of the upper south face give way to large debris-filled gullies that characterize the mountain's southern flank. The peak is located in the middle of the Stuart Range, between Colchuck and Sherpa peaks.

SOUTH ROUTE

This is high and dry scenery at its best, deep in the heart of the rugged Stuart Range. OK, there's some nasty brush and a lot of loose rock to contend with, but it's definitely worth the hardships. The view of Mount Stuart's north face from the summit is fantastic.

Argonaut Peak from the south Photo by Scott Stephenson

APPROACH

Time to camp	3–4 hours
Mileage	7 miles
Elevation change	+1,900 ft; -1,300 ft
GT 15-minute	Mount Stuart (No. 209)
Contact	Okanogan/Wenatchee NF, Cle Elum Ranger District

ROUTE

Difficulty	▲▲ Grade II; class 4 rock
Time to summit	4–5 hours
Elevation change	+4,300 ft; -0 ft
USGS 7.5-minute	Enchantment Lakes
Season	May–October

Approach: Backcountry self-registration permits are required for the Alpine Lakes Wilderness and may be obtained at the trailhead. A Northwest Forest Pass is required to park at the trailhead.

Drive Interstate 90 to Cle Elum (exit 85) and follow Highway 970, which becomes US 97, for 7 miles to Teanaway Road. Turn left onto Teanaway Road and follow it for 13.2 miles to a fork in the road where the pavement ends. Bear right at the fork onto Forest Road 9737 and drive 3.7 miles to the junction with Beverly Creek Road just before the bridge over the creek. Turn right onto Beverly Creek Road and follow it for 1.5 miles to its end at the trailhead for the Beverly Turnpike Trail (3,600 ft).

Rappelling Argonaut Peak's final summit gully Photo by Scott Stephenson

Cross the footbridge and hike the Beverly Turnpike Trail 2.7 miles to the junction with the Fourth Creek Trail (approx. 5,100 ft). Turn right onto the Fourth Creek Trail and hike 0.6 mile to a pass and the junction with the County Line Trail (approx. 5,500 ft). From here there are good views of the south face of Argonaut and the main central gully that provides the route (the one that ends at the smooth summit slabs). Stay left at the junction and continue on the Fourth Creek Trail for 3.6 miles to Ingalls Creek and good camping on the opposite bank (4,200 ft).

Route: Continue a short distance on the Fourth Creek Trail to the junction with the Ingalls Creek Trail (4,280 ft). Turn right (east) onto the Ingalls Creek Trail and hike approximately 250 yards to 4,200 feet. This point is just before where the trail crosses a small creek gully (often dry) that drains the south slopes of Argonaut Peak.

Leave the trail and ascend the forested, brushy slopes north-northwesterly. Stay left (west) of the creek gully along the edge of the forest to avoid the thick brush that chokes the gully, especially at lower elevations. Whenever the bushwhacking becomes too nasty, retreat left (west) back into the forest, making use of game trails wherever possible. Periodic views of Argonaut Peak's smooth summit slabs provide the key landmark: head straight for them. At approximately 5,100 feet, bushwhack up and right through dense alder, using overgrown game trails, to reach a clearing in the dense brush at approximately 5,200 feet. From here, wide game trails lead right (east) onto a broad south-trending ridge immediately west of Argonaut's central gully. Ascend the forested ridge northerly, then alp slopes to approximately 6,000 feet before dropping into the barren and rocky gully (snow-filled in early season).

Scramble up the gully, staying right of several small waterfalls (class 2). When the gully forks at approximately 7,000 feet, stay left and scramble (class 3) to the head of the gully and the base of the smooth summit slabs (approx. 8,200 ft). Locate a narrow 50-foot gully with two large chockstones at its head. The gully ends at a notch in the summit ridge approximately 50–75 yards right of the summit slabs. Scramble (class 4) up the gully, passing the chockstones on the right. Turn left (west) and scramble a short distance along the ridge crest (class 3) to the base of the large leaning summit rock. Either scramble through a broad gap at the base of the summit rock or along an exposed ledge on its left (south) side to reach easier terrain on the west side. Scramble up a short distance (class 3) to the summit (8,453 ft).

Descent: Rappel or downclimb the narrow 50-foot gully back to the base of the summit slabs and descend the remainder of the route.

CASCADE VOLCANOES

•

WASHINGTON'S VOLCANOES ARE, FOR MANY, THE ESSENCE of the Cascade Range: from Mount St. Helens, whose violent 1980 eruption sent ash clouds around the world; to hulking Mount Rainier, whose immense glaciers, gaping crevasses, and unpredictable weather have earned it the nickname "Everyman's Everest." These majestic ice-clad summits are part of a 1,000-mile-long chain of volcanoes that stretches from northern California to southern British Columbia. The chain forms a segment of the Ring of Fire, a hotbed of volcanic and seismic activity that encircles the entire Pacific Ocean. Many of these volcanoes have erupted in the recent past and will undoubtably do so again in the future. Although beautiful, these peaks are also potentially very dangerous. Mount Rainier is particularly so due to its close proximity to the major metropolitan areas of Western Washington. Should a cataclysmic eruption occur, the large volume of ice on its flanks could melt to form devastating mudslides (called lahars), which can travel for long distances, obliterating everything in their paths.

Of the five Cascade volcanoes and one subpeak in Washington, two of them can be climbed in a single Slam itinerary, leaving four Free Agent peaks to be climbed individually.

● Grand Slam

Peaks & routes Mount Rainier (Ingraham Glacier Direct or Disappointment Cleaver), Little Tahoma (Whitman Glacier via Paradise)

Max difficulty ▲▲▲ Grade III; steep snow and ice; glacier travel; class 3 rock

Duration 5 days

Roundtrip to camp 12 miles

Elevation gain +12,400 ft

USGS 7.5-minute Mount Rainier East, Mount Rainier West

GT 15-minute Mount Rainier East (No. 270) or Paradise (No. 270S)

Trailhead Skyline Trail

Season May–August

Mount Rainier stands as a testament to the dynamic environment of the Pacific Northwest. Climb the peaks of this Slam and witness, firsthand, the results of the dueling forces of fire and ice that have shaped our planet for millions of years and still continue to do so. This is perhaps the most physically demanding outing in this guidebook. For those of you who are gluttons for punishment, this is your Slam. For the rest of us, split it into two trips.

ITINERARY

Day	Elevation change	Instructions
1	+4,700 ft; -0 ft	Follow the approach for Mount Rainier to Camp Muir and camp (10,080 ft).
2	+4,400 ft; -4,400 ft	Climb Mount Rainier and return to camp.
3	+0 ft; -0 ft	Rest day at Camp Muir.
4	+0 ft; -1,700 ft	Descend the Muir Snowfield to below Anvil Rock and join the route for Little Tahoma. Camp below the col in lower Cathedral Rocks (8,400 ft).
5	+3,400 ft; -6,400 ft	Climb Little Tahoma and hike out.

Notes: It almost goes without saying that this is a very strenuous Slam. The climb of Mount Rainier alone is a full outing. Enough said.

95 Mount Rainier

14,410 ft; highest

Mount Rainier truly needs no introduction. This crowning achievement of the Cascade Range forms the awesome backdrop for the major metropolitan areas of Western Washington. The expansive flanks harbor immense glaciers, gaping crevasses, ancient old-growth forests, raging rivers, and seemingly end-less meadows overflowing with wildflowers. If you summit Mount Rainier, you'll have journeyed through a microcosm of the best the Cascade Range has to offer. It's a challenging climb by any route and should not be attempted by the inexperienced. Fortunately, for those less experienced, excellent guide services can help to bring the summit within reach.

INGRAHAM GLACIER DIRECT OR DISAPPOINTMENT CLEAVER

These routes are the most popular on the mountain so don't expect a wilder-ness experience. Guides lead several thousand climbers up the DC (Disap-pointment Cleaver) every year. However, these routes can offer great views of Little Tahoma, Gibraltar Rock, Mount Adams, Mount St. Helens, and, higher up the route, Glacier Peak and Mount Stuart.

APPROACH

Time to camp	4–5 hours
Mileage	5 miles
Elevation change	+4,700 ft; -0 ft
GT 15-minute	Mount Rainier East (No. 270) or Paradise (No. 270S)
Contact	Mount Rainier National Park

ROUTE

Difficulty	▲▲▲ Grade III; steep snow and ice; glacier travel
Time to summit	5–7 hours
Elevation change	+4,400 ft; -0 ft
USGS 7.5-minute	Mount Rainier East, Mount Rainier West
Season	May–September

Ascending to Camp Muir in spring Photo by Scott Stephenson

Approach: Permits are required to camp or climb on Mount Rainier and can be hard to get in peak season, so consider reserving one in advance by contacting the park. Either way, get or pick up your climbing permit at the ranger station at the upper Paradise parking lot. If the ranger station is closed, get your permit at the Henry M. Jackson Visitor Center a quarter mile back down the road. (Be sure to inquire about route conditions.)

From Tacoma, drive 40 miles south on Highway 7 to Elbe. Join Highway 706 and follow it 10 miles east to the Mount Rainier National Park Nisqually Entrance Station. Continue to the upper Paradise parking lot (5,420 ft).

From the parking lot, take the Skyline Trail 1.5 miles to Panorama Point (6,900 ft). In summer, continue 0.5 mile on the trail to Pebble Creek (7,200 ft) and the start of the Muir Snowfield. If the trail is snow-covered, continue along the broad ridge above Panorama Point staying west of McClure Rock (7,385 ft) to the Muir Snowfield.

Once on the snowfield, ascend north-northwesterly past Anvil Rock (9,584 ft) to Camp Muir (10,080 ft) and good camping, approximately 4.5 miles from the parking lot. This section is difficult to navigate in low visibility, so be sure to have your map and compass handy. Once at Camp Muir, talk with rangers or other climbers for route-condition information.

Route: From Camp Muir, cross the Cowlitz Glacier north-northeasterly to Cathedral Gap (10,600 ft) and access the Ingraham Glacier. Continue up and left (west-northwesterly) on the glacier to reach Ingraham Flats and additional camping (11,100 ft). (Note that there are no toilets at the Flats so blue-bag disposal is required.) From here there are two recommended routes: Ingraham Glacier Direct and Disappointment Cleaver.

In early season (before June/July), most climbers choose the Ingraham Glacier Direct route because it's shorter and less avalanche prone (see Gauthier, p. 84). From Ingraham Flats, ascend the glacier west-northwesterly (watching out for icefall), passing through the Ingraham Icefall, to reach the head of Disappointment Cleaver (12,300 ft).

In later season (after June/July), the Ingraham Glacier melts out and becomes difficult to navigate, making the Disappointment Cleaver the route of choice. From Ingraham Flats, ascend the glacier west-northwesterly (watching out for icefall) to its right (north) side at 11,400 feet. Gain a loose ledge system on the cleaver and follow the ledges westerly (watching out for rockfall) to reach the head of the cleaver (12,300 ft) (see Gauthier, p. 84).

From the head of Disappointment Cleaver, ascend westerly up the Ingraham/Emmons glaciers to reach the crater rim (14,100 ft). There are numerous crevasses in this section. Cross the flat crater westerly before making a final climb up snowslopes to reach Columbia Crest and the summit (14,410 ft).

Descent: Descend the route.

96 Little Tahoma

11,138 ft; 3rd highest

Little Tahoma is a satellite peak of Mount Rainier. Its ranking as the third-highest peak is belittled by its enormous neighbor, but this is a serious climb with huge active glaciers, gaping crevasses, challenging routefinding, a physically demanding approach, highly changeable weather, and often poor visibility.

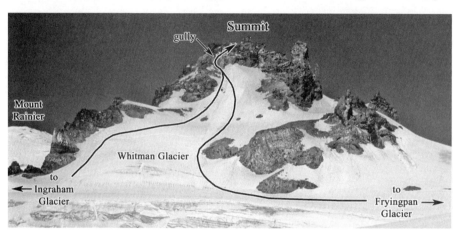

Little Tahoma from the east Photo by Lowell Skoog

WHITMAN GLACIER VIA SUMMERLAND

This route has all the elements of a Cascade classic with the added "delight" of dreadful volcanic rock. The glacier travel on this route is quite straightforward, with very few crevasses.

APPROACH

Time to camp	4–5 hours
Mileage	5 miles
Elevation change	+3,600 ft; -0 ft
GT 15-minute	Mount Rainier East (No. 270)
Contact	Mount Rainier National Park

ROUTE

Difficulty	▲▲ Grade II +; steep snow and ice; glacier travel; class 3 rock
Time to summit	4–5 hours
Elevation change	+3,700 ft; -0 ft
USGS 7.5-minute	Mount Rainier East
Season	May–September

Little Tahoma approach from Summerland Photo by Scott Stephenson

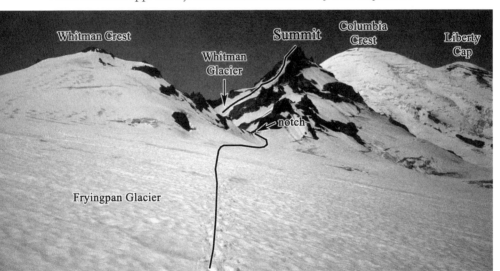

Little Tahoma from the west-southwest Photo by Scott Stephenson

Approach: Permits are required to camp or climb on Mount Rainier and can be hard to get in peak season, so consider reserving one in advance by contacting the park. Either way, get or pick up your climbing permit at the White River Entrance Station. (Be sure to inquire about route conditions.)

From Enumclaw, drive 43 miles east on Highway 410 to the Mount

Rainier National Park White River Entrance Station. Continue 3 miles to the parking area on the right near the Fryingpan Creek Bridge. The trailhead for the Wonderland Trail (3,900 ft) is across the road.

Hike the Wonderland Trail 4 miles along Fryingpan Creek to Summerland (5,900 ft). Bear south-southwesterly across the flats, then ascend southerly, staying right of cliffs, to Meany Crest (7,500 ft) and good camping on existing tent platforms.

Route: From Meany Crest, ascend the Fryingpan Glacier west-southwesterly (250 degrees) aiming for a prominent notch in Whitman Crest (9,000 ft). Cross the notch and descend a short way to the Whitman Glacier. Contour southwesterly past a rock outcrop before turning right (west) and climbing steep snowslopes to the top of the glacier (10,500 ft).

From the top of the glacier, stay left of the crest and ascend a loose rock- and snow-filled gully for approximately 400 feet. Bear left through a gap in the rocks and then ascend rightward to the crest. Follow the crest to a small, very exposed notch just below the summit. Cross the notch (belay recommended) and scramble loose rock to the summit (11,138 ft).

Descent: Descend the route.

WHITMAN GLACIER VIA PARADISE

This route joins the Whitman Glacier via Summerland route high on the Whitman Glacier. However, because this route crosses the Cowlitz and Ingraham glaciers first, it's treated as a distinct route rather than a variation. This route gives you a real alpine wilderness experience with fantastic scenery and some challenging glacier routefinding. This route up Little Tahoma doesn't see a lot of traffic, so once you depart the crowded snow slog of the Muir Snowfield, you'll probably have the whole place to yourself.

APPROACH

Time to camp	4–5 hours
Mileage	5 miles
Elevation change	+3,200 ft; -200 ft
GT 15-minute	Mount Rainier East (No. 270) or Paradise (No. 270S)
Contact	Mount Rainier National Park

ROUTE

Difficulty	▲▲▲ Grade III; steep snow and ice; glacier travel; class 3 rock
Time to summit	4–5 hours
Elevation change	+3,000 ft; -200 ft
USGS 7.5-minute	Mount Rainier East
Season	May–August

Ingraham Glacier crossing from the Cathedral Rocks ridge Photo by Brian Bongiovanni

Approach: Follow the approach for Mount Rainier to below Anvil Rock at 8,500 feet. Rope up and traverse the Cowlitz Glacier easterly at 8,600 feet, being careful to stay above the major crevasse field below. Negotiate the icefall aiming for a prominent notch in the Cathedral Rocks ridge at 8,400 feet. There's good camping just east of this notch, but it can be extremely windy so be sure to anchor your tent well.

Route: From just east of Cathedral Rocks, descend 200 feet to a flat area on the Ingraham Glacier. Traverse northeasterly across the glacier to below a prominent notch in the ridge above. Ascend a snow finger and/or loose slabs to the notch (approx. 8,800 ft) and access the Whitman Glacier. Contour northeasterly on the glacier past a rock outcrop before turning left (northwest) and ascending steep snowslopes to the top of the glacier (10,500 ft).

From the top of the glacier, stay left of the crest and ascend a loose rock- and snow-filled gully for approximately 400 feet. Bear left through a gap in the rocks and then ascend rightward to the crest. Follow the crest to a small, very exposed notch just below the summit. Cross the notch (belay recommended) and scramble loose rock to the summit (11,138 ft).

Descent: Descend the route.

▶ Free Agents

97 Mount Adams

12,276 ft; 2nd highest

Mount Adams, Washington's second-highest peak, is a very popular summit due to its high elevation and technically easy South Route. The mountain has some fancifully named geologic features bestowed by imaginative miners, including Battlement Ridge and The Castle, Victory Ridge, Ridge of Wonders, Hellroaring Meadow, and Devils Garden. If you're new to Washington or the Cascades, Adams makes a great introduction to the unique rigors of high-altitude climbing in the Northwest minus the extensive glacier travel. You'll definitely have a physically demanding outing and chances are good that you'll get at least a taste of highly changeable weather and poor visibility. All in all, Adams makes a great place to cut your Cascade volcano teeth.

SOUTH ROUTE

This is a busy route, so don't expect a wilderness experience. The ascent poses no technical difficulties but should not be undertaken lightly, as altitude and highly changeable weather can be a dangerous combination.

APPROACH

Time to camp	4 hours
Mileage	5 miles
Elevation change	+3,400 ft; -0 ft
GT 15-minute	Mount Adams (No. 367S)
Contact	Gifford Pinchot NF, Mount Adams Ranger Station

ROUTE

Difficulty	▲ Grade I+; moderate snow; glacier travel
Time to summit	3–4 hours
Elevation change	+3,300 ft; -0 ft
USGS 7.5-minute	Mount Adams East
Season	May–October

Approach: A Cascade Volcano Pass is required to climb above 7,000 feet between June 1 and September 30 and costs $15 per person (annual permits are also available). Stiff fines are handed out for those climbing without a pass.

From Highway 141 at Trout Lake, drive approximately 5 miles north on Mount Adams Recreation Area Road to the junction with Forest Road 80. Bear left onto Forest Road 80 and continue north to the junction with Forest Road 8040. Bear right onto Forest Road 8040 and drive north, past Morrison Creek Campground, to the end of the road at Cold Springs Campground, approximately 15 miles from Highway 141. The trailhead for the South Climb Trail (5,600 ft) leaves from the parking area.

From the campground, hike 3.5 miles up the South Climb Trail to the toe of the Crescent Glacier. Ascend the snowslopes of the generally crevasse-free glacier northerly to reach the Lunch Counter, a flat area with good camping (9,000 ft).

Route: From the Lunch Counter, climb the snowslopes northerly to Pikers Peak, the false south summit (11,657 ft). Traverse north-northwesterly across the flat south peak for a couple of hundred yards before making the final ascent up easy, but tiring, snowslopes to the middle and true summit (12,276 ft).

Descent: Descend the route.

98 Mount Baker

10,781 ft; 4th highest

Mount Baker's extreme prominence and unshadowed proximity to the ocean result in tremendous amounts of precipitation. The Mount Baker Ski Resort set a world record for annual snowfall! All this snow results in huge glaciers, making the mountain the second iciest of Washington's volcanoes, surpassed only by the much larger Mount Rainier. Depending on how you count, there are no less than ten major glaciers covering all flanks of the mountain. It's a truly incredible alpine spectacle and an ascent of any route on this Cascade classic should be on every climber's list. If you make your ascent on a summer weekend with a stable weather forecast, you'll definitely have a lot of company.

EASTON GLACIER

This is a moderate glacier route, particularly for a Washington Cascade volcano. Keep an eye out for hidden crevasses in the glacier and changes in weather, which can deteriorate rapidly. Perhaps the biggest drawback of this route is that it lies within the Mount Baker National Recreation Area, so snowmobiles may be present in large numbers (until approximately late May). If this will bother you, ascend the Coleman-Deming Glacier route for a slightly more peaceful (but more technical) experience.

APPROACH

Time to camp	3–4 hours
Mileage	3–4 miles
Elevation change	+2,800 ft; -0 ft
GT 15-minute	Mount Baker (No. 13), Hamilton (No. 45)
Contact	Mount Baker–Snoqualmie NF, Mount Baker Ranger District

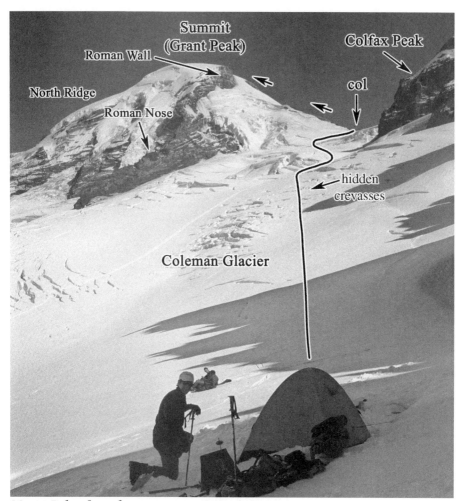

Mount Baker from the west Photo by Brian Bongiovanni

ROUTE

Difficulty   ▲▲ Grade II; moderate snow; glacier travel
Time to summit 4–6 hours
Elevation change + 4,800 ft; -0 ft
USGS 7.5-minute Baker Pass, Mount Baker
Season   May–September

Approach: Permits are not required to camp or climb in the Mount Baker Recreation Area. A Northwest Forest Pass is required to part at the trailhead.

From Interstate 5 north of Mount Vernon, take exit 230 (Anacortes/ Burlington). Turn east on Highway 20 and drive 7 miles to Sedro-Woolley. Continue another 14.5 miles to Baker Lake–Grandy Road. Turn left onto

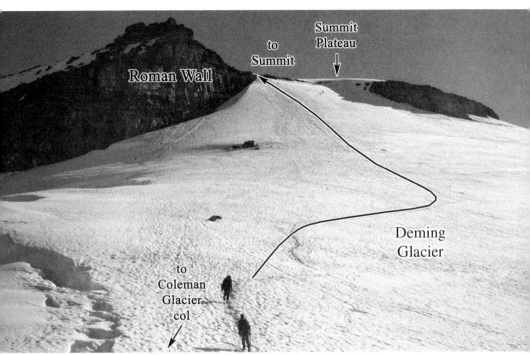

Mount Baker final snowslopes from the southwest Photo by Brian Bongiovanni

Baker Lake–Grandy Road and drive 12.5 miles to South Fork Nooksack Road (Forest Road 12). Turn left onto South Fork Nooksack Road and drive 3.5 miles to Sulphur Creek Road (Forest Road 13). Turn right onto Sulphur Creek Road and continue approximately 5.5 miles to its end at the trailhead for the Baker Pass Trail near the creek (3,200 ft).

Follow the Baker Pass Trail through Schriebers Meadow, across the Easton Glacier stream (Sulphur Creek) suspension bridge, and through forest to Morovitz Meadow (4,500 ft). Continue through the meadows and take the right-hand fork to the Railroad Grade Trail. Continue up the moraine on the Railroad Grade Trail to timberline and good camping (5,600 ft). (In early season you can ascend snowfields below the moraine.) Additional camping can be found along the edges of the moraine at 6,000 feet and 7,000 feet.

Route: From camp at 6,000 feet, continue northerly up the moraine to 7,000 feet. Rope up and ascend the Easton Glacier northerly, bearing a little west of Sherman Peak, to reach a saddle on the west rim of Sherman Crater (approx. 9,600 ft). Continue up 30-degree snowslopes to the summit plateau (10,600 ft). Mark this spot clearly with wands to avoid confusion on the descent. Walk easterly for several hundred yards to the summit (10,781 ft), which is a pronounced knoll.

Descent: Descend the route.

COLEMAN-DEMING GLACIER

This route is more of a wilderness experience than the Easton Glacier because snowmobiles are not allowed on this side of the mountain. Added treats are views of the heavily crevassed lower Coleman Glacier, the classic North Ridge, and the daunting Coleman Glacier headwall.

APPROACH

Time to camp	4 hours
Mileage	4 miles
Elevation change	+3,300 ft; -0 ft
GT 15-minute	Mount Baker (No. 13)
Contact	Mount Baker–Snoqualmie NF, Mount Baker Ranger District or Glacier Public Service Center

ROUTE

Difficulty	▲▲ Grade II +; moderate snow; glacier travel
Time to summit	4–5 hours
Elevation change	+3,800 ft; -0 ft
USGS 7.5-minute	Baker Pass, Mount Baker
Season	May–September

Approach: Permits are not required to camp or climb in the Mount Baker Wilderness. A Northwest Forest Pass is required to park at the trailhead. Registration at the Glacier Public Service Center (summer only) is recommended.

From Interstate 5 near Bellingham, take exit 255 (Mount Baker). Drive 31 miles east to the town of Glacier. Continue 1 mile farther east from town, past the Glacier Public Service Center on the right, and turn right onto Glacier Creek Road (Forest Road 39). Follow Glacier Creek Road for 8 miles to the parking area on the left and the trailhead for the Heliotrope Ridge Trail (3,700 ft).

Follow the Heliotrope Ridge Trail to approach the Coleman Glacier. When the trail forks at approximately 5,200 feet, stay right and ascend to campsites at timberline (often full). Continue ascending to reach additional camping on the top of The Hogback (approx. 6,000 ft) or, for an even shorter summit day, rope up and ascend the Coleman Glacier southerly to a flat area and good glacier camping (7,000 ft).

Route: From camp at 7,000 feet, ascend the glacier east-southeasterly aiming for a broad col between Colfax Peak and the summit cone (9,000 ft). Watch for hidden crevasses on this section. From the col, ascend a pumice ridge east-northeasterly for approximately 700 feet (depending on snow cover), then move right (east) onto the upper Deming Glacier. Continue up 30-degree snowslopes, staying well right (east) of the unstable cliffs of the Roman Wall, to reach the summit plateau (10,600 ft). Mark this spot clearly with wands to avoid confusion on the descent. Walk easterly for several hundred yards to the summit (10,781 ft), which is a pronounced knoll.

Descent: Descend the route.

99 Glacier Peak

10,520 ft; 5th highest

Called "DaKobed" or "Great Parent" by some Native Americans, Glacier Peak is the most remote of the Cascade volcanoes and is the crown jewel of the outstanding Glacier Peak Wilderness. The mountain's location deep in the heart of Puget Sound's Convergence Zone results in huge annual snowfall and large glaciers. There are no less than seven major glaciers blanketing all the flanks of the mountain. Definitely get in here and climb this peak—it's one of the most spectacularly scenic outings in the Cascades.

SITKUM GLACIER

Despite the long approach, this is a popular route in high season so don't expect a wilderness experience. The beauty of the country and the great alpine scenery somehow keep the crowds from negatively affecting the experience. They have heavily affected the base camp in Boulder Basin however, so please take extra care to practice minimum-impact camping.

APPROACH

Time to camp	5–6 hours
Mileage	9 miles
Elevation change	+3,200 ft; -0 ft
GT 15-minute	Sloan Peak (No. 111), Glacier Peak (No. 112)
Contact	Mount Baker–Snoqualmie NF, Darrington Ranger District

ROUTE

Difficulty	▲▲ Grade II +; moderate snow; glacier travel
Time to summit	5–6 hours
Elevation change	+5,100 ft; -0 ft
USGS 7.5-minute	Glacier Peak East, Glacier Peak West
Season	June–October

Approach: Permits are not required to camp or climb in the Glacier Peak Wilderness. A Northwest Forest Pass is required to park at the trailhead. Registration at the Darrington Ranger District is recommended.

From Interstate 5 near Arlington, take Highway 530 east for 32 miles to Darrington and the junction with the Mountain Loop Highway. Turn right (south) onto the Mountain Loop Highway and drive 10.5 miles to the junction with White Chuck Road (Forest Road 23). Turn left (east) onto White Chuck Road (Forest Road 23) and drive 11 miles to the end of the road and the trailhead for the White Chuck Trail (2,300 ft). (The White Chuck Road was severely damaged in the October 2003 floods and repairs may take some time. The alternate route via Forest Road 27 over Rat Trap Pass is also unusable; call ahead.)

Hike the White Chuck Trail 5.1 miles to Kennedy Hot Springs and the junction with the Upper White Chuck Trail (3,300 ft). (The hot springs and trail were buried beneath tons of debris in the October 2003 floods; it may take some time to repair or reroute the trail.) Continue 1.8 miles southeasterly on the Upper White Chuck Trail to Sitkum Creek and the junction with the Pacific Crest Trail (3,900 ft). Turn left (north) onto the Pacific Crest Trail and hike approximately 0.5 mile to 4,100 feet where a climber's trail leads off to the right (east) onto Sitkum Ridge. Follow the climber's trail for approximately 1 mile up Sitkum Ridge, staying right (south) of Sitkum Creek, to reach Boulder Basin and good camping at timberline (5,500 ft).

Route: From camp in Boulder Basin, ascend slopes east-southeasterly to gain the lower Sitkum Glacier. Ascend the glacier easterly to 7,600 feet. Bear slightly right (south) and then ascend a narrow corridor, keeping just left (north) of a cleaver, to reach the upper Sitkum Glacier. Climb northeasterly up the glacier aiming for a saddle (9,300 ft) in Glacier Peak's west ridge just right (east) of the Sitkum Spire (Point 9355). Turn right (east) and follow a loose pumice ridge toward the summit. From the top of the pumice ridge, continue easterly for several hundred yards, staying right (south) of a prominent rock outcrop, to reach a snow-filled gully. Climb the gully to the summit area and walk to the summit (10,520 ft).

Descent: Descend the route.

100 Mount St. Helens

8,365 ft; 82nd highest

Called "Louwala-Clough" or "Smoking Mountain" by some Native Americans, Mount St. Helens is famous worldwide for its tremendous 1980 eruption that completely destroyed the northern flank of the mountain and vaporized its largest glaciers. From the summit there are excellent views of the devastation as well as of the ever-growing lava dome in the center of the crater. Perhaps nowhere else in the Cascades is the power of nature so readily apparent.

SOUTH ROUTE (SUMMER)

This is a nontechnical, but strenuous, hike to the summit. After snow cover has melted, it's primarily a tedious and dusty scree and ash slog.

APPROACH

Time to camp	n/a (done as a day trip)
Mileage	n/a
Elevation change	n/a
GT 15-minute	Mount St. Helens (No. 364) or Mount St. Helens NW (No. 364S)
Contact	Gifford Pinchot NF, Mount St. Helens National Volcanic Monument

ROUTE

Difficulty	▲ Grade I + ; hiking
Time to summit	4–6 hours
Elevation change	+ 4,700 ft; -0 ft
USGS 7.5-minute	Mount St. Helens
Season	May–October

Approach: A permit is required to climb above 4,800 feet between April 1 and October 31 and costs $15 per person. From May 15 to October 31, climbing is limited to 100 people per day, so permits can be hard to come by in peak season. Reserve in advance, or risk it and try to get a permit on the spot from Jack's Restaurant and Store 23 miles east of Woodland on Highway 503. Stiff fines are handed out for those climbing without a permit. The Climbing Information Line is updated frequently and is a useful source of route and road-condition information.

From Interstate 5 at Woodland, take exit 21 and drive east on Highway 503 to Cougar. Continue 7 miles past Cougar to the junction with Forest Road 83. Turn left onto Forest Road 83 and drive 3 miles to a fork at the junction with Forest Road 81. Turn left onto Forest Road 81 and drive 1.5 miles to another fork at the junction with Forest Road 830. Turn right onto Forest Road 830 and drive approximately 3 miles to the end of the road at Climber's Bivouac (approx. 3,700 ft) and car camping (no water).

Route: From Climber's Bivouac, follow the Ptarmigan Trail for 2.1 miles through forest to the junction with the Loowit Trail (4,700 ft). Leave the trail at the junction and ascend northerly up Monitor Ridge (scree and ash in late season; follow the wooden posts) to reach the crater rim, approximately 4.5 miles from the trailhead. Turn left (west) and follow the crater rim 0.5 mile, staying well back from the very unstable edge, to the summit (8,365 ft). Beware of cornices in early season.

Descent: Descend the route.

SOUTH ROUTE (WINTER)

This ascent poses few technical difficulties, but keep an eye on the weather. The route is very popular with ski mountaineers, providing an uninterrupted descent from summit to car.

APPROACH

Time to camp	n/a (done as a day trip)
Mileage	n/a
Elevation change	n/a
GT 15-minute	Mount St. Helens (No. 364) or Mount St. Helens NW (No. 364S)
Contact	Gifford Pinchot NF, Mount St. Helens National Volcanic Monument

ROUTE

Difficulty	▲ Grade I + ; moderate snow
Time to summit	5–6 hours
Elevation change	+ 5,700 ft; -0 ft
USGS 7.5-minute	Mount St. Helens
Season	December–April

Approach: From November 1 to March 31, there is no fee for permits and no daily quota for people climbing the mountain.

Follow the approach for the South Route (summer) to the junction with Forest Road 83, 7 miles east of Cougar. Turn left onto Forest Road 83 and continue to the end of the road at the Marble Mountain SnoPark and the trailhead for the Swift Creek Trail (2,700 ft).

Route: Follow the Swift Creek Trail northerly to timberline (6,600 ft), approximately 2.5 miles from the trailhead. Ascend the obvious ridge northerly, then north-northwesterly to where it joins Monitor Ridge (approx. 7,600 ft). Climb avalanche-prone snowslopes northerly to the crater rim. Turn left (west) and follow the crater rim for 0.5 mile, staying well back from the very unstable and heavily corniced edge, to the summit (8,365 ft).

Descent: Descend the route; skis are highly recommended.

Find a Slam

ALL SLAMS BY DIFFICULTY

The following lists categorize the Slams alphabetically by climbing grade with duration in days given for each in parentheses. Use these lists to find a Slam that fits your experience, skills, and available time.

▲ Easier: Grade I–I+

Azurite Slam (4)

Cathedral Slam (4)

Chelan Slam (5)

Craggy Slam (2)

Enchanted Slam (3)

Gardner Slam (3)

Lago Slam (3)

Sawtooth Slam (3)

Spirit Slam (2)

Wish Slam (3)

▲▲ Intermediate: Grade II–II+

Chickamin Slam (3)

Chinook Slam (5)

Copper Slam (3)

DaKobed Slam (3)

Devore Slam (5)

Dragon Slam (2)

Dumbell Slam (2)

Entiat Slam (4)

Fortress Slam (3)

Golden Slam (3)

Monumental Slam (3)

Ptarmigan Slam (6)

Sahale Slam (3)

Stuart Slam (3)

Thunder Slam (5)

Twisp Slam (2)

▲▲▲ Advanced: Grade III

Bonanza Slam (3)

Chilliwack Slam (6)

Grand Slam (5)

Icecap Slam (5)

ALL SLAMS BY DURATION

The following lists categorize the Slams alphabetically by duration in days with the climbing grade given for each in parentheses. Use these lists to find a Slam that fits your available time, skills, and experience.

Short: 2 days

Craggy Slam (I+)

Dragon Slam (II)

Dumbell Slam (II)

Spirit Slam (I+)

Twisp Slam (II)

Medium: 3–4 days

Azurite Slam (I+)

Bonanza Slam (III)

Cathedral Slam (I+)

Chickamin Slam (II+)

Copper Slam (II)

DaKobed Slam (II)

Enchanted Slam (I+)

Entiat Slam (II)

Fortress Slam (II)

Gardner Slam (I+)

Golden Slam (II)

Lago Slam (I+)

Monumental Slam (II)

Sahale Slam (II)

Sawtooth Slam (I+)

Stuart Slam (II)

Wish Slam (I+)

Long: 5–6 days

Chelan Slam (I+)

Chilliwack Slam (III)

Chinook Slam (II)

Devore Slam (II)

Grand Slam (III)

Icecap Slam (III)

Ptarmigan Slam (II)

Thunder Slam (II+)

Appendix B:

Find a High Point

ALL HIGH POINTS BY DIFFICULTY

The following lists categorize the peaks alphabetically by climbing grade with duration in days given for each in parentheses. Use these lists to find a peak that fits your experience, skills, and available time.

▲ Easier: Grade I–I+

Abernathy Peak (1)

Mount Adams (1–2)

Amphitheater Mountain (4)

Andrews Peak (3)

Apex Mountain (3)

Azurite Peak (3)

Mount Ballard (3)

Big Craggy Peak (1–2)

Mount Bigelow (2)

Blackcap Mountain (3)

Cardinal Peak (2)

Mount Carru (3)

Cashmere Mountain (2)

Cathedral Peak (4)

Colchuck Peak, South
    Route (2)

Copper Peak (2)

Cosho Peak (3)

Courtney Peak (2)

Dumbell Mountain (2)

Emerald Peak (2)

Enchantment Peak (2)

Flora Mountain (3)

Fortress Mountain,
    Southwest Route (2)

Gardner Mountain (2–3)

Hoodoo Peak (1–2)

Kimtah Peak (3)

Mount Lago (3)

Lake Mountain (2)

Lost Peak (4–5)

Martin Peak (Lake Chelan–
    Sawtooth Wilderness) (2)

Mount Maude (2)

McClellan Peak (2)

North Gardner
    Mountain (2–3)

Osceola Peak (3)

Oval Peak (2)

Pinnacle Mountain (3)

Raven Ridge (1–2)

Remmel Mountain (3)

Robinson Mountain (1–2)

Saska Peak (2–3)

Seven Fingered Jack (2)

Mount St. Helens (1)

Star Peak (2)

Switchback Peak (2)

West Craggy Peak (1–2)

Windy Peak (1)

▲▲ Intermediate: Grade II–II+

Argonaut Peak (2–3)
Austera Peak (3–4)
Mount Baker (2)
Big Snagtooth (1)
Black Peak (2)
Boston Peak (2)
Buck Mountain (3)
Mount Buckner (2)
Cannon Mountain (1)
Castle Peak (4–5)
Chiwawa Mountain (2)
Clark Mountain (2)
Colchuck Peak, Colchuck
    Glacier (1–2)
Mount Custer (3)
Devore Peak (3)
Dome Peak (3)
Dragontail Peak (1–2)
Eldorado Peak (2)

Mount Fernow (2)
Mount Formidable (3)
Fortress Mountain,
    Southeast Route (2)
Glacier Peak (3)
Golden Horn (2)
Mount Goode (3)
Greenwood Mountain (2)
Jack Mountain (3)
Katsuk Peak (2–3)
Klawatti Peak (2)
Little Tahoma,
    Whitman Glacier via
    Summerland (2)
Mount Logan (3)
Luahna Peak (3)
Luna Peak (3–4)
Martin Peak (Glacier Peak
    Wilderness) (2)

Mesahchie Peak (2–3)
Monument Peak (3)
Primus Peak (3–4)
Ptarmigan Peak (4–5)
Mount Redoubt (3)
Reynolds Peak (1)
Sherpa Peak (2)
Mount Shuksan (2)
Silver Star Mountain (1–2)
Sinister Peak (3)
Snowfield Peak (3)
South Spectacle Butte
    (2–3)
Mount Spickard (3)
Storm King Mountain (3)
Mount Stuart (2)
Tower Mountain (2)
Tupshin Peak (3)

▲▲▲ Advanced: Grade III

Bonanza Peak (3)
Dorado Needle (2)
Forbidden Peak (2)

Little Tahoma, Whitman
    Glacier via Paradise (2)
Mox Peaks–Northwest
    Spire (3)

Mox Peaks–Southeast
    Spire (3)
Mount Rainier (2–3)

ALL HIGH POINTS BY DURATION

The following lists categorize the peaks alphabetically by duration in days with the climbing grade given for each in parentheses. Use these lists to find a peak that fits your available time, skills, and experience.

Short: 1–2 days

Abernathy Peak (I+)
Mount Adams (I+)
Argonaut Peak (II)
Mount Baker, Coleman-
    Deming Glacier (II+)
Mount Baker, Easton
    Glacier (II)

Big Craggy Peak (I+)
Big Snagtooth (II)
Mount Bigelow (I+)
Black Peak (II)
Boston Peak (II)
Mount Buckner (II)
Cannon Mountain (II)

Cardinal Peak (I+)
Cashmere Mountain (I+)
Chiwawa Mountain (II)
Clark Mountain (II)
Colchuck Peak, Colchuck
    Glacier (II)

Colchuck Peak,
  South Route (I+)
Copper Peak (I+)
Courtney Peak (I+)
Dorado Needle (III)
Dragontail Peak (II)
Dumbell Mountain (I+)
Eldorado Peak (II)
Emerald Peak (I+)
Enchantment Peak (I+)
Mount Fernow (II)
Forbidden Peak (III)
Fortress Mountain,
  Southeast Route (II)
Fortress Mountain,
  Southwest Route (I+)
Gardner Mountain (I+)
Golden Horn (II)
Greenwood Mountain (II)
Hoodoo Peak (I+)

Katsuk Peak (II)
Klawatti Peak (II)
Lake Mountain (I+)
Little Tahoma,
  Whitman Glacier via
  Paradise (III)
Little Tahoma,
  Whitman Glacier via
  Summerland (II+)
Martin Peak (Glacier Peak
  Wilderness) (II)
Martin Peak (Lake
  Chelan–Sawtooth
  Wilderness) (I+)
Mount Maude (I+)
McClellan Peak (I+)
Mesahchie Peak (II)
North Gardner
  Mountain (I+)
Oval Peak (I+)

Mount Rainier (III)
Raven Ridge (I+)
Reynolds Peak (II)
Robinson Mountain (I+)
Saska Peak (I+)
Seven Fingered Jack (I+)
Sherpa Peak (II)
Mount Shuksan (II+)
Silver Star Mountain (II)
South Spectacle Butte (II)
Mount St. Helens (I+)
Star Peak (I+)
Mount Stuart (II)
Switchback Peak (I)
Tower Mountain (II)
West Craggy Peak (I+)
Windy Peak (I)

Medium: 3 days

Andrews Peak (I+)
Apex Mountain (I)
Austera Peak (II)
Azurite Peak (I+)
Mount Ballard (I+)
Blackcap Mountain (I+)
Bonanza Peak (III)
Buck Mountain (II)
Mount Carru (I+)
Cosho Peak (I+)
Mount Custer (II)
Devore Peak (II)
Dome Peak (II+)

Flora Mountain (I+)
Mount Formidable (II+)
Glacier Peak (II+)
Mount Goode (II+)
Jack Mountain (II)
Kimtah Peak (I+)
Mount Lago (I+)
Mount Logan (II)
Luahna Peak (II)
Monument Peak (II)
Mox Peaks–Northwest
  Spire (III)

Mox Peaks–Southeast
  Spire (III)
Osceola Peak (I+)
Pinnacle Mountain (I+)
Primus Peak (II)
Mount Redoubt (II+)
Remmel Mountain (I)
Sinister Peak (II+)
Snowfield Peak (II)
Mount Spickard (II)
Storm King Mountain (II)
Tupshin Peak (II)

Long: 4–5 days

Amphitheater Mountain (I)
Castle Peak (II)

Cathedral Peak (I+)
Lost Peak (I+)

Luna Peak (II)
Ptarmigan Peak (II)

Appendix C:

Topographic Maps

GREEN TRAILS 15-MINUTE MAPS

The following Green Trails maps, listed by number, cover the approaches for all the routes in this guide.

Mount Baker (No. 13)
Mount Shuksan (No. 14)
Ross Lake (No. 16)
Jack Mountain (No. 17)
Pasayten Peak (No. 18)
Billy Goat Mountain (No. 19)
Coleman Peak (No. 20)
Horseshoe Basin (No. 21)
Hamilton (No. 45)
Diablo Dam (No. 48)
Mount Logan (No. 49)
Washington Pass (No. 50)
Mazama (No. 51)
Cascade Pass (No. 80)
McGregor Mountain (No. 81)

Stehekin (No. 82)
Buttermilk Butte (No. 83)
Sloan Peak (No. 111)
Glacier Peak (No. 112)
Holden (No. 113)
Lucerne (No. 114)
Prince Creek (No. 115)
Wenatchee Lake (No. 145)
Mount Stuart (No. 209)
The Enchantments (No. 209S)
Mount Rainier East (No. 270) or
    Paradise (No. 270S)
Mount St Helens (No. 364) or Mount
    St Helens NW (No. 364S)
Mount Adams (No. 367S)

USGS 7.5-MINUTE QUADRANGLES

The following quads, listed alphabetically, cover all the routes in this guide.

Azurite Peak

Baker Pass

Billy Goat Mountain

Cascade Pass

Cashmere Mountain

Castle Peak

Clark Mountain

Crater Mountain

Diablo Dam

Dome Peak

Downey Mountain

Eldorado Peak

Enchantment Lakes

Forbidden Peak

Gilbert

Glacier Peak East

Glacier Peak West

Goode Mountain

Holden

Hoodoo Peak

Horseshoe Basin

Jack Mountain

Lost Peak

Martin Peak

Mazama

Midnight Mountain

Mount Adams East

Mount Arriva

Mount Baker

Mount Challenger

Mount Lago

Mount Logan

Mount Lyall

Mount Prophet

Mount Rainier East

Mount Rainier West

Mount Redoubt

Mount Shuksan

Mount Spickard

Mount St. Helens

Mount Stuart

Oval Peak

Pinnacle Mountain

Prince Creek

Pyramid Mountain

Remmel Mountain

Robinson Mountain

Ross Dam

Saska Peak

Silver Star Mountain

Skagit Peak

Slate Peak

Stehekin

Suiattle Pass

Sun Mountain

Trinity

Washington Pass

Appendix D:

High Points Personal Log

Rank	High Point	Elevation	Comments
1	Mount Rainier	14,410 ft	
2	Mount Adams	12,276 ft	
3	Little Tahoma	11,138 ft	
4	Mount Baker	10,781 ft	
5	Glacier Peak	10,520 ft	
6	Bonanza Peak	9,511 ft	
7	Mount Stuart	9,415 ft	
8	Mount Fernow	9,249 ft	
9	Mount Goode	9,200 ft	
10	Mount Shuksan	9,131 ft	
11	Mount Buckner	9,112 ft	
12	Seven Fingered Jack	9,100 ft	
13	Mount Logan	9,087 ft	
14	Jack Mountain	9,066 ft	
15	Mount Maude	9,040 ft	
16	Mount Spickard	8,979 ft	
17	Black Peak	8,970 ft	
18	Mount Redoubt	8,969 ft	
19	Copper Peak	8,964 ft	
20	North Gardner Mountain	8,956 ft	
21	Dome Peak	8,920 ft	
22	Gardner Mountain	8,898 ft	
23	Boston Peak	8,894 ft	
24	Silver Star Mountain	8,876 ft	
25	Eldorado Peak	8,868 ft	
26	Dragontail Peak	8,840 ft	

Rank	High Point	Elevation	Comments
27	Forbidden Peak	8,815 ft	
28	Mesahchie Peak	8,795 ft	
28	Oval Peak	8,795 ft	
30	Fortress Mountain	8,760 ft	
31	Mount Lago	8,745 ft	
32	Robinson Mountain	8,726 ft	
33	Colchuck Peak	8,705 ft	
34	Star Peak	8,690 ft	
35	Remmel Mountain	8,685 ft	
36	Katsuk Peak	8,680 ft	
37	Cannon Mountain	8,638 ft	
38	Mount Custer	8,630 ft	
39	Ptarmigan Peak	8,614 ft	
40	Sherpa Peak	8,605 ft	
41	Clark Mountain	8,602 ft	
42	Cathedral Peak	8,601 ft	
43	Kimtah Peak	8,600 ft	
44	Mount Carru	8,595 ft	
45	Monument Peak	8,592 ft	
46	Cardinal Peak	8,590 ft	
47	Osceola Peak	8,587 ft	
48	Raven Ridge	8,572 ft	
49	Buck Mountain	8,528 ft	
50	Enchantment Peak	8,520 ft	
50	Storm King Mountain	8,520 ft	
52	Reynolds Peak	8,512 ft	
53	Martin Peak (Glacier Peak Wilderness)	8,511 ft	
54	Primus Peak	8,508 ft	
55	Mox Peaks—Southeast Spire	8,504 ft	
56	Cashmere Mountain	8,501 ft	
57	Klawatti Peak	8,485 ft	
58	Big Craggy Peak	8,470 ft	
59	Hoodoo Peak	8,464 ft	
59	Lost Peak	8,464 ft	
61	Chiwawa Mountain	8,459 ft	
62	Argonaut Peak	8,453 ft	
63	Tower Mountain	8,444 ft	
64	Mount Bigelow	8,440 ft	
64	Dorado Needle	8,440 ft	
64	Sinister Peak	8,440 ft	

Rank	High Point	Elevation	Comments
67	Emerald Peak	8,422 ft	
68	Dumbell Mountain	8,421 ft	
69	Greenwood Mountain	8,415 ft	
70	Mox Peaks—Northwest Spire	8,407 ft	
71	Saska Peak	8,404 ft	
72	Azurite Peak	8,400 ft	
72	Luahna Peak	8,400 ft	
72	Pinnacle Mountain	8,400 ft	
75	Blackcap Mountain	8,397 ft	
76	Courtney Peak	8,392 ft	
77	South Spectacle Butte	8,392 ft	
78	Martin Peak (Lake Chelan–Sawtooth Wilderness)	8,375 ft	
79	Lake Mountain	8,371 ft	
80	Golden Horn	8,366 ft	
80	West Craggy Peak	8,366 ft	
82	Mount St. Helens	8,365 ft	
83	McClellan Peak	8,364 ft	
84	Devore Peak	8,360 ft	
85	Amphitheater Mountain	8,358 ft	
86	Snowfield Peak	8,347 ft	
87	Mount Ballard	8,340 ft	
88	Austera Peak	8,334 ft	
89	Windy Peak	8,333 ft	
90	Cosho Peak	8,332 ft	
91	Big Snagtooth	8,330 ft	
92	Mount Formidable	8,325 ft	
93	Abernathy Peak	8,321 ft	
93	Switchback Peak	8,321 ft	
95	Flora Mountain	8,320 ft	
95	Tupshin Peak	8,320 ft	
97	Luna Peak	8,311 ft	
98	Castle Peak	8,306 ft	
99	Andrews Peak	8,301 ft	
100	Apex Mountain	8,297 ft	

Appendix E:

Contact Information

NATIONAL FORESTS
Gifford Pinchot National Forest
www.fs.fed.us/gpnf/
Mount Adams Ranger Station
2455 Highway 141
Trout Lake, WA 98650
(509) 395-3400
Mount St. Helens National
Volcanic Monument
42218 NE Yale Bridge Road
Amboy, WA 98601
(360) 449-7800
Climbing Information Line (360)
449-7861

Mount Baker–Snoqualmie National Forest
www.fs.fed.us/r6/mbs/
Darrington Ranger District
1405 Emmens Street
Darrington, WA 98241
(360) 436-1155
Glacier Public Service Center
(summer only)
1094 Mount Baker Highway
Glacier, WA 98244
(360) 599-2714

Mount Baker Ranger District
810 State Route 20
Sedro-Woolley, WA 98284
(360) 856-5700

Okanogan and Wenatchee National Forests
www.fs.fed.us/r6/oka/
www.fs.fed.us/r6/wenatchee/
Chelan Ranger District
PO Box 549
428 W. Woodin Avenue
Chelan, WA 98816
(509) 682-2576
Cle Elum Ranger District
803 W 2nd Street
Cle Elum, WA 98922
(509) 852-1100
Entiat Ranger District
2108 Entiat Way
Entiat, WA 98822
(509) 784-1511
Lake Wenatchee Ranger District
22976 State Highway 207
Leavenworth, WA 98826
(509) 763-3103

LEAVENWORTH RANGER DISTRICT
600 Sherbourne Street
Leavenworth, WA 98826
(509) 548-6977

METHOW VALLEY RANGER DISTRICT
24 W Chewuch Road
Winthrop, WA 98862
(509) 996-4003

TONASKET RANGER DISTRICT
1 W Winesap
Tonasket, WA 98855
(509) 486-2186

NATIONAL PARKS
Mount Rainier National Park
www.nps.gov/mora/
MOUNT RAINIER NATIONAL PARK
Tahoma Woods, Star Route
Ashford, WA 98304
(360) 569-2211

North Cascades National Park
www.nps.gov/noca/
HEADQUARTERS
810 State Route 20
Sedro-Woolley, WA 98284
(360) 856-5700

GOLDEN WEST VISITOR CENTER
Stehekin, WA 98852
(360) 856-5700, ext. 340 then 14

MARBLEMOUNT RANGER STATION
7280 Ranger Station Road
Marblemount, WA 98267
(360) 873-4500, ext. 39

BOAT AND PLANE SERVICES
Boat
LAKE CHELAN BOAT COMPANY
1418 W Woodin Avenue
Chelan, WA 98816
(509) 682-4584
www.ladyofthelake.com

ROSS LAKE RESORT WATER TAXI
(206) 386-4437
www.rosslakeresort.com

Plane
CHELAN AIRWAYS
Box W
Chelan, WA 98816
(509) 682-5555
www.chelanairways.com

KENMORE AIR
6321 NE 175th Street
Kenmore, WA 98028
(425) 486-1257 or (800) 543-9595
www.kenmoreair.com

SEATTLE SEAPLANES
1325 Fairview Avenue E
Seattle, WA 98102
(206) 329-9638
www.seattleseaplanes.com

References

Beckey, Fred. *Cascade Alpine Guide: Climbing and High Routes, Vol. 1; Columbia River to Stevens Pass.* 3rd ed. Seattle: The Mountaineers Books, 2000.

———. *Cascade Alpine Guide: Climbing and High Routes, Vol. 2; Stevens Pass to Rainy Pass.* 3rd ed. Seattle: The Mountaineers Books, 2003.

———. *Cascade Alpine Guide: Climbing and High Routes, Vol. 3; Rainy Pass to Fraser River.* 2nd ed. Seattle: The Mountaineers Books, 1995.

Gauthier, Mike. *Mount Rainier: A Climbing Guide.* Seattle: The Mountaineers Books, 1999.

Goldman, Peggy. *75 Scrambles in Washington: Classic Routes to the Summits.* 1st ed. Seattle: The Mountaineers Books, 2001.

Nelson, Jim, and Peter Potterfield. *Selected Climbs in the Cascades, Vol.1.* 1st ed. Seattle: The Mountaineers Books, 1993.

———. *Selected Climbs in the Cascades, Vol.2.* 1st ed. Seattle: The Mountaineers Books, 2000.

Phillips, W. S. *The Chinook Book.* Seattle: R. L. Davis Printing Co., 1912.

Shaw, George. *The Chinook Jargon and How to Use It.* Seattle: Rainier Printing Company, Inc., 1909.

Index

About the Authors

SCOTT STEPHENSON IS A NATIONAL OUTDOOR LEADERSHIP SCHOOL (NOLS) graduate and an avid weekend climber who has climbed extensively in the mountains of the Pacific Northwest. He has crossed South Georgia Island following the famous Shackleton Route and has twice climbed Mount Kilimanjaro. He has also climbed in the Indian Himalayas, the Alps, the Sierras, and the Rockies of Colorado and Wyoming. He makes his home in Seattle.

Scott on the summit of McClellan Peak Photo by Brian Bongiovanni

BRIAN "BONGI" BONGIOVANNI IS AN ACTIVE MEMBER of and instructor for the Seattle Mountaineers. He is an avid climber and has climbed extensively in the mountains of the Pacific Northwest. He has also climbed in the Alps, Alaska, South America, and the Rockies of Colorado, Montana, and Wyoming. He has climbed the high points of the fifty U.S. states, the Adirondack 46 in winter, and three of the Seven Summits, including multiple ascents of Denali and a solo of Aconcagua.

Bongi on the summit of Austera Peak Photo by Grant Meyers

Other Titles by AlpenBooks

(AS OF SEPTEMBER 2004)

Bicycle Design
Mike Burrows
0966979524
November 2000

Sea Kayak Navigation Simplified
Lee Moyer
0966979532
May 2001

The River Chasers
Susan Taft
0966979516
September 2001

Classic Climbs of the Northwest
Alan Kearney
0966979559
May 2002

Canoeing in Tennessee, 2nd edition
Holly Sherwin
0966979540
August 2002

Encycleopedia 2002-03
Alan Davidson, editor
0966979567
September 2002

Cooking with Sourdough in the Backcountry
Scott E. Power
0966979575
July 2004

For more information, contact
AlpenBooks Press, LLC
4602 Chennault Beach Road, B-1
Mukilteo, WA 98275 USA
(425) 493-6380
www.alpenbooks.com